Ginger,
May your
deeper and deeper. I pray as
your faith grows stronger, your
trust grows deeper.

Tom

THE

CRUCIBLE

OF TRUST

THE
CRUCIBLE
OF TRUST

By Tommy Pierce, D. Min.

XULON PRESS

Xulon Press
2301 Lucien Way #415
Maitland, FL 32751
407.339.4217
www.xulonpress.com

Unless otherwise indicated, Scripture quotations taken from the New
King James Version (NKJV). Copyright © 1982 by Thomas Nelson,
Inc. Used by permission. All rights reserved.

Other translations also accessed from PC Study Bible 4.2 B: New
American Standard; New International Version.

All italics are my own.

Printed in the United States of America.

ISBN-13: 978-1-6312-9113-5

Acknowledgements

First and foremost, I acknowledge God Almighty: Our Father, Precious Lord Jesus Christ and Awesome Holy Spirit, Who inspired me, motivated me to write and led me to the right people to help me in this journey.

Robin, my precious wife, has stood by me with much encouragement and loving support. Her belief in me and in what God has called me to do truly give me freedom to grow and mature as a man of God and as a writer. Our eldest son, Nathan helped me tremendously in many research papers in my graduate work, which honed my ability to write.

Don Bradford, my very good friend with whom I worked for many years in the steel mill would read my early spiritual essays. He would often tell me after reading them, "Tom, you will write books; you have a gift." His words always stirred my faith to write.

Lizabet Nix was my first editor; we worked together for many months. However, over time, she realized her other life-commitments were interfering with her ability to focus on my book, so she introduced me to Bethany Swoboda. Beth and I collaborated back and forth with my manuscript for some time until she suggested that I would benefit from a writing coach. She introduced me to Abigail Geiger. Abigail was very instrumental in guiding me through some vital principles in the craft of writing. Her counsel was invaluable as she helped me to better grasp how to communicate instead of just writing. Then I amended the entire manuscript and sent it back to Beth. Her final editing was just what I needed, really catching what I was trying to say and helping tremendously with corrections and adjustments to express my thoughts.

Ron Pennell is another good friend, a retired school teacher, who proofread my manuscript. His acumen in grammar and sentence structure helped me further sharpen my ability to communicate as a writer.

Brian Daniels caught my vision of the cover art. He worked diligently with his graphic art skills and created the wonderful image.

There are many others not mentioned here. Thanks to all my family and friends, teachers, and mentors who encouraged and guided me for the development of *The Crucible of Trust*.

ENDORSEMENTS

"Learning to trust God comes from hearing His voice and deepening your experience of Him as your Wonderful Counselor. This book, <u>The Crucible of Trust</u> will guide you into deeper trust of Almighty God, by leading you into a deeper encounter with Him and His marvelous grace. May your heart be strengthened as your spiritually intimacy is enhanced."

Dr. Mark Virkler,
Author of *4 Keys to Hearing God's Voice*

"My friend Tommy Pierce has written <u>The Crucible of Trust</u> to help you grow stronger and deeper in faith. The powerful story of his own conversion and spiritual growth is reason enough to read it! But it also contains his encouragement to you to walk with the Lord and follow His direction for your life. I commend it to you and pray God uses it to help you build a deeper faith in every situation and circumstance of life!"

Dr. Doug Munton,
Author and Senior Pastor, FBC O'Fallon, IL

"It is a privilege in knowing the author of this book for many years. Dr. Tommy is man who endeavors doing God's best at all times. He has a strong love for God and a willingness to do what is right in God's eyes. Tommy has come through many trials of different kinds, but at the end always willing to allow God have His way. His heart is tender towards God and very motivated following God's voice for his personal life.

"Dr. Tommy is known for a heart that is quick to repent in re-aligning his thoughts with the mind of Christ. Tommy has walked through furnaces of affliction and his trust in God always brought him through triumphantly.

This book is a great reflection of the author's life and his relationship with God through Christ Jesus."

Andries van Schalkwyk, PhD. CLC. PLC,
Pastor of Crossroads Church of God, Mt. Vernon, IL

TABLE OF CONTENTS

SECTION III: WAITING IN TRUST

INTRODUCTION

"Trust in the LORD with all your heart,
and lean not on your own understanding;
in all your ways acknowledge Him,
And He shall direct your paths."
Proverbs 3:5-6

Dear Reader,

Do you realize, along with me, the need to grow in your trust of God, and in that need it is essential that we desire to trust Him wholeheartedly? Trust is absolutely necessary in any relationship, especially the one we have with our Heavenly Father. Hopefully, we all know instinctively that trusting God pleases Him, and learning to trust Him completely is in constant development. Indeed, it is a process of growth, an ongoing journey, and whether we realize it or not God has wired each one of us in such a way that we truly need to trust Him.

Almighty God created us for His good pleasure, and it is our faith that pleases Him. As we learn to walk in faith, there comes forth an added need to trust Him as life unfolds. What a wonderful experience it can be as we grow in our trust of God, but at times it can be rather a challenge. Of course God's ultimate purpose for each of us individually is maturity as sons and daughters by being transformed into the image of His own dear Son, Jesus Christ. God uses all of life's experiences in His plan and purpose by somehow taking both the good and the bad in our lives—as we learn to trust Him wholeheartedly—and works them out for our good.

However, life's experiences are very often more of a trial, or a whole series of trials. Brennan Manning speaks of this in *Ruthless Trust*: "Without exception trust must be purified in the crucible of trial" (2000, 9). The concept of "crucible of trial" just jumped out at me as I read Manning's book, because I had chosen the title *The Crucible of Trust* in my original essay written long before I had ever heard of Manning or read his books. At the outset of writing my essay I was beginning to realize that my personal trust in God is often revealed during trials, so Manning's words were poignant and congruent with my original effort to express my thoughts regarding trials of faith and trust.

The first promptings to write on the subject of the crucible of trust came as I was meditating upon Proverbs 3:5-6. I realized that my trust was important to God, but I also knew my trust was shallow because I was trying to figure it all out on my own. The Lord impressed upon me that I was going through the testing of my heart, of my faith, and of my trust in Him. This was not so inviting to my immature heart. I liked God's love, His grace and His mercy, but His testings (which also could include chastening) were not so inviting or comfortable. I also began to see many places in Scripture that speak to the testing of hearts. Holy Spirit (as I refer to Him as "Holy Spirit" throughout most of this book) seemed to be leading me to the truth regarding the tests of my heart almost every time I read the Word. However, I also realized that He was testing my faith and trust. So in my immaturity, I told Him, "Lord, I am sick and tired of being tested." God was (and continues to be) so gracious to me in my childish responses. So I began to put my thoughts down on paper, deciding to write the essay on the subject, thinking maybe others could read it and find encouragement. That

Introduction

essay sat in a file in my laptop for several years, but eventually, as I entered retirement and receiving encouragement from others, it became a stirring in my heart to explore the idea of the crucible of trust more fully.

I have written from my ongoing journey of faith, and the process toward total trust in God. My path has taken me through many ups and downs—with more to come—in learning to trust the Lord. My hope and prayer is that in reading this book, it will draw you closer to the Lord Jesus, to God's Fatherly love, and to His Spirit. I pray that God's guidance and comfort be your experience. Personally, I have a way to go myself in this "process of maturity" department, but I have learned one thing. God is absolutely trustworthy, even when I struggle.

One sleepless night I was wrestling in my mind and heart—having doubts about writing this book. So I got up to pray in the wee hours of the morning. I had allowed myself to be stressed to that point of thinking that I did not have the ability to finish a book. As I was praying and waiting on the Lord, all of a sudden an inner witness and a revelation came—God sees my book as complete. I had to repent of doubt and to trust that the vision to write was a reality from Him. It was His assignment to me, already accomplished in His mind and heart. I had to catch up with His vision with obedience and willingness.

So just what will you gain from this book? Will taking the time to read this book be worth it? I believe it will. As I wrote this book, I sought the leading of Holy Spirit in every chapter, every sub chapter and every paragraph. Through tears and laughter and through joys and sorrows this book has been written.

Reading *The Crucible of Trust* will take you on a journey—reading of mine and sensing your own—from faith to trust. Drawing from my own experiences and many from the Bible, I believe this book will speak to you regarding your own personal faith and trust in God. Whether you are a seasoned disciple of the Lord Jesus Christ, a struggling Christian, or a new Christian, the truths in this book will lead you to deeper trust.

Trials can be very uncomfortable and challenging because going through them often feels like we are being grated, squeezed, pressed, or refined, like being in a crucible. I realize this "crucible of trial" is not an isolated event. Yet learning to trust the Lord is vital in finding meaning in life, in experiencing His love, joy, peace, and in fulfillment as a mature child of God. The difficulty is the problem of "leaning upon my own understanding" when going through life's challenges: things that are troublesome, demanding, or demeaning. Perhaps you have this same struggle. But be assured, God has these under His loving observation and guidance as He is very involved in all our struggles, challenges, and trials.

As you read this book, among many other insights, you will:
- Gain understanding as to the reason for trials
- Learn why we need to crucify the flesh
- Understand God's silence
- Learn to draw near to God's rest
- Gain trust and love while conquering fear
- Learn how to go through trials with trust in your heart
- Learn how to enjoy your journey

I humbly invite you to join me by reading this book, even as you are on your own adventure of trust in this ongoing journey of life on which we all find ourselves. I encourage you to begin in prayer, asking Holy Spirit to lead your own journey each time you read. I warn you, however, it might make you rejoice and it may frustrate you a little at times. You may cry or you might laugh. But Holy Spirit will lead in deepening your love for and your trust in our Wonderful God and our Lord and Savior, Jesus Christ, because

He always directs us to, "Trust in the LORD with all your heart" (Proverbs 3:5a).

Your brother in the journey,
    Tom Pierce

SECTION I

REPENTANCE
PRODUCES TRUST

Therefore bear fruits worthy of repentance.
Matthew 3:8

THE CRUCIBLE

The crucible is for silver and the furnace for gold,
And a man is tested by the praise accorded him.
Proverbs 27:21 NASB

The refining pot is for silver and the furnace for gold,
But the LORD tests the hearts.
Proverbs 17:3

I used to work in a steel mill, starting just few months after high school graduation. I was not a Christian then. That came some years later. I was employed there for 43 years, retiring January, 2017. Over the years I got to know some very colorful and interesting individuals as I worked in various areas within the mill. I starting out in a finishing department, but eventually, I moved over to the steel making department, where the steel is produced and then poured. I worked in the steel pouring area called the caster until retirement.

My early experiences in steel pouring were a little intimidating, since it is a very tough, daunting environment, and some steel mill employees are often intimidating as well. I learned to trust some of these threatening, but seasoned individuals. Several of these guys took me under their wings teaching me what to do in the many dangerous situations that occur during the steel pouring process. I learned to trust their experience and judgment, and when I look back over those years in the steel mill, I realize God's Spirit was teaching me to trust in the acumen of others so I would learn to trust Him.

The furnace where the steel is produced is also called the vessel, which is actually a refining pot or a crucible. This vessel is as large as a small house and its purpose is to melt and purify the metal placed in it, which is a combination of scrap steel and molten iron. Oxygen flows through a probe or a lance which is submerged into this mixture, working sort of like a straw in a soda as one blows creating bubbles. Intense heat is produced as the oxygen is blown into the furnace's molten content. As other elements are added, all these ingredients amalgamating together make steel. Extreme temperature is essential in producing the quality necessary for the end product in steel applications.

In many ways, the steel making process is similar to how God works in our lives as Christians. Holy Spirit, the Breath of God, is sort of like the oxygen creating the heat as He purifies our hearts, at the same time exposing and burning out impurities. Jesus said the Holy Spirit will "bring conviction of sin, of righteousness, and of judgment" (John 16:8-11). These convictions work as a process of revealing our heart to ourselves, exposing the sin and impurities in our lives, and the struggles we have with our faith. Conviction either reveals our faith and trust in Christ, or exposes the lack thereof. While the Spirit of God is our comforter, guide and teacher, He is also the refining fire of God purifying our hearts and bringing us to maturity, which is God's purpose, and during this ongoing development, we must learn to trust Him.

The word for crucible and refining pot is the same in the original Hebrew language, which is a vessel used for refining metal, particularly gold and silver. The analogy of being in a crucible is a demonstration of just how vital our pure personal faith and trust is to God, because He knows the condition of our hearts. Faith and trust in God are tested and refined in the crucible of life, just as precious metals are heated for purity in a refining pot. The Lord knows exactly what needs to be refined and purified within each of our souls. In the New Testament, the apostle Peter, inspired by the Spirit of God writes about this purifying process:

> In this you greatly rejoice, though now for a little while, if need be, you have been grieved by various trials, that the genuineness of your faith, being much more precious [to God] than gold that perishes, *though it is tested by fire*, may be found to praise, honor, and glory at the revelation of Jesus Christ, whom having not seen you love. Though now you do not see Him, yet believing, you rejoice with joy inexpressible and full of glory, receiving the end of your faith — the salvation of your souls (1Peter 1:6-9).

As steel is refined in extreme heat, so we experience trials and tests in the refinement of our faith and trust in God. John of Kronstadt (1829-1908 or 1909?), a Russian Orthodox priest speaks of this refinement this way: "Our faith, trust and love are proved and revealed in adversities, that is, in difficult and grievous outward and inward circumstances." Or as Peter says, "tested by fire."

Ongoing faith and trust are necessary for God's purposes to be revealed in our lives, because the end of our faith is the salvation of our souls. Our love for God and others is also refined and established in the crucible, because trust is an aspect of love which is revealed as we go through various trying experiences. Love and trust work together in our relationship with our Heavenly Father. Admittedly, it is God's grace that brings about His purposes, but we must have faith, without which we cannot please God. Are we willing to allow our faith, our trust, and our love for God to go through times of testing? Do we truly desire His purposes to be revealed His way? Through experiences, we are in this crucible of life where our belief in God is challenged to validate our trust in God, which stems from our love for Him. Our trust in God is forged and strengthened through fiery trials only as we rely upon Him. We do not necessarily like it, but our emotions, our thinking, our attitudes, and our character all need to be purified in these fiery trials in what I call the crucible of trust, so that, as Peter wrote, we can be found in the praise and glory of God.

Scriptures of the Process

For the word of God is living and powerful, and sharper than
any two-edged sword,
piercing even to the division of soul and spirit, and of joints
and marrow,
and is a discerner of the thoughts and intents of the heart.
And there is no creature hidden from His sight,
but all things are naked and open to the eyes of Him
to whom we must give account.
Hebrews 4:12-13

One of my mentors in the faith, Frans Du Plessis (who has since gone on to be with the Lord) used to say, "Read your Bible; it will read you." Scripture has a way of truly piercing into our hearts. The following Scriptures, along with accompanying thoughts, are the foundation for the theme of this book. Some are repeated for illustrations throughout this book. While many other Scriptures are used, the following provide the basis for *The Crucible of Trust* message. Each one emphasizes different aspects of what it means to experience the trials of faith while learning to trust the Lord—which is the essence of what it means to be in the crucible of trust.

- Isaiah 48:9-10a says, "Behold, I have refined you, but not as silver; I have tested you in the furnace of affliction. For My own sake, for My own sake, I will do it."

Almighty God (for His own sake) allows, and then uses our life experiences, which can include afflictions and refinement, to test the heart. The furnace is of course the crucible of trust in which we experience God's grace, goodness, faithfulness, and comfort while going through trials.

- Romans 8:28-30 says, "And we know that all things work together for good to those who love God, to those who are the called according to His purpose. For whom He foreknew, He also predestined to be conformed to the image of His Son, that He might be the firstborn among many brethren. Moreover whom He predestined, these He also called; whom He called, these He also justified; and whom He justified, these He also glorified."

All of our life experiences, whether afflictions or blessings, are God's instruments in working out the good intentions of His will for our lives. We learn to trust God continually and grow in our love for Him regardless of our experiences in life or how many times He tests that trust. His eternal plans are activated in everyday life initiating our conformity to Christ's image leading us to eventual glory in His will.

> · 1 Peter 4:12-13 says, "Beloved, do not think it strange concerning the fiery trial which is to try you, as though some strange thing happened to you; but rejoice to the extent that you partake of Christ's sufferings, that when His glory is revealed, you may also be glad with exceeding joy."

We all face these fiery trials as disciples, and in a small way identify with our Lord's sufferings as He endured the pain and agony of the cross. We accept and trust that He did this for us. In order for us to not think it strange when fiery trials come to us we learn to develop that deep, abiding trust that everything we go through will be worth it, and it will. To rejoice as one who partakes in Christ's sufferings is a true response of the person who trusts the Lord. Our focus is to be on Him, not trials. Hebrews 12:2-3 encourages us to keep looking onto Jesus, the Author and Finisher of our faith, to consider Him who endured the cross. If we do not keep our focus on Jesus we will grow weary.

Consider many Christians today in foreign lands who suffer dire persecutions for their faith in Jesus Christ. I must admit, I have not really suffered compared to these, who are truly partakers of Christ's sufferings. I encourage all of us to pray regularly for our brothers and sisters in Christ in those countries and cultures that persecute Christians, for the Lord to extend His grace into their hearts to withstand and overcome in their suffering. In America, we enjoy great freedom for the most part as far as our Christian faith is concerned.

Another very small way we suffer is through self-denial, taking up our cross and dying daily, but this involves little physical suffering. I am not minimizing self denial, but maturity comes when our focus is on Christ through whatever we face. We must lay aside ourselves as living sacrifices, lay aside our rights, thus becoming more Christlike. We are not our own; we are bought with His blood. When trials come we are encouraged to rejoice in the Spirit.

- James 1:2-5 says, "My brethren, count it all joy when you fall into various trials, knowing that the testing of your faith produces patience. But let patience have its perfect work, that you may be perfect and complete, lacking nothing."

There is a perfect work transpiring in our hearts as we face various trials. Counting it all joy in these trials moves us toward maturity as disciples of Jesus Christ, who tells us in Luke 21:19, "By your patience possess your souls." What does Jesus mean by possessing our souls? The Greek word for possess is *khaomai*, which means "to own" (Strong). I believe He means we conquer our souls, our tendency to sin, our selfishness and our pride in exercising self-control and self-denial, taking up our cross in following Jesus. We learn to stand in faith while trusting God by the power of Holy Spirit. This does not mean we possess our soul as in ownership. It bears repeating that we are not our own; we are bought with the price of Jesus' blood (1 Corinthians 6:19). In our maturity and patience, God leads us to possess our souls with godly self-control, in wise choices, in how we treat others, and in being led by Holy Spirit. It means we seek God's will, not our will. It takes trust to acknowledge we are not our own and that in His will we are taken care of, that our needs are met, and that we have hope and a future. It takes trust to count it all joy during the trials of life. I have faced many trials in my life and admit to not having such a joyous attitude, but God is patient. Let us all be patient with ourselves and with one another, because God is not finished just yet.

He is continually working to develop our lives toward transformation into the image of His dear Son. Let's let Him have His way.

· Romans 5:1-5 reads, "Therefore, having been justified by faith, we have peace with God through our Lord Jesus Christ, through whom also we have access by faith into this grace in which we stand, and rejoice in hope of the glory of God. And not only that, but we also glory in tribulations, knowing that tribulation produces perseverance; and perseverance, character; and character, hope. Now hope does not disappoint, because the love of God has been poured out in our hearts by the Holy Spirit who was given to us."

This passage is a progressive description of going through the crucible of trust. We come into relationship with God through faith, gaining peace with Him because our sins are forgiven—we are justified. We have access into His grace to stand before Him as righteous because of Jesus' atonement for sin. Great rejoicing results as a wonderful hope wells up in our hearts. In our relationship with God, He gives grace to our hearts, in which we learn to rejoice during trials and tests. Patience and perseverance are the result in our hearts, leading into character development, from which hope arises. The promise from God is that hope will not dissatisfy. His love is released into our hearts by His Spirit. Love endures long and is kind, does not envy, does not parade itself, is not puffed up. Love is hopeful, trustful, and bears all things. Love never fails (1 Corinthians 13:4-8). Indeed, God is love and He pours out His love into our hearts by His Spirit. The love of God then becomes our motivating factor, involving love for Him and love for others as it becomes our lifestyles in trusting the Living God. Our love for God leads us to trust Him.

What is trust?

Preserve me, O God.
For in you I put my trust.
Psalm 16:1

In an early season of my Christian walk, I was greatly encouraged by a song called "Learning to Trust," composed and sung by David Meece. He sang, "I'm learning to trust in You, but at times it is so hard to do" (1989). I had come to a place in my walk with the Lord where trusting Him was difficult, and these words uplifted me as I heard Meese's heart cry in them. I realized progressive trust was absolutely necessary in my journey with Jesus. Why was it so difficult on occasion? I really had to examine my trust level and my need to cry out to God about my lack in this area.

We all can identify with David's psalm above in asking God to preserve us, especially when we struggle while learning to trust. Preservation happens over time, as does gaining knowledge. Learning to trust God while waiting on Him to come through in whatever we need is a challenge but very important in our journey of trust.

Trust can be defined as a firm belief in the reliability, truth, ability, and strength of something or someone. Our trust is in our Heavenly Father, in Jesus Christ, and in Holy Spirit. Our trust is also in God's written Word, which establishes and builds our trust in who He is for us. Faith, reliance, hope, conviction, confidence, and yieldedness are all part of what trust encompasses. Yet when we trust, we are vulnerable to the one we trust—God. Allowing ourselves to be vulnerable can be difficult. We have to rely upon *another*, expecting and relying upon Him who is unseen to help us get through life's challenges, trials, and struggles, and He absolutely will. In another of Meece's songs he refers to God's love and help reaching out to him with an "invisible hand" (1987). That is part of why trust can be so challenging; God works very often in ways we cannot see during the trial, but He is there and the answer or resolution is always available by His grace. He is absolutely trustworthy. By His Spirit, who dwells within us, we are empowered by grace for everything we face.

That's why Scripture, which was inspired by Holy Spirit, is so important for the renewing of our minds. In Psalm 23, David used word pictures depicting God's trustfulness. "The LORD is my shepherd. I shall not want. He makes me lie down in green pastures. He leads me beside still waters. He restores my soul." David was a shepherd who was often unseen and unnoticed by the sheep, so these concepts were very real to him because he knew that sheep needed him to do these things, to protect and to provide for them. David had the revelation that God, who was his Shepherd and not seen, should be and can be trusted likewise. In reading any of David's psalms, one cannot help but notice how he trusted God, even when he was uncertain of what was happening; he knew God would guide him and was trustworthy. Trust, for David was truly a journey of learning to trust God during life's challenges and relying upon his Shepherd, loving Him intimately, whether during great trials and battles or in victory and celebration. We are compelled to follow David's example of reliance upon God.

RECEIVING CHRIST: THE BEGINNING OF TRUST

Whoever falls on that stone will be broken; but
on whomever it falls, it will grind him to powder.
Luke 20:18

When I first came to trust Christ I literally fell to my knees in brokenness and tears of contrition, for God had been working on my heart and I did not even realize it. The previous Friday night I had been out drinking beer and smoking pot, but when I came home around midnight I was drawn to stay outside. It was a beautifully clear early September night in 1977, so I decided to lie down on the grass to look up at the stars. As I observed those stars, recognizing the wonder of the heavens I began to ponder about my life. Who am I? Why am I here? What is the reason for living? Is there a purpose in all this?

I realized I did not have any purpose. Why were all these questions flooding my mind? I thought I was doing all right, yet there were longings in my heart and there were no meaningful relationships in my life. I had a few casual friends, but no real close relationships. I was not married and had no steady girl friend. At a month short of my 22nd birthday, I was lonely; there was emptiness inside my heart. I did not know how to trust anyone, not even God.

As I lay there, I began to think about my dad, my family and upbringing. I had been raised in a Christian home, attending church regularly. And looking back on that night I perceive now that I was trying to fill that emptiness with alcohol, pot, and other things. Interestingly, I had little thoughts of God that night. However, Holy Spirit was doing work on my unsaved heart in drawing me to the Lord Jesus. I just did not recognize it at the time. I mentally knew that Jesus had died on the cross for my sins, but it had never dawned on me that I had never accepted Christ into my life. In my rebellious, mid-teenage years I had decided to quit going to church. My parents capitulated to my whims and did not force the issue. Six or seven years had passed since I had even attended a church service.

During that season of my life in 1977 I had been very interested and involved in martial arts. My instructor told me that, though I was strong and fast, I did not have the spirit of a fighter and that I needed to reach into my spirit to stir the heart of a fighter in order to improve, so I had been thinking about these things as well. But God had other plans for my heart. As I think back, I had sensed the Lord on occasion in my life, but I had not recognized it as Him. However, others were praying for me, particularly my maternal grandparents, Papa Bud and Grandma Lucy, who loved the Lord wholeheartedly and were mighty prayer warriors. They had been interceding for me to be saved since I was born and though I was oblivious at the time, their prayers were at work bringing me to a place of realization of my need for Jesus Christ and His wonderful grace.

While looking up at the stars that night I had an interesting thought: "Call Dad and ask to go to church with him on Sunday." Somehow, even in a somewhat drunken state it actually seemed like a good idea, so I called him the next day. He was delighted, and that Sunday I went to church for the first time in many years. Dad was the teacher of the college and career Sunday school class, so I attended with him, meeting Christians around my own age. Then later, when the main church service took place, I looked around seeing those young people and all the others, thinking this is just what I needed, to be involved in church. I really did not hear anything the preacher said during his sermon, because I was pondering the whole time about this experience of going to church. I realize I needed change, thinking church attendance was the answer.

At the end of his sermon, the minister offered an altar call. I was compelled to respond and went forward, determined that I needed to be involved in church again. It was an intellectual decision more than a heart decision, or so I thought. My intent was to say to the pastor, "I would like to join the church." However, when I got to him my words came out completely different than planned. As I shook his hand something very strange took place. I exclaimed, "I want to give my heart to Jesus!" and as I did I fell to my knees crying out to God, weeping, sobbing, and groaning. Something wonderful and powerful took place because even as there was contrition, brokenness, and a great release of emotion with tears, there was gladness and sorrow at the same time. It is hard to explain. I could feel the Lord's love, His drawing me to Himself, and His acceptance of me just as I was, even though I knew I was a sinner. I fell on the Rock of Jesus as the above Scripture indicates and experienced being broken inside, but even in that brokenness, something felt very good because I knew that what was happening was good and right. I thought the thing I needed was to be involved in church again, but I really needed the Lord Jesus Christ in my life. I needed a Savior in the center of my heart and soul, in that place of preeminence, so I surrendered to Jesus that day, giving Him my heart. The Bible calls that being born again or born of the Spirit of God, and that is exactly what happened to me.

That same day I met Jesus, I also met Robin, a sweet and gentle nineteen-year-old young lady. She had been in Dad's Sunday school class. That night at church she invited me to a hay ride taking place soon, which I accepted. Then we started dating a week or so later. In the months following, our dating became more serious as our hearts really began to knit together, so about five months into our relationship I went to her dad and asked for her hand in marriage. He was delighted and asked, "What took you so long?" Her parents were so gracious to me because we all knew it was God's will for Robin and me to be together. One year from the day I was born again we were married. We have been married since 1978, and our relationship is a testimony to God's goodness. Even our being together has been part of the crucible of trust as we have both gone through many ups and downs in our life together.

Admittedly and sadly, Christ has not always been the center of our relationship. But God's grace has always kept us together in Him. Later, when I was not right with the Lord, the grace of God was there, and He brought her through some very tough times with me. He has always been the strength of our marriage, even when I was not drawing from that strength. But though it has not always been the case, I can say He is now the Center of everything Robin and I live for, everything we do.

When I first gave my heart to Christ I experienced that newness that only comes with being born again. Even though it had been accompanied with brokenness and contrition, things were wonderfully different as I knew something fantastic had taken place. I felt brand new because I was brand new. There was a feeling in my heart, sort of like I was returning home from a long and arduous journey. I had fallen in love with Jesus Christ, the Son of the Living God, who not only cleansed me of all sin, but also gave me a brand new life; and He gave me His Spirit. I was a new creature. If you have never given your heart to Jesus Christ, I urge you to ask the Lord to come into your life right now. Give your heart to Him. Repent of sin and selfishness, turning to Jesus. Confess and believe Him as Lord of your life; believe in your heart that God has raised Him from the dead and you shall be saved. Look up John 3:16-18, Romans 10:9-10, and Ephesians 2:8-9 in the Bible. Think deeply about these truths and follow through. If you do these with a true heart of repentance, you are born again. Then ask Him to fill you with His Holy Spirit, because He loves to give of Himself (Luke 11:13).

Grace is defined as unmerited favor, but can also be defined as "especially the divine influence upon the heart, and its reflection in the life; including gratitude" (Strong). I walked the aisle that day not realizing that I was under a divine influence. God had been invariably working on my heart, and I responded, thus beginning my life of faith and trust with Jesus as my Savior. Little did I know that I had only begun my real journey of faith and entering the crucible of trust in life as a disciple of Jesus. I had accepted Jesus as my Savior, and I had to learn to accept His as my Lord. I was to gain the understanding that God always intended me (and all of us) to totally trust and rely upon Him irrespective of life's circumstances or situations, because God is totally and absolutely trustworthy, no matter what comes our way.

Approaching God

Let us therefore come boldly to the throne of grace,
that we may obtain mercy and find grace
to help in time of need.
Hebrews 4:1

If we were invited to have an audience with the queen of England, or the king of a sovereign nation, we would be instructed, counseled, and prepared by staff and advisers in just how to properly address royalty and the correct approach in meeting with them. What about approaching a face to face audience with Almighty God? We will all literally face Him one day. Until that actually happens God invites us right now to come unto Him just as we are. Because of His great mercy He accepts us with grace and compassion, and with love that surpasses understanding. With confidence we can approach Him. Because His love for us is so great that, when we come to Him broken and sinful, and with a repentant heart, He desires to activate grace to forgive us, to cleanse our hearts, and to transform us into being complete in Him. Because of what Jesus did on Calvary we have access to the Father, to all His wonderful and marvelous grace by which we may live. To approach God in repentance leads us to having peace with Him through Jesus Christ as He opens the entrance into His grace in which we stand (Romans 5:2). And as long as we live in this flesh, standing in His grace is where we must position ourselves to approach Him.

May I suggest that the reason for the tests, trials, and temptations not only have to do with our lives now, but also when we actually face Almighty God in His full glory and majesty? How could one describe the indescribable? God, in all His omnipotence, omnipresence, and omniscience is absolutely sovereign, Self-existent, totally immutable, never changing. Nothing in existence can compare to Him, because He created the universe and everything that exists. And our sin has separated us from Him. Yet even in all His power He loves us so much that He desires what is best for us. He wants us to be prepared to face Him in all His holiness and splendor, so in this life He takes us on a journey of faith and trust to lead us to His glory, to transform us into the image of His Son Jesus so we may become sons, and so when we behold

Him in all His power, glory, and holiness, we will be ready. His purpose is that in Christ we are now and will be prepared. Consider these thoughts in light of the two following Scriptures:

The first is 1 Timothy 6:13-16. "I urge you in the sight of God who gives life to all things, and before Christ Jesus who witnessed the good confession before Pontius Pilate, that you keep this commandment without spot, blameless until our Lord Jesus Christ's appearing, which He will manifest in His own time, He who is the blessed and only Potentate, the King of kings and Lord of lords, who alone has immortality, dwelling in unapproachable light, whom no man has seen or can see, to whom be honor and everlasting power. Amen."

The second is Jude 24-25. "Now to Him who is able to keep you from stumbling, And to *present you faultless* before the presence of His glory with exceeding joy, To God our Savior, Who alone is wise, Be glory and majesty dominion and power, both now and forever. Amen."

What juxtaposition. God dwells in unapproachable light, yet he is able to keep us from stumbling, presenting us faultless before His glorious presence. So who is this One who is able to make us stand? It is Jesus Christ Himself, our Precious Lord and Savior. Almighty God is holy. Scripture says no one in their flesh can see God and live (Exodus 33:20). But Jesus Christ is the Bridge between God and mankind, the Wonderful Mediator and the express image of Almighty God in human form (Hebrews 1:3). He reveals the Father to whomever He wills, which is all who desire this, and according to John 6:37-38, He will not cast anyone away who comes to Him. Jesus Christ, on the Father's behalf, accepts sinners who approach Him in faith, and in willingness to repent, trusting that what He did by going to the cross brings full salvation to all who call upon His Name. This is great news! This is the Gospel of Jesus Christ.

Do we really understand that? He will not reject *anyone* who comes to Him. Whoever calls upon the Name of the Lord will be saved (Romans 10:14). He is gentle and kind with us, wanting to guide us into all truth by His Spirit, leading us to grow in the grace and knowledge of Jesus Christ, becoming mature children of the Most High God. As we grow in faith He lovingly initiates this wonderful process of transformation to prepare us to see Him in all His glory.

This is the purpose of God as He tests our faith and trust in Him during our development. He also lovingly chastens those whom He loves. While we dwell in our bodies He purifies our hearts and leads us to purify ourselves, so we may draw nearer to Him. As 2 Corinthians 7:1 says, "Therefore, having these promises, beloved, let us cleanse ourselves from all filthiness of the flesh and spirit, perfecting holiness in the fear of God." What promises? The verses just before this in 2 Corinthians 6:16-18 speak of His dwelling among us, of us separating from sinners, and of His promises that we are His people, His sons and daughters.

Scriptures speak of God as a consuming fire (Deuteronomy 4:24; 9:3; Hebrews 12:29). Scriptures also encourages us in how to approach God while we live this earthly tabernacle called flesh. "Let us therefore come boldly to the throne of grace, that we may obtain mercy and find grace to help in time of need" (Hebrews 4:16). We can approach God in confidence, but we also must approach Him with reverence and faith.

Hebrews 10:22-25 also instructs us in how we are to approach God.

> Let us draw near with a true heart in full assurance of faith, having our hearts sprinkled from an evil conscience and our bodies washed with pure water. Let us hold fast the confession of our hope

without wavering, for He who promised is faithful. And let us consider one another in order to stir up love and good works, not forsaking the assembling of ourselves together, as is the manner of some, but exhorting one another, and so much the more as you see the Day approaching.

The sprinkling indicates the blood of Jesus that cleanses us from sin, while the washing in pure water involves the power of the Word of God that washes over our thought life, which can only come as we think and meditate upon its truths. Our thought life is who we are internally. We must consider every thought in light of God's thoughts, which are His principles, precepts, judgments, and testimonies found in Scripture. As we think, so we will be (Proverbs 23:7).

God tests our ability to allow His Word to renew our minds and our thoughts, so we are encouraged to think on whatever is true, right, good, pure, virtuous, and praiseworthy (Philippians 4:8). We choose what we think about. Even as we approach God we are to present ourselves to Him as living sacrifices, and in our current condition our minds need washing and renewal by the truths in Scripture (Romans 12:1-2). He is the one who invites us to do just that.

James 4:8 says, "Draw near to God and He will draw near to you; cleanse your hands you sinners; and purify your hearts." When we draw near to God and His Spirit draws near to us, we begin to recognize His holiness and our need for the cleansing of our heart condition before Him. The blood of Jesus cleanses from all sin (1 John 1:7). All of us sin, because 1 John 1: 8-9 mentions that if we claim to have no sin, we deceive ourselves and the truth is not in us. But if we confess our sins, God is faithful and righteous to do His part to forgive us of all sin and cleanse us of all unrighteousness.

Confession and repentance of sin need to take place regularly as our lives progress and as we continually approach God in faith. We turn from our sin as we understand His holiness juxtaposed with our sinfulness. But let us emphasize His holiness and not so much our sinfulness. Not that we ignore our transgressions, but in our repentance we should have no more consciousness of sin by focusing only on our shortcomings (read Hebrews 10 asking Holy Spirit to reveal this truth). When we only focus upon our sin, we get to a place where we feel condemned. That is what the devil wants, to make us feel unworthy of being saved. But God desires our hearts to be righteous; He has made us righteous with the provision of Jesus' blood, so that our focus is not to be on sin, but on His righteousness and the refining of our hearts toward transformation.

We *were saved* by grace through faith; we are *being saved* through sanctification at the same time as we work out that salvation in fear and trembling (Philippians 2:12). And when we finally face God in all His holiness, we will be *completely saved* in order to be able to stand in His glorious presence. Activating faith and trust is our part in this process of purification as we make choices to turn away from sin by seeking His help and grace. God does His part as we do our part in cooperation with Him, trusting His loving refinement. God lovingly cleanses our hearts, and in the process He leads us in becoming holy, and He allows us to go through tests to purify our hearts so we may stand, and eventually dwell in His glorious, holy presence.

The Trustworthiness of God

Great is Thy faithfulness, O God my Father.
There is no shadow of turning with Thee.
Thou changest not, Thy compassions they fail not.

As Thou hast been Thou forever will be.
Great is Thy Faithfulness, Lord unto me.
Chisholm

The words above from the great song, "Great is Thy Faithfulness" have always stirred my heart toward deeper faith and trust in God (1923). These lyrics flow with the fundamental truth that God is absolutely faithful, providing for needs, compassion, and comfort. History is filled with testimonies of the lives of trusting believers who experienced God's faithfulness. The great thing about God is that His trustworthiness applies to everyone, whether they trust Him or not. Throughout Scripture God promises that we can trust Him and we can believe His promises as uncompromisingly true. Indeed, He is faithful to His people to the uttermost. Scriptures record His trustworthiness in wonderful and miraculous ways to all His people who call upon His Name. He shows this same loyalty to all who seek His Face, His will, and His purpose, and while we are in our crucibles of trust we experience His trustworthiness, going through trials, struggles and challenges *with* God, not apart from Him.

God is really pleased with our faith in Him and since His very Nature is love, it includes trustworthiness. Because He made us to have fellowship with Him in a trusting relationship which He initiates, it benefits us to seek His Face and trust Him. The more we trust Him—whether we do it well or blow it, or whether in good or bad situations—the better off we are in our lives. Trust leads to obedience and obedience opens the blessings and favor of God.

His trustworthiness toward us, particularly as we grow cognizant of it, compels us to love Him, to trust Him, to trust His promises, and to trust His Word. Our relationship with Him is initiated by Him and based upon His pure love for us, not upon our behavior. Of course, if we truly love Him, we will repent from our sinful behavior seeking His grace to live obediently and righteously. God always forgives when we ask with repentance in our hearts. Thus we have ongoing experiences of His grace where God comes through while in our crucibles of trust. The knowledge gained from our sensing and encountering His wonderful grace opens our understanding to the truth that God is absolutely trustworthy.

Part of the trustworthiness of God is revealed in His promises, and we can be assured He will follow through with them as we seek His help and grace. The Bible is filled with His promises. The Old Testament promises from God to His people are many and great, but we have far better promises through Christ in the New Covenant, and we are recipients of the former promises as well. Even the promises have a promise—with a seal—to all who believe and trust in Jesus Christ. God's precious Holy Spirit is our security of His commitment to keep His Word. "For all the promises of God in Him are Yes, and in Him Amen, to the glory of God through us. Now He who establishes us with you in Christ and has anointed us is God, who also has sealed us and given us the Spirit in our hearts as a guarantee" (2 Corinthians 1:20).

Everlasting life is the best promise of God and Jesus said eternal life is to know God and Jesus Christ whom He has sent (John 17:3). Knowing Him, intimately and personally, is what this wonderful promise involves. His Spirit leads us into all truth and knowledge of God, and He seals us by His Spirit in our acceptance of Christ as our assurance for everything promised. This means these promises are all dependent with our relationship with Jesus Christ and His Spirit, and that we accept and agree with the promises. We trust that God backs them up. When we are in Christ, every promise is ours, and we must rely on these promises during all trials, tribulations, and testing of our hearts. The promises were given so we would exercise our faith and learn to trust God and His Word. While relying on them, we often find ourselves in the crucible of trust and while in the crucible, we stand on the promises of God, and we will find that He is always faithful to us in the midst of anything and everything we face in life.

Here are just a few of His wonderful and precious promises enumerated. He promises:

- That those who wholeheartedly seek Him will find Him (Jeremiah 29:13-14).
- To meet every need according to His riches in glory by Christ Jesus (Philippians 4:19).
- To guide us into all truth by His Spirit (John 16:13).
- That we can hear His Voice and follow Him (John 10:27).
- To never leave us nor forsake us (Deuteronomy 31:6; Hebrews 13:5).
- That He will not allow us to go through more than we can handle, but will provide a way out of every trial, test, and temptation (1 Corinthians 10:13).
- To save us to the uttermost (Hebrews 7:25).
- That we may have and enjoy His Divine nature (2 Peter 1:4).
- His joy to be in us and that our joy will be complete (John 15:11).
- To be faithful to bring our call (assignment) to pass (1 Thessalonians 5:24).

All the promised blessings found throughout Scripture are ours through faith in Christ. The whole counsel of God, in all His promises, is one of liberation from sin which leads to victorious living and a release of His favor with a richer and more abundant life in Christ. The greatest blessing, I believe is the love relationship in communion and intimacy with God Himself: Father, Son and Holy Spirit.

God promised Abraham that He would be his shield and his exceedingly great reward (Genesis 15:1). That promise is ours as well. Indeed, God is our prize; and to know Him and His Son Jesus Christ intimately is eternal life (John 17:3). He promises that in knowing Him we will become like Him; that we are His sons and daughters; that we are his royal priests; that we have been blessed with every spiritual blessing in the heavenly realm in Christ Jesus; that we are seated with Him in the heavenly places; and that we will reign with Him eternally. All of these are promises in Scripture. God, in His trustworthiness to these promises, is refining us so we can experience and walk in all these blessings progressively. He uses every circumstance and situation, good or bad, in order to bring us into conformity to the image of His Son, Jesus (Romans 8:28-29), which is His ultimate purpose in all His promises.

CRUSHING THE OLD SELF–
EMBRACING THE NEW

And those who are Christ's have crucified the flesh
with its passions and desires.
If we live in the Spirit, let us also walk in the Spirit.
Galatians 5:24-25

But God forbid that I should boast except in the
cross of our Lord Jesus Christ,
by whom the world has been crucified to me,
and I to the world.
Galatians 6:14

B efore Christ set me free, I was a slave to sin. Tragically, after
accepting Christ my old sin habits slowly returned back
into my life, causing me again to become a servant to this sin. I
was bound by lust. Thank God I am free of this now because of the
blood of Jesus and His marvelous grace.

The sin of lust resurfaced time and time again in my journey
with Christ. This habitual sin started during early puberty before
I knew Jesus and transitioned into my adult life even after I was

born again, after being filled with Holy Spirit, and after receiving God's call into ministry. I failed my Lord miserably and repeatedly by continuing in this habitual sin of lust through self-gratification and pornography—and how I hated this about myself.

Like so many men this sin drew me into its web of bondage and there was no one to blame except myself and my own sinfulness and desires (James 1:13-15). The subtle allurement of this sin is Satan's attempt to trap anyone. He will use whatever it takes, the lust of the eye, the lust of the flesh, and the pride of life, to draw us away from God and back into the world of sin (1 John 2:15-17). This is what happened to me, and I knew I needed deliverance. So I sought the Lord wholeheartedly. He showed me how this developed in my life by taking me all the way back to the root of the problem. I had experienced rejection and abandonment as a young boy of four or so when my birth mother left my dad in divorce, leaving me and my younger brother with him. I did not see her during childhood, and she played no role in my life. From this abandonment, a void and a deep wound were created in my young, confused heart, and while in my teenage years, and beyond, I was attempting to comfort that wound with whatever made me feel good.

Only God can fill the void to heal a wounded heart. He truly will as we seek Him. But we have to let Him heal us His way. Unfortunately, in our sexually charged society it is acceptable to follow through with sensual desires outside holy matrimony. As Christian disciples we must be vigilant, because Satan attempts to allure us into a sense of false intimacy with pornography, illicit affairs, and all sorts of sexual activities. Outside of marriage, sexual desires acted upon are sinful. Only within the bounds of holy matrimony between one man and one woman is sexual desire pure and holy. God created male and female for this purpose in reveling what intimacy, true spiritual intimacy, involves. Paul, the apostle writes of this mystery of intimacy between a husband and wife as a picture of intimacy between Christ and the church (Ephesians 5:25-33).

After earnestly seeking and being set free, the Lord revealed to me that in cases like mine, a spirit of lust is attempting to destroy by filling this void and wounded heart with sin instead of a mother's love and God's love. I was exposed to this spirit at the age of eight when a teen-aged male relative visited our farm. He took my siblings and me to the barn several times masturbating in front of us and encouraging us to touch ourselves inappropriately. The Spirit of God revealed to me years later that he was bound to this sin as the spirit of lust was on him.

I am not blaming him, my birth mother, or the evil spirit for my personal sin. Nonetheless, being curious and drawn to it, I started this habit of self-gratification at a very early age and continued it well into my adult life. The Lord showed me that every time this sin was acted out by using pornography, I was subconsciously trying to medicate the pain in my wounded heart by filling the void with something that temporarily felt very pleasant, but was very immature, sensual, sinful, and wrong.

As I grew into manhood, I tried to suppress this habit, but these sinful desires would attack me at my weakest moments—especially when alone. No one knew but me (and God). I would fall victim to my own sinfulness, which resulted in an inward loathing of myself and thinking I was unworthy of salvation and particularly of my call from God. Satan's strategy is whatever it takes to get a person to feel separate from their relationship to God and others, to hate their life, to actually blame God, or to blame anyone or anything, and refusing to take personal responsibility by bringing it before the Lord in true repentance. This is exactly why I needed to experience deliverance. Praise God He brought liberation as I took personal responsibility for and repentance from my sin and also submitting myself to my spiritual mentor.

For me this also meant I had to admit this sin of lust to my wife, which was extremely painful, embarrassing, and humiliating. Exposing this sin was really difficult, because it broke her heart and mine while I witnessed her reaction. She felt betrayed, violated as I, with tears and brokenness, confessed my transgressions. Failing the Lord is the worst thing I could have done, but hurting my wife is a very close second, and I truly hurt her. But in order for God to bring healing to her and liberty to me from this sin I had to humble myself to her and be completely honest. I was ashamed of what I had allowed to develop in my life. I was supposed to be a loving and loyal husband, a man of God and yet behaved as if I was not even saved.

The only way to live a life of holiness, to be an effective witness, and to be a minister of the Gospel is to be a pure vessel. The Lord still loved me and spoke to my heart, and His loving chastisements led me to true contrition and a deep inner heart change. However, I knew I needed to be delivered from this habitual sin and could not do it on my own.

Jesus Christ is the Anointed One who sets captives free. I was trapped in a yoke of bondage, captive to sin. I needed the anointing of Holy Spirit to set me free from this bondage of sin (Isaiah 10:27). So how does the anointing of Jesus work? The removal of this sinful desire started with the confession to my Lord and then to my wife. I had fasted; I had made confessions; I had confided in several brothers to be accountable; I had purchased books and even a specific training on how to break this bondage. But I was in a deep hole of my own making with layers of wounds, hurts, and dysfunctional behavior. To be set completely free, I required not only true repentance, but submission to my spiritual mentor, ongoing accountability, and specifically, I needed deliverance from spiritual bondage. God healed my heart and Christ set me free by the anointing in a faithful man of God to activate that deliverance into total freedom; a person who modeled God's love and who carries the anointing of Jesus, operating in great faith. I needed someone who was willing to accept me with all my faults, pray for me and with me, someone who loved me enough to stand with me till the bondage broke. So I was compelled to go to my mentor, a precious, loving man of God who is blessed with the anointing of Holy Spirit in leading others to freedom by the power of God.

I went to him privately and humbly and with vulnerability. I confessed to him. He responded to me with love, grace, and compassion. I acknowledged and activated his loving admonition by renouncing this hidden thing of shame. He prayed, and then laid hands on me to cast off any demonic spiritual influence, breaking any soul ties that I had allowed. Soul ties come into effect because a false intimacy is created with this habitual sin and the imagery of pornography. He did this in the authority of the Name of Jesus and in the power of Holy Spirit. We prayed together and contended for the promise of being set free until I experienced breakthrough, and I did. The anointing of the Spirit of God was released into me and broke the yoke of bondage. In great tears of repentance, crucifying the flesh, and deliverance, I was set free that day. Hallelujah! I am forever free in Christ Jesus, my Lord!

Prone to Wander—Desirous to be Faithful

> For if you live according to the flesh you will die;
> but if by the Spirit you put to death the
> deeds of the body, you will live.
> Romans 8:13-14

There is a powerful story told by Jesus of a prodigal son (Luke 15:11-31). In the immaturity and presumptuousness of his youth, this son demanded his inheritance from his father. Having received it, he went off to a foreign land and squandered it all away, and had reached such a low that he was eating food with pigs to keep from going hungry. He in time came to his senses, realizing even the servants back home had it better, so he decided to return to his father to ask for forgiveness and to become a servant.

The father's love was so strong he had believed for his son's return. He often watched the road for him, and when he saw his son from a distance, he ran and grabbed him in a loving embrace. He put a ring on his finger and a robe upon his shoulders, and then called for the servants to make a feast for his returning son. There was gracious forgiveness in the father's heart for his son's transgressions. Jesus tells this parable to illustrate our Heavenly Father's yearning heart for all His children as they come to Him in repentance for wandering.

In 1758 Robert Robinson wrote the words of the hymn, "Come Thou Fount of Every Blessing" (1975). He penned these words while 22 years old, and even at that young season of life, there was a depth of spiritual maturity that was reflected in his life, in his ministry, and in the hymns he wrote. Consider the original fourth verse in light of the prodigal son's story. Perhaps this is your experience. It was definitely mine:

> O to grace how great a debtor
> Daily I'm constrained to be!
> Let Thy goodness, like a fetter,
> Bind my wandering heart to Thee.
> Prone to wander, Lord, I feel it,
> Prone to leave the God I love;
> Here's my heart, O take and seal it,
> Seal it for Thy courts above.

We are all apt to stray if not careful because apart from Christ, our hearts are sinful and desperately wicked. This proneness to wander often takes place while we are in the crucible of trust. Proneness means disposed to do something or a tendency toward a certain way. Prone to wander means the proclivity to sinful behavior. We must trust God to keep us from wandering, by putting on the Lord Jesus, walking in His Spirit, and standing on His Word. If not, we allow our old sin nature to reappear, manifesting as we wander back into sinful patterns.

But in Christ we have been given a brand new heart. We continually receive Christ's wonderful gift as debtors to His grace, and we must persistently negate the proneness to wander by presenting our bodies to Him as living sacrifices. The song's phrases speak truth in respect to our human condition and the need to present our hearts to God constantly. We are to be living sacrifices, sealed—set apart—for His courts above, while also experiencing the reality of living for Jesus and His eternal Kingdom while here on earth. The members (parts) of our bodies are to be presented to God as instruments of righteousness as we present ourselves to Him as alive from the dead (Romans 6:13). He has given us a new life and our lives are in His hands.

We must be vigilant, or else we will be tempted to stray. Consider the progression found in James 1:14-15. "But each one is tempted when he is drawn away by his own desires and enticed. Then, when desire has conceived, it gives birth to sin; and sin, when it is full-grown, brings forth death." That is why we must be attentive and alert to our own tendencies, which are used by the devil in attempt to trip us up and lead us to destruction (1 Peter 5:8). The devil tries to lure us with our old nature, which we must acknowledge has been crucified with Christ, away from our walk in the Spirit of Christ. That is why we are given the privilege (promise) to reckon our old nature as dead and that we are alive in Christ

(Romans 6:11). We must be vigilant in our faith to put off the old-man tendencies toward sin.

Putting off the Old Man

Since you have put off the old man with his deeds,
and have put on the new man who is renewed in knowledge
according to the image of Him who created him,
Colossians 3:9-11

I used to smoke marijuana. Before being born again I lived for getting high. When I was born again I stopped, but after a time fell right back into the fleshly tendency of smoking pot. It took several years for me to surrender my desire for pot to God. He wanted me to eliminate this habit, because it was detrimental to my spiritual growth. Eventually, I received the grace He was extending to me and made the commitment to stop. I put this old inclination off by realizing the need to deny myself. With grace God led me in the renewing of my mind with His Word, learning to walk in His Spirit. I also sought godly accountability with others. It was not easy, but He truly helped me change my desires as I finally embraced and experienced the fact that He set me absolutely free.

Jesus sets us free from sin so we can live in righteousness, but it takes a committed decision to accept His liberation of our souls, being vigilant and resolute to live for Him. "He breaks the power of canceled sin; He sets the prisoners free" is a very powerful truth from the hymn, "O for a Thousand Tongues to Sing" (1975). That is what happened in my life; His grace is what empowered me to eventually overcome this sin. Christ canceled all our sin with His shed blood and His obedience to go to the cross. Because I had wandered into sin again and again, I needed to let Him set me free by breaking the hold of that sin over my will. He breaks the control of sin over all of us as we deny ourselves and take up our cross in following Him.

Addressing the disposition to wander, Jesus suggested in Matthew 18:8-9 that if your hand offends you, cut it off; if your eye offends you, pluck it out. Of course He did not literally mean to physically abuse our bodies. Jesus' admonition was further expressed years later through Paul the apostle: "Those who are Christ's have crucified the flesh with its passions and desires" (Galatians 5:24). Scripture says that our old man "was crucified with Christ" so that the body of sin is done away with (Romans 6:6), and our part is putting off the old man submitting it to Him.

Because we are in Christ, we are set free spiritually. Now we must learn to appropriate our freedom while we dwell in this flesh. That's why Paul wrote "work out your own salvation in fear and trembling" (Philippians 2:12). Not that we work to earn it, but that we are engaged in the process of cooperation with Holy Spirit in our salvation day by day. We apply ourselves in working with Him to yield in obedience as He is working in us to form Christ.

In light of Jesus' words regarding cutting off our hand, or plucking out our eye, we need to crucify and renounce whatever keeps us from living righteously. Before Jesus set our hearts free, our own deeds were sinful, desperately wicked, needing to be crushed. Though we are free from sin in Christ, we still must be vigilant by regularly and consistently putting to death any sinful deeds of the flesh that try to creep back into our lives and this is done by an act of our will to allow His Spirit to be in control as we cooperate with Him (Romans 8:13-14).

But even in the need to put to death the deeds of the flesh, we are alive in Christ in our spirit man because Jesus died in our stead. Hallelujah! Let us rejoice in the Lord for the new heart and the new mind He gives us in Christ. That's exactly what is provided to all who come to Him in repentance. The crushing, or the crucifying of the flesh is really nothing more than repentance with a vigilance to please God wholeheartedly by resisting the old tendencies.

The condition of the sinner's heart is wicked before Christ enters and dwells there (Jeremiah 17:9). Before our born again experience we were sinners, "For all have sinned and come short of the glory of God" (Romans 3:23). Because we repent from our sins we are born again accepting salvation and God gives us a new heart and a new spirit (Ezekiel 11:19; 36:26). We actually become a new creation in Christ as the old is passed away and all things become new (2 Corinthians 5:17). That is why Jesus came declaring, "You must be born again." Being born again is the activation of His new creation in us.

Jesus went to the cross to provide for our new birth in His Spirit. He offers forgiveness and reconciliation and then reveals the spiritual dynamic of self-denial so we can metaphorically take up our own cross as we follow Him. Taking up our cross literally means to crucify our old self, reckoning ourselves as dead to sin, knowing we were crucified with Him.

The Word of God says those in Christ *have crucified the flesh* with its evil passions. It is quite a mystery but we were crucified with Christ. "I have been crucified with Christ; it is no longer I who live, but Christ lives in me; and the life which I now live in the flesh I live by faith in the Son of God, who loved me and gave Himself for me" (Galatians 2:20). While He was on that cross, we were with Him spiritually. He took our sins upon Himself and identified with our sinful hearts, even though He was pure, spotless and without sin. What is so miraculous is what I call the great exchange; we give Him our hearts and we acknowledge our sins as forgiven, then we receive His pure and spotless life as our own by faith.

Scripture tells us to put off the old self, or old man (Ephesians 4:22; Colossians 2:11; 3:9). The truth is that by the Spirit we must daily put to death—crucify—the deeds of the flesh, which simply means to stop sinning and obey the Lord. To stop sinning means repentance and it is a choice, a commitment, and a discipline. We turn from the old way of sinning, turning to God in faith and believing Him for His help, and then the Spirit of God empowers us with grace and self control to live righteously. Let us all be cautious to present ourselves to God, because if the old-self tendencies to sin are not addressed with faith in the renewal of our minds, by submission to the Holy Spirit, prayer, and godly determination, they will negate new man transformation (Romans 6:1-12; 12:1-2). When we are vigilant in this process God delights to help us become like Christ.

Put another way, when the old sinfulness of self is not dealt with—by self denial and taking up the cross—it will resurface in ways that lead to old sinful patterns, as in my case with lust and smoking pot. This is what the Bible calls the old man, which is the unregenerate soul of each person, male or female, that was dead in sin and now crucified with Christ. I had allowed old-man tendencies to creep back into my life. Even though the old man (outer temporal self) is perishing, the new man is being renewed daily (2 Corinthians 4:16). In effect, the old man is the sin nature. Even though the phrase "sin nature" is not found in the Bible, it is inferred. Since Scripture promises there is a divine nature provided in the giving of a new heart and a new spirit, there must be a sin nature which is in need to be put off or dispelled.

Jeremiah 17:9-10 says regarding the innate sin nature characteristic, "The heart is deceitful above all things, and desperately wicked .Who can know it? I, the LORD, search the heart; I test the mind, even to give every man according to his ways, according to the fruit of his doings." This passage is a brief snapshot of the old nature of sin. In His love for us the Lord searches our hearts so we will realize our need for change. Under His loving examination we experience the crucible of trust as He refines our hearts.

Paul's words to the Galatians are important for us to understand as they refer to the old self in terms of the flesh juxtaposed to the Spirit:

> I say then: Walk in the Spirit, and you shall not fulfill the lust of the flesh. For the flesh lusts against the Spirit and the Spirit against the flesh; and these are contrary to one another, so that you do not do the things that you wish. But if you are led by the Spirit, you are not under the law. Now the works of the flesh are evident, which are: adultery, fornication, uncleanness, lewdness, idolatry, sorcery, hatred, contentions, jealousies, outbursts of wrath, selfish ambitions, dissensions, heresies, envy, murders, drunkenness, revelries, and the like; of which I tell you beforehand, just as I also told you in time past, that those who practice such things will not inherit the kingdom of God (Galatians 5:19-21).

This list is of old nature tendencies written for Christians to avoid, in other words, put off from their lives by walking in the Spirit.

Regarding old self tendencies within disciples, let us properly represent Christ. Even though the behaviors listed above might not be prevalent or filthy language may not flow readily out of some Christian's mouths, what about being overly casual in the use of our precious Lord's Name as it becomes all too easy in saying, "Oh Christ!" or "Oh my God!" when exasperated or under stress? Or how about gossip, backbiting, slander, complaining or grumbling? These are all forms of filthy language in God's eyes. Perhaps we all have sinned in these ways. Will you pray with me? "Oh Lord, lead us to walk in your Spirit and have our tongues baptized in your Holy Spirit and fire and in your love."

We are commanded and given the opportunity to be filled with the Spirit of God. Therefore we must walk in the Spirit so we will not fulfill the lusts of the flesh (Galatians 5:16). Because we dwell in this flesh, we need to continuously seek Holy Spirit's influence over our lives as Ephesians 5:18 encourages. The Greek wording there infers being under His control and literally means "to make replete, to cram, to level up" (Strong). This indicates a continual need of being filled. As disciples of Jesus, we constantly receive grace to activate discipline by yielding to Holy Spirit. This wonderful grace always affords us the ability to deny, renounce, and put off anything of the old that hinders our relationship with God.

Holy Spirit inspired John, Jesus' beloved disciple to write of three areas pertaining to the old self. "Do not love the world or the things in the world. If anyone loves the world, the love of the Father is not in him. For all that is in the world — *the lust of the flesh, the lust of the eyes, and the pride of life* — is not of the Father but is of the world. And the world is passing away, and the lust of it; but he who does the will of God abides forever" (1 John 2:15-17).

Jesus conquered all three of these areas of sin when He was tempted of the devil in the wilderness; He did so by quoting the Word of God, saying, "It is written" and always deferring to the Word of God, not Himself (Matthew 4:1-11). This was His lifestyle and we follow Jesus' pattern and example as His disciples. His victory is ours as we are in Him. Vigilance is necessary in order to stay pure in saying, "It is written" when we are confronted by trials, temptation, or tests. In living by and quoting the Word, we are activating and putting on the new way of life in Christ.

Putting on the New Man

And that you put on the new man
which was created according to God,
in true righteousness and holiness.
Ephesians 4:24

After I was born again I felt brand new inside and wanted that to reflect on the outside. So I decided to buy a new suit. I would wear it to church; when I wore it I really felt sharp. My dad would say to me with a smile, "Son, you really clean up nice." He was proud of me for turning my life around, away from the old man of sin and becoming a new Tom. In Christ I became a new person.

When anyone experiences being born again, they are completely cleansed by the blood of Jesus and experience a sense of vitality. "Repent therefore and be converted, that your sins may be blotted out, so that *times of refreshing* may come from the presence of the Lord" (Acts 3:19). From this new sense of aliveness we enter a life of continuously putting on the new. "Therefore if anyone is in Christ, he is a new creation; old things have passed away; behold all things have become new" (2 Corinthians 5: 17). Off with the old nature, on with the new nature. Oh, what a privilege to put on the new because we really are putting on Christ, the Person of Jesus. We put on His robe of righteousness, His light, His joy, His very nature.

Times of refreshing enter our hearts by the power of Holy Spirit as a gift from our gracious Heavenly Father, who loves to bring us into His joy. In the Old Testament, David wrote, "You will show me the path of life; in Your presence is fullness of joy. At Your right hand are pleasures forevermore" (Psalm 16:11). In the New Testament, our Lord Jesus said, "These things I have spoken to you, that My joy may remain in you, and that your joy may be full" (John 15:11). The Joy of the LORD is truly our strength.

Our God dwells in perpetual joy and by putting on the new man we are afforded an invitation into His joy. Experiencing God's joy is often spontaneous, but at times we need to make joy a choice practicing it with rejoicing and an act of our will. Even though we do not now see the Lord Jesus, we rejoice in Him with unspeakable joy filled with glory (1 Peter 1:8).

What happens when we do not spontaneously experience the joy of the Lord? We find ourselves in the crucible of trust and needing to put on the new man in Christ Jesus to reactivate His joy, to count it all joy as we face every trial or whatever seems to block our joy. By the way, joy is not always only emotional; it is also volitional. Joy leads into the oil of gladness that flows from our hearts. Jesus' joy becomes our experience because—as we are in Him—His Spirit produces the Fruit of joy in our lives.

God is so gracious to His children. Because we have been born again by His Spirit, He dwells in our hearts, and by faith we not only receive from Him, we acknowledge and embrace His presence as absolute fact. Holy Spirit's influence produces fruit within our hearts: love, joy, peace, patience, kindness, goodness, gentleness, faithfulness, and self-control (Galatians 5:22-23). Each one of these wonderful characteristics is interposed and imparted into our hearts and activated because we abide with Jesus. He is the Vine and we are His branches drawing from His life-giving Spirit and the fruit of the Spirit that is produced in us activates His divine nature revealed in our character as we live in Him.

By allowing the fruit of the Spirit to be put into practice in our new nature we reveal we are truly abiding in Him. Because of His goodness and His exceedingly great and precious promises every born again disciple becomes a partaker of His divine nature (2 Peter 1:4). When we are born again, a new DNA—the very DNA of God—is introduced and interposed by grace into the inner essence of our being. And as Jeremiah 31:33 says of the New Covenant, God will put His Law in our hearts and our minds. Then we will instinctively obey by the power of His Spirit from our hearts. Therefore, as we put on the new man in Christ, He initiates change in our hearts so we desire to obey and yearn to please our Heavenly Father.

As we put on the new man in Christ we identify with Jesus' very life. When we are born again we are also instructed to be baptized in water in obedience as well, which is a symbolic act depicting our identification with the death, burial, and resurrection of our Lord Jesus Christ. Baptism symbolizes the washing away of our sins. But it is much more as Romans 6:4 says, "Therefore we were buried with Him through baptism into death, that just as Christ was raised from the dead by the glory of the Father, even so we also should walk in newness of life."

As disciples of Jesus Christ, we are admonished to walk with newness of life, which then becomes a lifestyle change with freshness and newness in decision making, in how we treat others, and living righteously in our every day conduct. We are in a completely new paradigm of living. There is no such thing as instant maturity, but at the same time God's grace influences us to live in accordance with righteousness. We still must put on—daily—this new man as an act of our will. Grace not only saves, but empowers our development and growth toward godly maturity. We are given this newness in righteousness and it cannot to be earned, it is a wonderful gift to be accepted, then becoming our very life.

As we put on the new man of Christ, we also have the added benefit of spiritual warfare weapons. Vigilance is needed at times when putting on and retaining the new man. These weapons are provided for us by grace, mighty through God for pulling down strongholds in the mind, empowering us to cast down every imagination that exalts itself against the knowledge of God, and empowering us to take every thought captive subjecting it to the obedience of Christ (2 Corinthians 10:4-6). The need to take every thought captive is vital, because as we think so we become (Proverbs 23:7). Our spirit, as led by and in cooperation with Holy Spirit, must be ascendant over the old man, which will attempt to reappear at any given provocation. We must be aware of our heart's condition so we may constantly walk as a new man activated by faith.

We are also encouraged to take up the whole armor of God to stand against the wiles of the devil (Ephesians 6:10-18). These truths regarding spiritual warfare involve putting off the old and putting on the new man. Christ is the Greater One that dwells within our hearts, the One initiating our new-man activation. He has made us alive by His Spirit and it is our responsibility to abide in Him, causing us to be vigilant in living out our new man status. We are, after all, children of God; He has provided His Spirit in us and expects us to live accordingly.

Alive unto God

> Likewise you also, reckon yourselves
> to be dead indeed to sin,
> but alive to God in Christ Jesus our Lord.
> Romans 6:11

Praise God! Because we are born again we are raised to life from the death of sin. We have truly passed from death to life in Christ (1 John 3:14). By considering ourselves as dead to sin, we are in a place to be enveloped with the very life of Christ. Romans 6:13 encourages us to actually present ourselves to God as alive from the dead, because when we are in Christ we are alive with His life.

The Father sees us in Christ, so our faith in what Jesus did for us establishes our relationship with Him based upon the life of Christ within our hearts, and establishes our own sense of being alive in Christ Jesus. God has given us new life, and He wants us to know that life is within us, by faith and by experience. While we consider our old selves as dead to sin, our main focus must be the fact that we are indeed alive in Christ. We are in a place where we actually should have no more consciousness of sin (Hebrews 10:2). Instead, we are to live embracing our new life in the power of God that is actively working within (Ephesians 3:20).

Certainly God created all of us for His own good pleasure, but He also desires we enjoy the life He gave us as His dear children. When life hits us in ways that negate this principle, we are in our crucible of trust. The devil attacks us, attempting to pull us back into sinful ways and we are often down on ourselves. God uses these times to stretch our trust in Him. By faith we continually present ourselves to God as alive. Let us not fall prey to being in the middle ground. We either yield to the life of Christ within, trusting we are truly alive as He lives in us, or we allow our old sin nature to live, which leads us to condemnation. Let us choose Christ's life within, not the old sinful life. There can be only one Lord over our lives, and in choosing His Lordship in every circumstance we are alive. We simply present ourselves by faith to Him as a living sacrifice (Romans 12:1). We must be cautious, however, because whatever is not presented to God, Satan will try to fill with sin, disobedience, and dysfunction (Dr. Mark Virkler). But whatever is presented to God becomes a blessing in His wonderful hands; He will fill every area of our lives that are presented to Him with His life. We become vessels filled with His Spirit, well pleasing in His sight, for which He created us, and bringing us into the abundant life Jesus promised, a life of fruitfulness, joy, and purpose.

I had been guilty of not presenting my manhood to God, which led to much pain and disappointment. But in repentance I presented myself to the Lord as alive from the death of this sin. I thank Him for His grace and forgiveness. In my case I tragically allowed my vessel (body) to be filled with sin. I had to learn to possess my vessel, submitting it to Christ in honor and sanctification, which is His will (1 Thessalonians 3:3-5). I am now growing in daily presenting my whole heart to God. I am pure in His sight because of Jesus' blood. In faith I keep presenting myself to Him as alive from the dead. Hallelujah! Will you join me?

BUT AS FOR ME

"But as for me, I trust in You, O LORD;
I say, 'You are my God.'"
Psalm 31:14

Life has its ups and downs. Our own worst enemy is not necessarily Satan but actually ourselves because our flesh is at enmity with the Spirit and the Spirit is at enmity with our flesh (Galatians 5:16-17). However, because of our trust in what Jesus did on the cross, we refute this enmity and nullify its effects. We do so by having faith in what Jesus accomplished on the cross and walking in the Spirit, denying ourselves while abiding in Christ.

We can, nonetheless, occasionally fall victim to sin or disobedience and when this happens our hearts enter into grief because of Holy Spirit's conviction; our conscience brings this to our attention. Unless we repent we will fall victim into a sense of condemnation. Our walk with Christ can be affected deeply. David expressed in Psalm 31:10, "For my life is spent in grief and my years in sighing. My strength fails because of my iniquity." Not repenting or not paying attention to our conscience will lead us to the point of weakness and inability.

To be forgiven by God is a wonderful thing, but we must accept His forgiveness, and forgive ourselves. How many times have we struggled in grief because we have not been able to forgive ourselves? Acknowledging forgiveness and experiencing forgiveness are often two different things. God has forgiven, but for some reason it is difficult to really forgive ourselves. This is where leaning upon our own understanding limits our ability to receive forgiveness, because we have not acknowledged and truly received God's marvelous grace. He sees our condition and in His mercy He truly forgives. What we must do is get to that place that David experienced when he processed forgiveness in His relationship with God. After writing of his life spent in grief and his strength failing due to iniquity, David wrote, "But as for me, I trust in you O LORD. I say, You are my God."

God's Word is true, now and forever! Jesus Christ is the Word and He is the Way, the Truth, and the Life for all who come to Him in faith. When we are unable to forgive ourselves, perhaps it is partly from a lack of trust and faith in the truth that Jesus Christ died on Calvary for *all* our sins, past, present, and future. Satan's lies of condemnation also can lead us to not forgive ourselves. This inability to forgive oneself could also be attributed to a lack of forgiveness in our hearts toward another. Jesus taught us that in order to experience His forgiveness, we must forgive others (Matthew 6:14-15).

Additionally, the inability to forgive ourselves also might come from a lack of true abiding in Him. In our place of abiding we are to learn to acknowledge His righteousness as our own righteous standing with the Father. How we perceive ourselves after we have been forgiven is directly related to the depth of our abiding in Christ. Do we see ourselves as righteous "in Christ" or do we see ourselves as a no-good sinner? Before being born again we were sinners, but now we are born by His Spirit; we are children of

God. Our sins and our lawless deeds He remembers no more. A spiritual truth is that our identities are as saints who do not have a lifestyle of sin but occasionally transgress. And when we do, we repent, because we have an advocate with the Father, Jesus Christ the Righteous One, who saves us to the uttermost.

Additionally, all too often self condemnation arises from the futility of trying to please God in our own strength. This leads to what has been labeled as the cycle of regret, which is harmful to our spiritual growth. This cycle goes something like this: we fall victim to sin; we ask for forgiveness; we acknowledge we are forgiven; we attempt to do the right things in repentance; we accomplish a certain level of doing right; then life and circumstances unfold; we get distracted spiritually; we compromise in small areas which escalate until we are in the same mess we were in before, maybe worse; we repent another time; we promise God we will never sin in this way again. And so this cycle is repeated as we transgress and repent again and again.

I have been in this whirlwind of regret more than I care to admit. Most of us have been on this whirlwind if we are truly honest with ourselves. A whirlwind of regret is certainly due to repeated sins with a lack of true repentance, but it also can become a spiritual attack from the enemy of our souls targeted at sins already atoned for by the blood of Jesus, and particularly to get us to feel condemned. Our attempts to please God in our own ability or from this place of condemnation will always end in frustration. But God is seeking our humble willingness to believe and trust Him.

In Matthew 9:17-25 there is story of the man whose son was demonized. Jesus said to this father, "If you can believe, all things are possible to him who believes." The response of this desperate man rings true for every one of us at one time or another, "Lord, I believe; help my unbelief." How many times have we cried out in this same desperation? Andrew Murray said in his classic book, *Absolute Surrender*, "Lord, I am willing that Thou would make me willing." In willingness and humility we entrust ourselves to the Lord, with all our faults; He deals with our faults and us, with love and grace to transform us to be more like Him in righteousness.

God is always ready to forgive all who repent. Then why do we not *feel* forgiven? Intellectually, we believe the Word of God which says if we confess our sins He is faithful and just to forgive us (1 John 1:9). But it needs to go deeper so we trust and believe Him from our hearts that we are cleansed of all unrighteousness. "For He made Him who knew no sin to be sin for us, that we might become the righteousness of God in Him" (2 Corinthians 5:21). There's always hope in Jesus Christ, a much better, more preferable choice than the cycle of regret.

The Cycle of Trust

Draw near to God and He will draw near to you.
Cleanse your hands, you sinners;
and purify your hearts, you double-minded.
James 4:8

Let us draw near with a true heart
in full assurance of faith,
having our hearts sprinkled from an evil conscience
and our bodies washed with pure water.
Hebrews 10:22

The antidote to the cycle of regret is found in the above Scriptures (and many others). We are invited by the Father Himself to continuously draw near to Him, and to what I call the cycle of trust. What a precious invitation from our loving Heavenly Father as

He compels us to draw near. Willingly we come to God in faith and trust, finding His gracious acceptance. We come boldly, yet reverently in repentance as we cleanse our hands and purify our hearts by accepting that the blood of Jesus cleanses us of our sins. The goodness and kindness of God leads to true, heartfelt repentance (Romans 2:4). Let us all get to a place where our repentance is based on trusting God's goodness, not on trying to do better. Of course we must confess and turn from our sinful actions, but we must refrain from beating ourselves up mentally and emotionally when we feel self-loathing over mistakes. Satan hates our right standing in Christ and attempts to minimize, hinder, or negate our righteousness in Christ. Instead we embrace God's delight in giving mercy and experience His forgiveness, acceptance and receive His righteousness as our own by faith, then in growth and maturity, we learn to trust Him.

Taking faith to the deeper level of trust is first based upon His love for us and then our love for Him. We allow our trust in His goodness to become our lifestyle, but our righteous standing with God is based on what Jesus did on the cross, not upon our behavior or in keeping the Ten Commandments, or the Law of the Old Testament. Yes, we do try to obey them, but not in our own strength. The Law is actually there as sort of a protective net or a standard, but we know in our hearts we cannot measure up to that standard on our own. Our part is to trust in God that we might "be found in Him, not having my [our] own righteousness, which is from the law, but that which is through faith in Christ, the righteousness which is from God by faith" (Philippians 3:9). Theologically and Scripturally, we are righteous based on our faith in Christ's finished work on the cross. The solution for not realizing and accepting forgiveness is to be found in complete trust in God, true heart-level repentance, and continually presenting ourselves to Him. We humbly draw near to God and keep drawing near to Him, regardless of mistakes, and He will draw near to us (James 4:8).

Jesus compels all of us to come to Him when we are weary and heavy burdened so we will find rest for our souls (Matthew 11:28-30). He did not qualify this as a onetime event. This invitation is constantly available and should be our first response during all of life's many challenges. In our humanity we cycle in many ways. But our spiritual cycle should always be to draw near to God who actually is inside us in the Person of Holy Spirit. We draw near to God by acknowledging and being cognizant of His presence. As one draws near to God with humility and contrition, an intimacy is activated with an honoring of Him, and He honors those who honor Him (1 Samuel 2:30). Does being in a cycle of regret honor God? I do not think so, because it does not lead to true repentance. But the cycle of trust honors God, and it becomes a paradigm of abiding and constantly drawing nearer as our default demeanor and behavior. We are actually being raised up in Him, because our direction in the cycle of trust becomes upward toward Him as we trust continually.

However, when we find ourselves caught in the ugly spiral of the cycle of regret, we are actually drifting away from the Lord. God does not want us to remain in an attitude of regret, but desires that we walk in His Spirit, activating His righteousness by faith in our lifestyle. When we continually practice the cycle of trust, we draw near to the Lord, even when we feel unworthy due to sin. We are invited to approach our Heavenly Father with confidence. "Let us therefore come boldly to the throne of grace that we may obtain mercy and find grace to help in time of need." (Hebrews 4:16). This is true repentance with grace in action, and it is Good News. Jesus accepts and forgives sinners, making them into saints. He was accused of being a friend to sinners (Luke 7:34). He was then, and He still is a friend to all sinners, drawing us into repentance and into relationship, leading us to this wonderful cycle of trust which draws us into a cycle of righteousness and sanctification.

Forgiving Ourselves

Sanctification is the ongoing progress of making us holy. In holiness we must grasp forgiveness God gives us and learn to forgive ourselves. Forgiving self involves realizing God's love is unconditional. We cannot do better or worse to increase His love. Because He loves us, we are to love ourselves (Matthew 22:39). The proper love we have for ourselves is not narcissistic or selfish, but because we are made in God's image. We all have sinned, falling short of His glory, and when we are born again we become new creations in Christ, children of God. He began the good work of transformation when we were saved and He completes what He starts. This is what the Word of God teaches, and applying these truths to our understanding in how we are to love ourselves brings proper perspective. We have faith in God's Word that says He loves us, so that we can love and forgive ourselves in the healthy way His Word describes.

However, it is vitally important that we confess our sins and repent from them by turning to God. Otherwise we will experience the heaviness of our sin and we will feel like we're under condemnation, which leads to the cycle of regret and the inability to forgive ourselves. But there is no condemnation in Christ if we walk according to His Spirit (Romans 8:1). Walking in the Spirit means abiding, which include heart surrender and intimacy, with an ongoing progression of becoming holy even as God is Holy.

In light of this, consider what David expresses in Psalm 32:1-5:

> Blessed is he whose transgression is forgiven,
> whose sin is covered. Blessed is the man to whom

the LORD does not impute iniquity, and in whose spirit there is no deceit. *When I kept silent, my bones grew old through my groaning all the day long. For day and night Your hand was heavy upon me; My vitality was turned into the drought of summer.* Selah. I acknowledged my sin to You, and my iniquity I have not hidden. I said, 'I will confess my transgressions to the LORD.' And You forgave the iniquity of my sin.

From the above passage it is obvious that David went for a period of time before he confessed his sin to God. Haven't we all done this? When he did finally admit his sins God released forgiveness and freedom to him. Because David experienced God's mercy, he learned to trust the Lord and declare his trust. We can also experience the same thing.

In Psalm 86:1-5 David again reiterates trust:

Bow down Your ear, O LORD; hear me, for I am poor and needy. Preserve my life, *for I am holy*; You are my God; *Save Your servant who trusts in You!* Be merciful to me, O Lord. For I cry to You all day long. Rejoice the soul of Your servant, For to You, O Lord, I lift up my soul. For You, Lord, are good, and ready to forgive, and abundant in mercy to all those who call upon You.

Notice David understood he was holy, that he acknowledged God and trusted Him. He knew his trust in God set him apart. The cycle of trust really is a lifestyle of trust in God and sets us apart, especially during trials.

David experienced many troubles and attacks on his soul, some of his own making that attempted to undermine his trust in God. The same is true for you and me. Difficulty comes from many fronts that attempt to distract us from God's trustworthiness. They are attacks upon the heart to weaken our trust so we will not embrace forgiveness.

These attacks on our heart target our soul. God's intent is the salvation of our soul and Satan's intent is its condemnation. Our soul is made up of our mind, will, and emotions. Scripturally, our heart is considered the center of our being. The heart and soul are so interrelated it is difficult to distinguish, but I believe there is a subtle difference. The heart acts like a conduit between our soul and our spirit. Our spirit can receive from God's Spirit, and these truths are transferred through our heart into our soul. In this way understanding and wisdom come from God. However, our soul can affect our heart and, in turn, affect our spirit's ability to hear from God's Spirit. It is from our heart that we trust God (Proverbs 3:5-6). It is from the heart we also doubt due to the soul's influences.

Our unregenerate mind (soul) rationalizes and reasons while seeking its own understanding. This is where we find difficulty, not only in forgiving ourselves, but in many other areas of our spirituality. But the renewed mind, which comes from meditation upon God's Word, when we present our minds to Him and abide with Him, is activated by Holy Spirit. Faith arises in our hearts from hearing the Word of God (Romans 10:17). The end result of faith is the salvation of our soul (1 Peter 1:9). Trust is what arises from our faith, which pleases God, and trust always leads to intimacy with God.

Scriptures delineate a distinction between body, soul and spirit (1 Thessalonians 5:23; Hebrews 4:12). Jesus said in the Garden of Gethsemane on the night before His crucifixion, "My soul is exceedingly sorrowful, even to death. Stay here and watch with Me"

(Matthew 26:38). When this passion came upon Jesus, He was a man of sorrows and acquainted with grief (Isaiah 53:3). These were experienced in His soul, but Jesus trusted the Father. For Jesus the cycle of trust was perpetual abiding with the Father, even when He felt in His soul that God was forsaking Him. He cried out from the cross, "My God, My God, why hast thou forsaken Me?" He also cried out to the Father, "Into your hands I commit my spirit" (Luke 23:46).

Jesus was quoting David from Psalm 31:5. I have cried out this same phrase many times to God when seeking grace in order to take up my own cross in following Jesus. While Jesus' body hung on that cross dying for my sins and yours, His soul was grief-stricken. He identified with the sorrows of all humanity and their separation from God due to sin, taking upon Himself that separation along with all the sins of the world. He bore in His body the punishment for our sin and the chastisement of our peace. He embraced all sorrow, pain, and sickness in His body and His soul so we could be set free from them and be comforted (Isaiah 53:3-5). Jesus faced the *ultimate crucible of trust* in going to the cross for the sins of all humanity. He was sinless, but on the cross He became sin for our sakes (2 Corinthians 5:21). He is the atonement and the propitiation (meaning it is enough to satisfy God) for all sin, past, present, and future. Because of His willingness to take our punishment, we can face anything now. How can we not forgive ourselves when we consider all He did for us? Jesus paid for forgiveness of sins. How can we not praise Him in adoration and worship?

Times of Refreshing

Repent therefore and be converted,
that your sins may be blotted out,
so that times of refreshing may come
from the presence of the Lord,
Acts 3:19-20

For several years I have traveled to New Orleans during Mardi Gras—with a group called, No Greater Love Ministries—for a five day mission trip. The objective of our trip is to reach out in love to any and all on the streets who will listen to our witness about Jesus Christ. Our base camp is in the gym and kitchen area of a local Baptist church. We meet as a large group for worship, exhortation and instructions throughout our stay. Then leadership assigns us to groups of 6 or 7 men. Our strategy involves getting on a bus traveling to the French Quarter of New Orleans. We then disperse with our small groups to pass out Gospel tracks to engage in conversations, do some street preaching, and some clown skits that lead into asking what it takes to become a Christian. Most people really like the clown skits. And our motive is love, for Jesus first, and then love for those who need the Lord.

Several other organizations of God's well-meaning people also go to witness during Mardi Gras with different ways to witness. They carry signs that say, "Turn or Burn," "Repent or go to hell." Some have bull horns or miniature PA systems with some very fiery preaching targeting the crowd about its sinful behavior. Their zeal is commendable. I agree with their message, but not in the way they convey it. Scripture expresses that God calls us as His ambassadors of Christ, to be ministers of reconciliation, not condemnation (2 Corinthians 5:18-19). Jesus Christ loves sinners, and so should we. Our heart attitude should always be of a redemptive nature, seeing people through the eyes of the cross. Encouraging repentance is better served with the truth spoken in love and acceptance when attempting to lead someone to Christ. The emphasis of repentance is to turn away from sin and selfishness and turn to Jesus. Doing so always brings times of refreshing and newness of life. In other words, I believe the main focus of repentance is to be on Jesus Christ, turning to Him and His love, mercy, grace, and forgiveness. We must mention our sin and hell in our message, but not overly focus upon them. Mercy triumphs over judgment (James 2:13).

When Jesus first came onto the scene, He proclaimed, "Repent, for the Kingdom of God is at hand." Three and a half years later Jesus died on the cross for our sins and He rose from the grave for our justification. Fifty days later, and shortly after the Day of Pentecost, Peter exclaims, "Repent therefore and be converted, that your sins may be blotted out, so that times of refreshing may come from the presence of the Lord" (Acts 3:19). True repentance always brings refreshing into the human heart. As people who lead others into true repentance, we should have a heart that loves others, one that senses the Lord's goodness and extends His gentle and loving invitation. Our job is to tell the Good News of forgiveness. It is the Gospel that is the power of God unto salvation. Conviction of sin is the job of Holy Spirit, leading people to true, heart change and repentance, which will result when the message is given with love. There are times when a holy fear of God touches the heart, but ultimately it is His goodness, grace, and mercy that affects our hearts toward change: "Or do you despise the riches of His goodness, forbearance, and longsuffering, not knowing that the goodness of God leads you to repentance?" (Romans 2:4-5).

We come to Jesus in repentance. His grace then encourages us to *learn* that we must desire, with an act of our will, to deny ourselves, to take up our cross and follow Him; then He provides the grace to empower this desire into reality. We then must learn to rely upon His Spirit to help us. The cycle of trust is our response to Jesus' invitation to a lifestyle of repentance and refreshing. "Come to Me, all you who labor and are heavy laden, and I will give you rest. Take My yoke upon you and learn from Me, for I am gentle and lowly in heart, and you will find rest for your souls. For My yoke is easy and My burden is light" (Matthew 11:28-30). Jesus truly desires more than just our approach to Him; He desires our trust, our intimacy, and our hearts in relationship abiding with Him and in Him. Taking His yoke is an ongoing proposition which involves being in the cycle of trust in true repentance, liberating and revitalizing to our souls.

Spiritual DNA

When we experience the revitalizing refreshment of repentance, there is another very important principle. We must avoid toxic relationships with others because people are like elevators, taking us up or taking us down. There is a very practical aspect that is vital if we are to stay in the cycle of trust and true repentance: be careful who you hang around with and with whom you allow to influence you. "Do not be deceived; evil company corrupts good habits" (1 Corinthians 15:33). The truth is that we really are influenced by others, and spending time with those who do not edify our faith can eventually lead us to sin and the cycle of regret all over again.

Everyone has a spiritual DNA, whether of being a child of God with deep abiding faith, no faith, or many varying degrees in between. We must be attentive when listening to and spending time with others—so we can discern their faith, wisdom, understanding, or their doubts, fears, and unbelief. Their words reveal their hearts. Jesus said out of the abundance of the heart, the mouth will speak and that we can know others by their fruit.

When we affiliate with those who are upright and wise we are influenced correctly. "He who walks with wise men will be wise, But the companion of fools will be destroyed" (Proverbs 13:20). I pray that God will help us find spiritually wise companions and mentors. Submit to them; spend time with them; interact with them. Scripture encourages submission unto one another in the Body of Christ. There is an element of equity at the foot of the cross, yet wisdom says to submit to someone more mature who models discipleship and true Christ-likeness (Hebrews 6:12). We become like those with whom we affiliate and spend time. Spending time with faithful, mature people enhances the cycle of trust.

As we walk with Christ, we recognize the need to change, which comes from the Spirit of God in leading our hearts toward transformation into the image of Christ. But we also recognize there is no such thing as instant maturity. His Grace is what empowers this change, leading us into the healthy cycle of trust, initiating incremental changes each and every day. Being drawn into this cycle by love and God's goodness is truly what discipleship is all about. Then, in turn, our behaviors change because our choices are now in line with His Word, His love for us, and our love for Him. That is true repentance from the heart. Then, in faith we confess to God any sins that creep back into our lives as Holy Spirit brings loving conviction, being remorseful in our heart over them. Repentance means humbly turning to the Lord and turning away from sinful attitudes and behaviors. Repentance truly brings renewal and times of refreshing that come from the presence of the Lord (Acts 3:19). He is the One who brings that delight and refreshment into our hearts. Due to our repentance, He restores our souls.

Because we are in Christ, we are sons of our Heavenly Father. He works with us as sons because we now have His nature (DNA). As our Father, His Word is to be our Guide and His Spirit is our teacher. His desire is for us to always turn in His direction in every aspect of our lives. Proverbs 1:23 speaks of repentance in this way. "Turn at my rebuke; surely I will pour out my spirit on you; I will make my words known to you." His rebuke is nothing else but His loving conviction upon our hearts to turn from that which harms us. Repentance is a good word. To trustfully turn at His loving rebuke is to please Him. He will pour out His Spirit of love and acceptance upon us. He will make known to us His thoughts of grace and mercy with His acceptance of us—making us righteous in His sight. Holy Spirit empowers us to live righteously. This is truly the grace of the Lord working in our lives. In experiencing His grace, with His nature as our own, we will certainly learn to trust Him all the more.

RIGHTEOUS CONSCIOUSNESS
VERSUS SIN CONSCIOUSNESS

For the worshippers once purified,
would have had no more consciousness of sins.
Hebrews 10:2

When trapped in sin and bondage, I was constantly aware of my sinfulness. I would act out in sinful behaviors, and then my whole focus for days would be my own desperate and sinful condition. I was overly sin conscious with a wounded heart, not realizing God had provided for me to become righteous, cleansed, and healed by the blood of Jesus. Even as I had confessed the sin, I simply needed to accept by faith what God offered and to acknowledge and embrace His love, acceptance, forgiveness, deliverance, and healing.

We are forgiven and healed by what He did on the cross and by accepting His forgiveness and healing in simple, child-like faith—trusting that righteousness comes only through the blood of Jesus. We must come to realize that our own consciousness of sin should *only* be to acknowledge it before God so that we can experience godly sorrow, which leads to repentance and times of refreshing—acquiring a righteousness consciousness over a sin consciousness. Excessive consciousness of our sin leads to guilt and condemnation, becoming an obsession.

Dietrich Bonheoffer, a pastor during the Nazi regime said, "Guilt is an idol; but when we dare to live as forgiven men and women, we join the wounded healers and draw closer to Jesus" (Manning 2015, 12). Guilt leads to self-condemnation which only leads to that dysfunctional cycle of regret, because its only focus is upon self, becoming an idol. But God would have us "dare to live as forgiven." This is not pride; it is true righteousness based on faith.

God is merciful, gracious, and forgiving. When by faith and trust we get over our guilt, apprehending forgiveness of ourselves from God, then in our pardon we experience healing, refreshing, and restoration. As we are willing, God's Spirit enables and empowers us to help others because we are now free of our own pain. In Christ we are clean and pure, reconciled unto God, and as we embrace our restoration a desire comes to bring the same to others. Our own deliverance then becomes His invitation for us to become His ministers of reconciliation (2 Corinthians 5:18-19). We do this from a sense of wounded forgiveness, drawing ever closer to Jesus, compelled by compassion to help others get free from their sin and woundedness, just as we got free from ours. This is the way of redemption, not earning it, but willingly answering the Lord's invitation to be co-laborers with God, who chooses and uses wounded healers.

Wounded healers were once wounded and in need of healing themselves before they can become ministers of reconciliation. For many of us, whether in our wounded condition, or in attempt to be forgiven, we sought God out of our heart's pain, but our minds were still mainly focused on the wounds, or the sin, feeling guilty. Instead of identifying with God's mercy, grace, and forgiveness, we identified with sin and woundedness.

This wrong focus comes from leaning on our own understanding and very often can be attributed to an attack from evil and deceptive spirits. These evil spirits are always reminding us of the wounds or sins of which we are already healed and forgiven. Their objective is to kill, steal, and destroy our lives in any way they can, and to keep our focus on our wounds or an offense or whatever draws us away from God's redemptive power.

The answer lies in coming to Jesus, and abiding with Him, recognizing that He is the source of healing and forgiveness. As we accept by faith His salvation and forgiveness, we are healed and restored. Our part is to also submit to and allow Holy Spirit to lead us in working through the pain. When we repent of and confess our sins, we are forgiven: however, some *healings* of the heart are instant and some take a little more time. What God promises initially He will eventually bring to pass in our lives. Our God is our Healer.

Satan, on the other hand is called the accuser of the brethren. And according to Scripture he and his minion demons have been cast down from heaven (Revelation 12:10). He attempts to accuse us continuously through demonic influences on the mind and heart as an attack upon our righteous standing in Christ. Due to a wrong focus we can believe and fall victim to Satan's accusations. We then digress spiritually into having a consciousness of sin rather than a consciousness of righteousness (Hebrews 10:2). And this very often comes from having an unhealed wounded heart. Through the atonement, based upon what Jesus accomplished on the cross, our wounds are healed and our sins are totally forgiven.

To concentrate upon the sin and not upon God's grace is very detrimental to our soul and spiritual progress, because it negates trust and faith in God by setting our focus on that which is destructive. We are to set our eyes on Jesus, the Author and Finisher of our faith (Hebrews 12:2). When our focus is on ourselves, we begin to think we are unworthy. But with our focus upon Jesus, we will not become weary; we will be more than able to overcome.

Often we need to be accountable to God for sins. We might need to make restitution like Zacchaeus modeled in Luke 19:1-8, who gave half his wealth to the poor and agreed to pay back four times the amount to those whom he had defrauded. God will lead and empower us by grace if we need to do something of this nature. But in our repentance and confession, we are clean and pure by the blood of Jesus Christ. In and of ourselves we know that we are not worthy. But "in Christ" we are clean and pure. He makes us righteous with His worthiness transferred to us by faith. God remembers our sins and lawless deeds no more (Hebrews 10:17). He cancels the certificate of debt, having nailed it to the cross (Colossians 2:14). Therefore, we must not have consciousness of sin, but of His righteousness in us based on faith in Him.

Work Out What God Is Working In

Scripture says to, "work out your own salvation in fear and trembling; for God is at work to will and to do according to His own pleasure" (Philippians 2:12-13). So just what is God's good pleasure? Is it not our transformation into the very image of His dear Son, Jesus Christ? He desires sons and daughters. He makes all things new in our lives as we allow Him to work in us based upon His love and intimacy toward us, which leads us to trust Him.

Our Heavenly Father is the Master Potter; we are the clay. He shapes us into vessels of honor for His glory. Working out our salvation is actually the journey of trust as we cooperate with Him, yielding to His loving work in our hearts, submitting to His required adjustments in our lives, as He supplies grace, which He always will. This is all part of the cycle of trust.

King David's life modeled this truth as he learned to process God's mercy into his own soul as well. He sought the Lord in his yearning to know Him: "One thing I have desired of the LORD, that will I seek: That I may dwell in the house of the LORD all the days of my life, to behold the beauty of the LORD, and to inquire in His temple" (Psalm 27:4).

David longed for the Lord and he continually kept his focus upon the Lord. "I have set the LORD always before me. Because He is at my right hand I shall not be moved" (Psalm 16:8). Consider also David's words from Psalm 17:15 in light of having set the Lord before him and of beholding the beauty of the Lord. "As for me, I will see Your face in righteousness; I shall be satisfied when I awake in Your likeness."

Apostle Paul wrote of this same truth in 2 Corinthians 3:18: "But we all, with unveiled face, beholding as in a mirror the glory of the Lord, are being transformed into the same image from glory to glory, just as by the Spirit of the Lord." Like David, we seek the face of the Lord, looking for Him, embracing His forgiveness, drawing near to His heart, becoming like Him as we are transformed in righteousness into His image.

I believe David began to understand that God's love for him as a person overshadowed God's demand to punish him due to sin. As we are in Christ, our understanding is to be the same. Yes, we must repent from sin, but God does not hold our sinfulness against us because Jesus shed His blood on the cross on our behalf. Our focus should always be toward God's marvelous grace and mercy. Micah 7:18 says, "God delights in mercy." James, Jesus' brother, also writes, "Mercy triumphs over judgment" (James 2:13). David's trust in God drew him to embrace and accept God's mercy and forgiveness. "Be merciful to me, O Lord, for I cry to You all day long. Rejoice the soul of Your servant, for to You, O Lord, I lift up my soul. For You, Lord, are good, and ready to forgive, and abundant in mercy to all those who call upon You" (Psalm 86:3-5). David's relationship with God was obviously intimate and personal. Our Father desires we enjoy the same. The truth is that God is always ready to forgive and cooperate with us to work out His righteousness as He is working it into our hearts.

Even in knowing all of this, I personally, on occasion, feel like saying, "Lord I trust you; help though my lack of trust." Perhaps for many of us, our trust level is shallow at times. Let us trust the Lord to grow our faith and increase its measure, from faith to faith (Romans 1:17). Therefore we must be open and honest, trusting God from our hearts in a lifestyle of repentance and in our journey of trust working out our salvation into deeper trust.

The beginning of repentance takes place as conviction in the heart, leading to confession of sins to God. The message of John the Baptist was to repent for the remission of sins, and Jesus preached repentance because the Kingdom of God was at hand. Peter proclaimed repentance to receive the gift of Holy Spirit and also times of refreshing from the Lord, and that our sins will be blotted out (Acts 2:38; 3:19).

True repentance is integral in our journey of trust and in our transformation as God is working His righteousness within us. We are imputed with His righteousness by faith. We repent by being gut-level honest with God and ourselves, turning away from sin and turning to God with an act of our will. David understood the need for total honesty with God and within himself regarding his sin, and everything else for that matter. God requires truth in our heart, our soul, and our motives (Psalm 51:6). Complete honesty in our hearts is vital in order to truly repent and work out our salvation. Cooperating with God is truly allowing His work to affect our hearts and inner lives toward righteousness and holiness, which will activate the joy of our salvation.

Joyful Living

You love righteousness and hate wickedness.
Therefore God, Your God, has anointed You
With the oil of gladness more than Your companions.
Psalm 45:7

One recent Wednesday night my wife and I attended prayer meeting. We were deeply involved in a time of prayer and intercession, when something wonderful took place. There was a unique release of laughter—deep belly laughter—shortly after someone prayed that the joy of the Lord would be our strength. We could feel the joy of the Lord in this much-needed release. It was not irreverent nor disrespectful, but precious. God was releasing His joy so we would be strengthened, heartened, encouraged and edified in our prayer time. There is true freedom and joy in the presence of the Lord.

We are also involved in another prayer group on Monday evenings. Our vision in this group is to activate a prayer movement. We desire to involve anyone who will join us in agreement before God in seeking for spiritual awakening with the purpose of interceding for leaders, pastors, churches, individuals, and for whatever else we sense from the Spirit. Our practice is to have quiet worship music in the background while we wait on the Spirit. One night we were pressing in with fervent prayer, sensing God's presence very strongly. Then the music shifted, thus the atmosphere, to a mellow but obvious bluegrass feel. The leader who put the music on the CD player is originally from Oklahoma, so someone softly and jokingly commented, "That must be Oklahoma soaking music." This was quite humorous at the time, so when she said it, I started to chuckle as she also was quietly laughing. We had a nice, short laugh together. We then moved on to more serious prayer. After

20 minutes or so, there was a quiet moment, when someone began to chuckle, then I started quietly laughing with the others joining. Then our quiet laughter became more and more intense developing into true belly laughter. We could sense God's presence with the joy of the Lord becoming so strong in the atmosphere we could not help but laugh hysterically. The joy of the Lord truly is our strength, and there are times when we absolutely need to experience His joy in wonderful laughter.

The psalm at the head of this section is also cited in Hebrews 1:9 in reference to our Lord Jesus, the Son of God: He is anointed with the oil of gladness. God's very nature is love and one of perpetual joy and delight, in His children and in Himself. God desires His children walk in His joy, to experience abundant life, and to enjoy the oil of gladness. There should be great joy in knowing God, knowing we are forgiven, knowing He delights in us, and knowing that we will spend eternity with Him. Joy is the second Fruit of the Holy Spirit, which is within us and developed in our lives as we walk in the Spirit. Jesus earnestly desires that His joy is infused in the hearts of all His disciples. Sense the expressed desire of Jesus in His words found in John 15:11. "These things I have spoken to you, that My joy may remain in you, and that your joy may be full." He wants His joy to be sustained within us and He wants our own joy to be made complete in Him.

However, at times when we come before the Lord there can be brokenness and contrition that overwhelms us. We are keenly aware of our sinfulness and unworthiness (apart from Christ) as we sense His holiness and righteousness. Yet His love ever draws us closer. The closer we grow toward God, He draws toward us and the more we grow to realize that while life often seems like a crucible of trust, He desires to reveal more of Himself in each situation. Abiding in Him is truly our Secret Place of trust. This can be a place of perpetual intimacy, joy and delight, and also a precious place of refuge when we are troubled and attacked. God invites and draws us into His joy, while at the same time purifying our hearts, cleaning all the dross of doubt, inward struggles, unbelief, sinfulness, and iniquity. Let us be sensitive to Holy Spirit and resist the tendency to assign ourselves as unworthy during these times, because Jesus earnestly yearns for us to have the oil of gladness He enjoys. He paid the price so we could have His joy.

The devil continually tries to steal our joy by making us feel unworthy in our hearts. But we have repented of sin, so any unworthiness has been crucified with Jesus. Our old nature has been nailed to the cross. We were with Him on that cross, spiritually. We no longer live, but Christ lives in us (Galatians 2:20). God continually makes us not only worthy, but holy. We rejoice that we sense these things, because we know we are new creatures in Christ Jesus. We have been given a new nature—His divine nature—which is love and perpetual joy. Old things have passed away and all things have been made new so we may enter into God's presence with experiencing all His benefits.

Because of the cross, we are now able to approach God in a worthy manner, reverently, respectfully, and joyfully. God wants us to embrace the righteousness of the Lord Jesus, as our own and with joy. Let us embrace these words from Scripture as our own: "O LORD, I will praise You; Though You were angry with me, Your anger is turned away, and You comfort me. Behold, God is my salvation, I will trust and not be afraid; for YAH, the LORD, is my strength and song; He also has become my salvation. Therefore *with joy you will draw water from the wells of salvation*" (Isaiah 12:1-3). Experiencing God's wonderful forgiveness not only cleanses, but it brings great joy in our salvation. David said something very similar many years before. "For His anger is but for a moment, His favor is for life; Weeping may endure for a night, But joy comes in the morning" (Psalm 30:5).

God has translated us out of the night of sin into His wonderful Light of a glorious morning. Jesus is the Bright and Morning Star of our soul. He is the Light and in His Light we have Life. In Christ Jesus, we are like the newness of the morning.

When sorrows of brokenness come upon us, whether because of past sin, a new sin, or trials we face, let us recognize the conviction of Holy Spirit through our intimate relationship with Him. James 1:2 encourages us to count it all joy when trials and temptations come our way. We can do so because we instantly want to repent which leads us to times of refreshing, because we love our Lord. We sense His love and present ourselves to Him.

God takes care of everything in our lives that we allow to be brought into the Light of His grace. (Psalm 138:7-8). As Dr. Mark Virkler teaches, "Whatever is not presented to God, the devil will attempt to fill." But, whatever is presented to Him God will fill, and He will restore, edify, and renew. So we present our minds, wills, and emotions to Him and He will beautify these in His likeness. The cycle of trust always draws us nearer to God and He always draws nearer to us with His joy in our willingness to submit to Him.

David drew near to God during trials and victories, experiencing the cycle and journey of trust. In Psalm 30:11 he writes of his experience, "You have turned for me my mourning into dancing; You have put off my sackcloth and clothed me with gladness." David modeled the cycle of trust.

The joy of the Lord is our strength! We embrace the joy of the Lord in our trust in Him. We rejoice in the Lord always. Joy and gladness are in the Secret Place of the Most High. "You will show me the path of life. In Your presence is fullness of joy. At Your right hand are pleasures forevermore" (Psalms 16:11). Our journey of trust is to be one of joy because His presence is with us and it is ours to enjoy, today and forever.

The Trail of Tears

Let my prayer come before You;
Incline Your ear to my cry.
For my soul is full of troubles,
And my life draws near to the grave.
I am counted with those who go down to the pit;
I am like a man who has no strength,
Psalm 88:2-4

Perhaps one may think it strange to consider a subject like, "The Trail of Tears" immediately after "Joyful Living," but God is always at work to bring us into His joy, even during our times of tears. He is actively busy behind the scenes of life lovingly guiding us into His plans. As we seek Him He will make a way where there seems to be no way.

A personal example is when, in 2006 the Lord led my wife, Robin and I to move to a nearby city, blessing us with a wonderful house. He had promised us this blessing was coming, and He was true to His word. Our new home was quite an upgrade, being much nicer than our previous home, with more space, closer to my place of employment, and to our church's location. After a few weeks' time, I was delighted to discover an access to a local bicycle trail just a short walk from our house. An old railway had been paved into a beautiful, tree-lined path that stretches for miles. Walks on this path became frequent; Robin and I continue to enjoy these, having precious times of fellowship and conversation. There are always birds flying overhead, and squirrels, and chipmunks scurry across the path occasionally. At times, owls hoot, and hawks are often soaring overhead. Much to Robin's chagrin, there are, at times, small snakes resting on the warm asphalt. This trail is also a place I walk or run alone, where a sense of God's presence has became very real, where I can hear His voice. It has become a place of abiding.

However, just after our move I was going through much emotional and spiritual conflict in my life. Ironically, among several other things pertaining to my call from Him, one of my issues was the very house God had blessed us with. I had allowed myself to become frustrated in this different house, being bigger, with more upkeep. I was not truly trusting God. Often I would take long walks alone on that trail crying out to God in conflict of soul. I had actually made it a trail of tears. Honestly, I would angrily yell at God in my aggravation, telling Him what was wrong according to my limited understanding. I neglected to remember His goodness and patience with me, to count it all joy while experiencing different trials and tests. The Lord was very patient with me, even though I was totally wrong and immature. He was actually leading me through, but I had been stubborn and doubtful, not believing or trusting His goodness.

How in the world could I have gotten to a place of being mad at Almighty God? How could I be irritated with my precious Lord Jesus Christ who died for my sins and loves me with an everlasting love? His love passes knowledge (Ephesians 3:19). His tender loving kindness and compassion are always there for me to embrace, while His grace is always sufficient to get me through. There was neglect on my part: taking His grace and goodness for granted, and I'd failed to remember that He delights in mercy, that His plans are to give a future and hope, not calamity (Jeremiah 29:11). My heart neglected to believe and stand upon His promises because I had very little trust. I became a victim to the very immature attitude of complaining and grumbling to Him, not to mention a lack of gratitude for all He had done for me. The joy of the Lord was foreign to me during this season.

It should be obvious why I was in this very dysfunctional place with all the grumbling and ingratitude in my heart. Yet our precious Lord was bringing me through His refining process as I was in this crucible of my own making, and Holy Spirit opened my eyes to finally recognize I was blaming God for something that was totally my own fault. I had disappointments in my life, and I allowed them to be my focus, blinded by my own adolescent handling of my emotions; God was gracious in His dealings with me. As I sought Him with an open heart, He revealed to me that I had allowed myself to fall victim to a deceitful spirit, deluding my heart, influencing my thoughts.

Never negate the power of the enemy of our souls in dispensing lies or anything that exalts itself against the knowledge of God. We must cast down all imaginations that exalt themselves against the knowledge of Christ and take all negative thoughts captive, subjecting them to the obedience of Christ (2 Corinthians 10:4-5). Then activate the mind of Christ by thinking on whatever is true, right, noble, trustworthy and praiseworthy (Philippians 4:8).

Evil spirits have strength (though limited) to influence, but mostly their power is in deception. God will only allow their activity to a point, but He will not permit attacks of trials and temptations beyond what He knows we can handle. He wants us to draw upon Him for help. His purpose in these eventualities is to lead us to repentance on the one hand, but truly He desires we entrust our lives over to Him, whereby we may grow in spiritual discernment and that we become overcomers. He gives grace to conquer every area of our lives in dealing with our mind, will, and emotions and the lies of the enemy. God is leading us in becoming mature sons and daughters tried in the fires of adversity, always triumphant over the wiles and schemes of the devil, and over our own selves in leading us in self-denial by taking up our cross to follow Jesus.

All who are born again by the Spirit of God, all disciples of Jesus Christ, are targets of the enemy to kill, steal, and destroy (John 10:10). Spiritual attacks always seem to come through some avenue of the mind or flesh, whether emotions, thought life, pride, lust, or any number of fleshly characteristics. For me personally, the attack was becoming overly concerned emotionally with the misguided understanding of God's call. Total neglect of my intimate-trust relationship with God was being revealed. The ability to hear the Spirit of God was hindered and clouded by negative emotions and by my own soulish understandings. For the most part, I was only hearing my own inner resounding cries of pain and disappointment. My lack of trust is what initiated those long walks into a trail of tears. I was a spiritual pity puppy in need of change in my attitude; I needed to repent, to grow up, to quit complaining and grumbling to God, and to cooperate with Him in surrender of my will.

Trust God and Stop Complaining

Do all things without grumbling or disputing;
Philippians 2:14 NASB

Dr. Mark Virkler has a great teaching called "How to Have Mountain Moving Faith," in which he makes an imaginative statement as from God to Abram before the promise of a son was realized: "I just want you to trust Me until you die and believe Me and not grumble and not moan." When I read this, I was convicted in my heart and it spoke truth in my immature mind.

Honestly, this truth applies to all of us, even though some are more mature than others, because trusting and grumbling are not compatible on any level. Indeed, to grumble and complain is sinful. Since my attitude led me to sin in this manner, the precious Holy Spirit began to convict me of the futility and harmfulness this was causing in my life by exposing this blind spot. The recognition of these attitude-sins was hindered by my emotions and wrong perspectives. Thank God He opened my eyes and led me to repentance.

In a total shift in my heart, Holy Spirit led me into a habit of speaking God's Word and promises out loud along with truly meditating upon His truths, not my own limited perceptions. This became my daily discipline as I had written out several dozens of promises, reading them out loud, which really began to enhance my faith and trust. At times there is still temptation to complain, but thank God temptation is not sin. How we respond to temptation is what matters. I learned to take my thoughts captive by using and quoting Scripture. What I realize now is that God will always provide a way of escape for any temptation, but I must be open to His Spirit, willing to take responsibility and be a doer of His Word.

The Lord revealed to me that complaining is basically leaning upon our own immature and limited understanding. Proverbs 14:12 says, "There is a way that seems right to a man, But its end is the way of death." When we assume we know and lean upon our own sense of what is right outside of God's ways, we actually enter a downward spiral of spiritual dysfunction—leading to spiritual defeat. When we correctly evaluate life's situations and circumstances according to God's Word we enter His way of life and victory. God's Word—heard and meditated upon—gives light, understanding, and enlightenment (Psalm 119:130). Grumbling and complaining contradict light because they are of darkness. Light is much more preferable.

Much of my complaining toward God was due to being impatient with God and His timing. I thought my call meant pastoral ministry and that seemed a million miles away. I failed to accept that my times were in God's hands, that any invitation or opportunity of entering into ministry was up to His will, not mine. I began to apply 1 Thessalonians 5:23 (NASB) to my thinking and it became one of my many confessions: "Faithful is He who calls you, and He also will bring it to pass." Timing involves embracing God's call, enduring and trusting until He causes things to work in life's circumstances. During this time, God works in our hearts for His good pleasure as He is working in us what is necessary for growth, development, and maturity. Complaining hinders our ability to embrace what God is doing in our hearts due to wrong focus which causes an inability to renew the mind.

Complaining and grumbling build doubt which negate trust, generate inner strife, and create selfishness. Allowing these is devastating to our character, and, more importantly is displeasing to God. Even though the reason for our complaining may have been real, evil spirits are alert to bring it to a spiritual attack; their attempts are to get our focus off God and onto ourselves. This becomes pride. The target of any spiritual assault is the unregenerate mind to get wrong thinking to manifest, which leads to wrong conclusions ending in full delusion.

In my case, my personal dreams had become an ungodly idol in my heart, due to focus upon myself and not on Christ. Because my attention was on self, I wrongfully attributed any disappointment—in the very call from God to be in the ministry—upon God. All this was, of course, my own fault because I had blatant misunderstandings in my heart about God, His refinement of my heart, and His process of preparation for ministry. God was working to renew my mind with the Mind of Christ, to open my heart to take responsibility. Thus my time on that trail began to shift to something wonderful.

Trail of Trust—Path of Light

You enlarged my path under me;
So my feet did not slip.
2 Samuel 22:37

But the path of the just is like the shining sun,
That shines ever brighter unto the perfect day.
Proverbs 4:18

It took some years (yes, sadly, years) of spending many sessions on that trail in crying and complaining, to finally wake up to what I was doing to myself and how I was allowing my heart to be deceived. I had finally learned that complaining is detrimental to any spiritual growth, and devastating to emotional and mental stability. God provides us with His Word and His Spirit so that our hearts can be steadfast by trust in them and Him, and I have now come to a place in my life where my heart-cries to God are less about myself and more about Him and His Kingdom. Jesus is absolutely correct when He says to gain our lives we must lose them for His sake (Matthew 10:39).

My cries to the Lord have also become more about how I may please Him, about my relationship with Him and about how *He feels*, thus my feelings are much more stable. I put into practice what Proverbs 3:5-6 says, trusting Him and acknowledging Him in everything—my emotions, my desires, my aspirations, my life as a disciple of Jesus, and my call from Him for ministry. I have learned that I must activate the cycle of trust over and over again, especially when things seem to be going wrong or not the way I perceive they should be going. I have come to realize that I must be vigilant when tempted to revert back to the trail of tears, which is really the cycle of regret. I absolutely must resist, so I seek the Lord and worship Him constantly. I press in to hear Holy Spirit as He is constantly speaking life and encouragement to all of us.

Now my excursions on the trail have become very precious times with the Lord. I have grown so fond of my times with him there. I commune with Holy Spirit when I walk or run alone. I pray. I sing. I shout praises. I proclaim God's Kingdom. I declare the manifold wisdom of God (Ephesians 3:10). I often get revelations and insights from Holy Spirit as well. I am actually writing right now after a run on the trail because I heard these words in my spirit: "You have turned the trail of tears into your trail of trust." God led me to a wonderful revelation of how this trail had become a place of refuge as I spend time with Him—finally learning deeper trust. The trail of trust has truly become a path of light for me. He will do the same for all of us.

I love to spend time alone with God in the Secret Place listening for His voice. Whether on the trail, driving alone in my car, or when I'm in my study, I enjoy communing with Holy Spirit. If I do not perceive any words from Holy Spirit, I worship the Lord and wait with Him.

As I have told my story in part throughout this book, it should be obvious that I needed loving rebuke. I was a spiritual mess several years ago. But God is absolutely faithful and trustworthy to take me through my own mess and make something good and useful out of this old earthen vessel. We have the Treasure of His

Spirit within our earthen vessels so that any empowerment must be acknowledged as from God and not ourselves (2 Corinthians 4:7). He does this for all His children. "Being confident of this very thing, that He who has begun a good work in you will complete it until the day of Jesus Christ" (Philippians 1:6). God completes what He starts.

God is consistently renewing us and making our lives beautiful. He leads us to change our immaturity and wrong attitudes of the past into maturity with the attitude of Christ as we trust and rely upon His Spirit—today and the rest of our lives. Psalm 149:4 affirms God's intent: "For the LORD takes pleasure in His people; He will beautify the humble with salvation."

In His grace God will often lead us to become more humble than we intend to be. Actually we must live a lifestyle of humility. As God works in the salvation of our soul, transformation is at work bringing beauty from the ashes, making all things new as we put on the new man in Christ (Ephesians 4:22-24). Praise the Lord! All of us can enjoy newness constantly, as God is renewing our inner man daily (2 Corinthians 4:16).

Thank God for His gracious way of bringing us to a place of humbling ourselves. Each day His grace and loving kindness seems to grow sweeter and sweeter. Proverbs 4:18 says, "But the path of the just is like the shining sun, that shines ever brighter unto the perfect day." Shining brighter only comes because of His radiance manifesting inside our spirits exuding outward in our lifestyle in Him. We are to let our lights shine (Matthew 5:16). God has brought us into His light so we may enjoy and extend His light: "For it is the God who commanded light to shine out of darkness, who has shone in our hearts to give the light of the knowledge of the glory of God in the face of Jesus Christ" (2 Corinthians 4:6). He took us out from the darkness of selfishness, grumbling, complaining, and disappointment into His marvelous light of love, compassion, and trust, which only comes from the knowledge of God in the face of Christ.

As we walk on God's path of life, we are growing in grace and an inner joy that cannot be taken away—the joy of the Lord— which is His gift to us in the Fruit of the Spirit in us. Perhaps we can give it up, but we choose His joy. We recognize more clearly that God is absolutely for us and His ways are always best, leading us into His joy. As we walk with the Lord, we experience more of Him as our daily reward. Because as we abide in His love and His Word abides in us, we are truly deepening our trust in Him.

God's purpose for our journey in life is to mature us in the grace and knowledge of Jesus Christ and to establish His Word in our hearts so we (all in the Body of Christ) will manifest His Word upon the earth. Jesus Christ was the Word made flesh, and because we are in Christ He becomes the Word made flesh in our lives. This truly is the path of the righteous and light, to walk with Christ, experiencing His love, redemption, and salvation while also allowing His light to shine through so others may see Him in our lives.

God is perfect and does not change, but He is perfecting us and our perceptions of Him as we change and are conformed into His image. As each of us walks daily on our individual trail of trust, learning to draw from God's Spirit, His radiance shines through us: "They looked to Him and were radiant, and their faces were not ashamed (Psalm 34:5).

SECTION II

THE TRIAL OF TRUST

If there were no night, we would not appreciate the day,
nor could we see the stars and the vastness of the heavens.
We must partake of the bitter with the sweet.
There is a divine purpose in the
adversities we encounter every day.
They prepare, they purge, they purify, and thus they bless.

James E. Faust

REFINING FIRE OF GOD

For our God is a consuming fire.
Hebrews 12:29

My wife is so gracious to me. She blesses me with the freedom to go on an annual golf vacation with a friend. Many years ago while on such a vacation, I had compromised my faith, again falling victim to the sin I mentioned in Chapter Three. I awoke the next morning to these convicting words in my heart: "I made you righteous to live righteous; so be righteous." I was chastised with deep conviction of sin and wept in contrition and repentance. God's reproof was gentle and loving, yet very strong in my heart. I knew I had been lovingly rebuked, but I did not feel condemnation, only the desire to please my Lord and to be clean for Him. The precious grace of God was so clear and obvious that morning.

As I prayed and meditated with Him, the Lord reminded me to put on His righteousness continually, to put on the Lord Jesus Christ (Romans 13:14). We put on Jesus Christ by surrendering ourselves to Him, acknowledging Him as Lord, submitting to His

Lordship and allowing His life to shine through our experiences each moment.

Because we are disciples of Jesus, we must consciously deny ourselves with constant vigilance. God wants to progressively sanctify our hearts, so we must choose, with an act of our will, to separate ourselves from the pulls of the flesh and the world's ways. Sanctification is the ongoing progression toward holiness that comes from being in Christ, surrendering to His refining fires that purify our hearts, and obeying His Word and His voice. This is the only way to walk in victory in His righteousness.

God is called a consuming fire, because He is holy, pure, perfect, and righteous. As we come before Him, as we draw near to him, He becomes like a refiner's fire to our hearts and leads us in the daily renewal of our inner man or our minds (2 Corinthians 2:14). In Christ our spirits are clean and pure, completely righteous in His sight, but in our souls, we are continuously being renewed, regenerated, and revived into His holiness. Scripture says that in Him we are to live and move and have our beings. Our beings exist as a spirit with an outer man of the flesh and an inner man of the soul, or the mind, the will and the emotions. This is the area that is being renewed and sanctified. God is opening our ability to allow Him, by His Spirit, to live and move, and have His being within our hearts, so we may be holy even as He is holy.

Our Father compels us to come before His throne of grace with confidence (Hebrews 4:16). He also desires that we dwell in His presence, but without holiness we cannot (Malachi 3:2; Hebrews 12:27-29). Even as we are considered righteous in Christ, our faith, and our trust have to be tested in God's refining fire. Then, as we consider ourselves as He sees us, we realize the need for change.

God knows our thoughts, the intents, and motives in our hearts (Hebrews 4:12). Yet He has pure and unconditional love for us, loving us just as we are now. Because He loves us so much, however, His desire is for us to enter His holiness by being conformed as His children into fullness, completeness, and maturity in the image of His own Son, Jesus Christ. He delights in us and dotes over us; He also delights in who we are becoming as we grow in His Spirit as His mature sons and daughters. As a small illustration, I loved my sons just as they were as my children. But they were childish and immature at times, and I did not want them to remain this way. So I taught them and led them to grow into manhood and maturity. Our Heavenly Father's eternal plans for us is the same, that we learn likewise by His Spirit, becoming mature, perfect, holy in heart, and soul, growing into the fullness of the measure of the statue of Christ (Romans 8:28-29; Ephesians 4:13-14; Hebrews 6:1-3).

As we meditate upon 2 Corinthians 3:17-18, it reveals what the Spirit of God is doing during this process of putting on Christ, which transpires as we behold Him. "Now the Lord is the Spirit; and where the Spirit of the Lord is, there is liberty. But we all, with unveiled face, beholding as in a mirror the glory of the Lord, are being transformed into the same image from glory to glory, just as by the Spirit of the Lord." We behold Him with the use of our imagination from what we learn of Him in Scripture and by focusing upon Him with faith, and then we grow little by little into His glory. Our Heavenly Father's goodness and His tender loving kindness activate His plans for our inheritance, initiated by His Spirit in us working to transform us through maturity and conformity into the likeness of His Son, Jesus Christ—as He lived as a man on earth and as He is in heaven (1 John 4:17). God sees us as complete already even as we are progressively transforming. During this ongoing process, He sees us as righteous because of the blood of Jesus, and because of His grace He compels and lovingly influences us to choose to live righteously.

The more we look to Jesus, the more we become like Him. The words of Dr. Mark Virkler speak very clearly to illustrate this all-important truth: "What we focus upon grows within; what grows within we become."

As we focus upon Jesus, we grow to be like more like Him, and during this process, and because of this process, we enter into many trials, tests, and temptations. We dwell in these mortal bodies, or our flesh, and Scripture says the flesh is at enmity with the Spirit of God and vice versa (Galatians 5:17). The Spirit's inner presence is transforming us into the image of Jesus, and our flesh often gets in the way, which is why we must crucify the flesh by denying ourselves. The devil hates our transformation, and because of that we actually become his targets. Since we potentially have tendencies to sin, along with the spiritual attacks of the devil, we must present ourselves to God—constantly. Our Father wants us to continually draw near to Him through every circumstance in life, allowing His refinement of our hearts, thus abiding in Him becomes our everyday lifestyle.

Following Jesus and His Example

Then Jesus said to His disciples,
"If anyone desires to come after Me,
let him deny himself, and take up his cross,
and follow Me."
Matthew 16:24

We follow Jesus because His simple, yet profound request compels us to. His infectious love, with His beautiful nature of grace, mercy, and peace, His heart of compassion, and His gentle and meek Spirit are ever calling to us. His disciples, as well as sinners, are drawn to His contagious nature. John particularly, mentions,

"And the Word became flesh and dwelt among us, and we beheld His glory, the glory as of the only begotten of the Father, full of grace and truth" (John 1:14). His grace and His love are so inviting and good for all who come to Him.

Jesus' example was in obeying the Father, by only doing and saying what He saw and heard from the Father and by going to the cross for our sins. He exemplified serving others, not to being served. These examples draw us to love Jesus, to do as He asks, to deny ourselves, and to take up our cross, and to follow Him.

We have been discussing the crucible of trust. One meaning of the word crucible comes from the Latin word, *crux*, "indicating a cross or from a figure of the cross" (Webster, 1828). Jesus was crucified on a cross as payment for the sins of all humanity. Facing that experience as a man—being falsely accused, going through all the pain of scourging and beatings, the crown of thorns forced upon His precious head, and the being nailed to a cross—was the ultimate crucible of trust, especially since He was not guilty of any sin. The Bible says He was tempted in all the same ways we are, yet without sin (Hebrews 4:15). He trusted the Father through these grueling and cruel experiences, even to His death. He truly was the pure and spotless Lamb of God, taking away our sins.

Furthermore, Jesus not only paid for our sins, He took upon Himself all our sins as He was on the cross, which means He took them completely away. He hung there on that cross completely innocent, but as one guilty on our behalf. Isaiah 53:4-6 says:

> Surely He has borne our griefs and carried our sorrows; yet we esteemed Him stricken, smitten by God, and afflicted. But He was wounded for our transgressions, he was bruised for our iniquities; the chastisement for our peace was upon Him, and by His stripes we are healed. All we like sheep have

gone astray; we have turned, every one, to his own way; and the LORD has laid on Him the iniquity of us all.

What an example: "For He made Him who knew no sin to be sin for us, that we might become the righteousness of God in Him" (2 Corinthians 5:21). Even though He was falsely accused, arrested, and forced into His crucifixion, Jesus said that no one takes His life, but that He laid it down willingly for you and me (Matthew 10:17). How can we not praise Him?

Consider Jesus in the Garden of Gethsemane the night before His crucifixion:

And He was withdrawn from them about a stone's throw, and He knelt down and prayed, saying, 'Father, if it is Your will, take this cup away from Me; nevertheless not My will, but Yours, be done.' Then an angel appeared to Him from heaven, strengthening Him. And being in agony, He prayed more earnestly. Then His sweat became like great drops of blood falling down to the ground (Luke 22:41-44).

He knew beforehand that He would be facing the most brutal and heinous death on a cross. He knew it was the Father's will for Him to die for the sins of the world. Yet how could inner turmoil and torment not be in His heart facing this cruel inevitability? In His passion, His sweat was mingled with drops of blood due to the inner anguish of His soul as He cried out to the Father that night. Yet He yielded willingly out of a love that is incomprehensible so all our sins could be forgiven, as He said as He hung on the cross, "Father forgive them for they do not know what they are doing." It bears repeating: Jesus faced the *ultimate* crucible of trust in all that He experienced that night just before the crucifixion and in going to the cross. As He was about to die, He cried out, "Father, into your hands I commit My Spirit." Jesus trusted the Father His whole life and that trust continued on the cross.

In a tiny way, as Jesus' disciples, the proposition is similar as we lay down our lives willingly for Him. Matthew 16:24-25 records,

> Then Jesus said to His disciples, 'If anyone desires to come after Me, let him deny himself, and take up his cross, and follow Me. For whoever desires to save his life will lose it, but whoever loses his life for My sake will find it.'

In obeying Jesus we deny ourselves and take up our cross, identifying with the reason He went to the cross. Because of this we can now reckon ourselves as dead to sin but alive unto God (Romans 6:11). When we obey His instructions, something takes place in our hearts and minds called grace, which not only saves us, but empowers us to live out our faith and convictions. We do so in response to His love as an act of worship, trust, love, and obedience. Yet at times an inner tension is the result of obedience. This is where denial of self should be activated. It is obvious that as Jesus obeyed, He experienced great stress in the Garden of Gethsemane in facing and going to His crucifixion. Obedience is truly a test of our hearts and is part of the experience of refining our faith—as in a fire—as we go through the crucible of trust.

Microsoft Word's internal dictionary, defines crucible as "testing circumstances: a place or set of circumstances where people or things are subjected to forces that test them and often make them change." This meaning actually defines our spiritual lives in Christ and expresses just exactly what God is doing in our hearts to change our inner man, or heart. God uses life's experiences as a crucible to build trust in Him in order to change and to transform His children into the image of Christ—to become sons of God (Galatians 3:26). As disciples, male or female, we are growing as sons. In the eternal Kingdom of God, Jesus said we will be like the angels, not giving and taking in marriage, calling us the "sons of the resurrection" (Luke 20:35-36). As children of God, ladies, we are all sons, and, men, as part of the Body of Christ we are also the Bride of Christ.

A crucible is defined in many modern dictionaries as a metaphor for a severe trial or testing. Whether metaphorically, physically, or spiritually, whatever is in a crucible becomes broken, melted, refined, and/or crushed so impurities are exposed to be removed and the purity of what is desired remains. God desires our faith and our hearts to be pure and holy to the degree that when Christ appears we can stand in His glorious presence (1Peter 1:7; 1 John 3:2; Jude 24). We need wholehearted trust during the purifying and refining process just as Jesus trusted in going to the cross.

Our Father earnestly desires we trust in Him just as Jesus modeled. The reason is because He yearns for our intimacy, an intimacy He, the Son and His Spirit have eternally enjoyed. He created us to enjoy that same fellowship and intimacy with Him in His holiness (John 17:20-23; 1 John 1:3). We are to be sanctified, to become holy in the growing process of ones being set apart. Jesus sanctified Himself so we could also be sanctified. "And for their sakes I sanctify Myself, that they also may be sanctified by the truth" (John 17:19). In sanctification we trust.

As disciples of Jesus, our sanctification involves entering the refining fires of trials, tests, and temptations in faith, which becomes our crucible of trust. God puts us through the process of purifying of our souls, as He works in us to will and to do according to His good pleasure (Philippians 2:13). Just as with Jesus in His trust and love of the Father, so trust is the way the Lord has designed for us to endure this purifying process.

God Builds Character

> But you know his proven character,
> that as a son with his father he
> served with me in the gospel.
> Philippians 2:22

One purpose of the purification of our hearts is the development of our character. The above verse is speaking about Timothy, Paul's young protégé. He was a man who had stood the tests of faithfulness, with integrity, trustworthiness and consistency, which are character traits of godliness—a result of our relationship with Holy Spirit. Paul trusted Timothy completely because he had proven himself as a loyal and faithful companion and fellow minister.

Regarding character, Dr. Bill Hamon (a seasoned and noted leader in the Body of Christ) has a teaching called, "The Ten M's of Ministry" based on years of personal experience and training others. He delineates how ten characteristics of personhood must be in line with God's Word: manhood, ministry, message, maturity, marriage, method, manners, money, morality, and motive. Because these are affected by character, our development in each one specifically affects the way God can use us. Each one of these areas is to be under the scrutiny and management of Holy Spirit, particularly in our cooperation with Him as He is working in our hearts to develop our character in them toward completion in Christ. Our part is in yielding each one to Him.

The godly development of the Ten M's leads us to the foundation of Christlike character. Hamon teaches God builds the character of the man (or woman) before He builds a ministry. God is shaping and forming the disposition of the person into the image of Christ. We are all being fashioned on the Master Potter's wheel of life (Jeremiah 18:1-10). During this process, patience with God and trust in Him are imperative or else frustration results, which is not of faith. We must also be patient with ourselves in this process of becoming complete. As the saying goes, "Rome was not built in a day." Neither is our character.

In my experience, patience with God's process and with myself has not always been easy. God has dealt with my impatience in grace and by putting me through various circumstances causing me to cry out to Him in trust. What I experienced was exactly what I needed to get me to a place of deeper trust. Holy Spirit was (and is) at work perfecting my life, and in all of our lives for God's purpose and call. God continually is working on our manhood\ womanhood along with the other nine of the 10 M's of ministry to bring us to purity of heart and character.

THE DEEP OF GOD'S VOICE

Deep calls unto deep at the noise of Your waterfalls;
All Your waves and billows have gone over me.
Psalm 42:7

God's ways are deep and often mysterious. He speaks through His Word and by His Spirit. He also speaks through various other ways, such as prayer, authorities, and life's circumstances. But mysteriously, He will also speak from silence. His voice sometimes comes to us as inner waterfalls, heard within and often louder than actual words. I have experienced encounters with the Lord in various ways at different times in my journey, but twice He specifically communicated with my heart in life-changing visitations regarding His call upon my life.

The first time was while traveling in my car on the way to work the afternoon shift at the steel mill. It was Sunday, so I had attended church that morning. As I was driving along that day I was silently contemplating the pastor's sermon, when all of a sudden something tremendous took place. An overwhelming sense of God's presence came upon me and I sensed these words reverberating in and through my entire being, "You are my chosen vessel; I have chosen you." I was immediately and literally undone and over-whelmed. I could not stop weeping from a flood of emotions, bro-kenness, and humility. I had to pull over to the side of the road as my tears blurred my sight. God's Spirit seemed to overshadow me completely; I was in awe experiencing the fear of the Lord, but at the same time I also felt such love and acceptance from Him. I felt as if I needed to hide, yet I also desired to draw near to Him. It is difficult to explain, but I know that I was in God's presence in a way I had never experienced before.

This encounter led me to realize God was presenting a call to me. Perhaps many have not experienced this type of encounter, but God reaches out to all of His children individually in a specific way that is pertinent to His call upon their lives. All disciples of Jesus Christ are called by God to become vessels of honor, filled with His Spirit to overflowing to be useful in His Kingdom as His chosen vessels. As vessels of God's Spirit we are to be His witnesses called to share Christ wherever we go. It is our place to acknowledge and heed that call, or we might miss His perfect will.

That day He said to *me*, "You are my chosen vessel." I have drawn from, and been affected by, this encounter ever since. I per-ceived His call was for ministry, to be a pastor or in leadership of some sort, but I was certainly not ready. Even though at the time I was a deacon in the church, and was serving in that capacity to the best of my faith and ability, I was not prepared for His assign-ment upon my life in the near future. I was His chosen vessel in need of change.

To be ready for God's purposes, whatever His call upon our lives may involve, we must be willing to go through the process of being prepared and trained, which always leads to going through the crucible of trust. An old saying is very applicable: "God does not call the qualified; He qualifies the called." I have previously addressed this truth regarding God making the man or woman before He makes a ministry. Being prepared and ready for ministry means growing in becoming like Christ, gaining understanding in the knowledge of God's Word, and how His Spirit works through us as we learn to hear His voice. Preparations also come through the deep of God resting upon and working within our hearts as we grow and mature while trusting Him, no matter what, especially in the crucible of life's experiences

God's voice often comes out of silence, but it is truly communication of the spirit. That day in my car I did not hear an audible voice. What I experienced seemed louder because it shook me to the very core of my being. I did not understand then, but God eventually brought understanding to my heart as I continuously presented this experience back to Him in prayer. I learned He desires trust and faith, that an experience of this type is His invitation to grow, becoming more like Him, to be intimate with Him, and so I could be equipped to touch others in His Name. God initiates the bond of love first, as He reaches out to each one of us, so we will draw ourselves to Him. Truly His invitation to us is, first and foremost, for relationship and intimacy that can only be found as we respond to Him in submission, spending quality time in quiet with Him to learn His ways, and sense and learn His Heart.

Brennan Manning wrote in *The Relentless Tenderness of Jesus* that Jesus is not only the Way, He is also the inner impulse of our journey along the way through life. He refers to the desire for silence and solitude with Jesus as "the gratuitous gift of a gracious God" (2004, 28). The inner impulse is His still small voice. We learn to be alone and quiet with Jesus, and His Spirit draws us continually into intimacy. This is precious because of God's gracious, loving condescendence, which means God graciously comes down to our level in ways we do not deserve and meets us just as we are with love and acceptance, drawing us with His heart of love so we may transcend back with Him as His children. Our cognitive and mental abilities usually can't determine all that God is doing. He will, however, eventually enlighten our understanding. It is the deep of God calling to the deep of our hearts and souls by the Spirit of God.

The second time I experienced the waterfalls of God's depths was also a Sunday, six years later. I had grown spiritually. I had been praying, fasting, and truly seeking the Lord wholeheartedly. His Word was becoming more alive to me each time I read it; His love and grace were touching and impacting my soul. He also had led me to become involved with a prison ministry, reaching out to inmates to preach the Gospel at the jail every other Saturday afternoon. Additionally, for about three months I had been sort of an interim minister at a small church whose pastor had resigned.

That particular Sunday morning I had been in a time of prayer and preparation for the sermon and ministry for the day. While getting ready for church I was brushing my teeth having thoughts of my sermon racing through my mind. Then with toothbrush in hand my mind shifted as I began to consider Almighty God, high and lifted up in all His glory. My thoughts were of worship and honor of Him as I envisioned Him seated upon His throne in splendor and majesty. All of a sudden, just like that day in my car years earlier, I experienced a visitation of the Spirit of God. I was again overwhelmed as toothpaste spewed out from my mouth all over the mirror; emotions flooded my heart and upheavals transpired out of my being. It was as if I was present in that very throne room I had imagined in my heart. These words rang into my spirit, "I have heard your cries. I will give you the desires of your heart; go minister in my Name." Again, I heard no audible voice, but I knew God had spoken. I perceived that He wanted me to become the pastor of that small church. Interestingly, the service that day was much the same, only during the altar call we sang the hymn, Take My Life and Let it Be, with the lyrics, "Here am I; send me

Lord Make my life useful to Thee." There seemed to be an atmosphere of expectancy. That afternoon I got a call from the leadership of the church to meet, which became an invitation to be their pastor. I accepted, truly entering another depth of the crucible of trust that day.

On the Hot Seat

O LORD, You have searched me and known me.
Psalm 139:1

I was now a bi-vocational pastor of a small Baptist church. This was what I had thought was God's reason for my calling, what I had dreamed and desired. For three years I served as pastor while also working full time at the steel mill. Up to that point, it was one of the most challenging, yet fulfilling times of my life. I had so much to learn about pastoral ministry, instead of being an just the interim minister, and God led me to experience many growing pains during this season. I learned to hear His voice regarding sermons, ministry, and service to the church.

At first I was doing pretty well, or so I thought. I sought the Lord in prayer for the leading of the church. I learned early to get on my knees asking the Spirit of God what He desired before I began to prepare for sermons. Additionally, I sought counsel from experienced pastors on a regular basis. God was so gracious in leading me to have relationships with several seasoned men of God who took me under their wings. Their love, counsel, and encouragement were invaluable.

As an inexperienced pastor, I made many mistakes and could write a whole book on those missteps. One in particular came as a result of my lack of mature people-relationship skills. Being a steelworker I would make the mistake of resorting back to approaching people as I would at work. In my naiveté I was not aware of my gruff manners—another blind spot God needed to expose. I was not an unloving man, but my choice of words with others was in dire need of refining.

For example, the leadership agreed that the church needed to run an underground electric line out to our sign on the highway. Of course, as pastor of a small church, very often these types of projects fell to me. The nephew of one of our elderly ladies was gracious to volunteer and bring his trencher. As we worked together the conversation went to his aunt. I said something to the effect that his aunt was a strong-minded woman, which she was. I realized later that my choice of words could unfortunately have been misconstrued. He was not a member of the church and I certainly should have guarded my tongue better. In my heart I meant no disrespect nor was I criticizing her. But I did not realize he heard differently and would embellish my words; he later went to his aunt and told her that I said she was a stubborn old lady who was hard to get along with. I did not say those exact words, but apparently he took them that way.

Before church service that next Sunday this aunt asked to speak to me in my office. She was obviously very upset and proceeded to chew me out very sternly. I smiled sheepishly assuring her I did not actually say those words and apologized, asking her forgiveness for any misunderstanding regarding my words and her nephew's perceptions. As she left I shut the door and literally fell on my face before the Lord in brokenness and repentance. I felt devastated regarding my own lack of judgment and immaturity in speaking about a person. Even though at the time I felt like I had not done wrong, I had spoken out of turn in a manner that was misunderstood, so it was inappropriate for a Christian, or more particularly, for a man of God.

Our Father is very gracious to us when we repent. As I was before Him on my face, I knew I was still responsible to lead the Sunday service. So I got up and went into the sanctuary of the church. I was truly in a crucible of trust, and God provided me with great grace during that service. In my weakened and humbled condition, I felt the strength of the Lord in ministering that day. His Spirit encouraged and empowered me as I preached and led the church service.

Most everyone has been in embarrassing situations, confronted by a well-meaning friend, or even accused and exposed in a wrong doing like in this case. It feels like a hot seat because it is unpleasant, and it is often somewhat embarrassing. None of us like to be called out as wrong nor exposed when attempting to cover it up. Our egos and our humanness are on the carpet, under the spotlight. Experiences of this type truly reveal our attitude and character, whether on the hot seat or just going through life's struggles. Faith and trust, along with our character are either revealed, or the lack of them is exposed during trials and temptations.

Faith comes by hearing and hearing by the Word of God, while trust originates from the heart's response in that faith. As Proverbs 17:3 mentions, "The LORD tests the heart." He tests us on the hot seat of life for our good, so we can be afforded the opportunity to see ourselves as we really are—as He sees us. God always gives us the opportunity to repent and adjust, refining our hearts toward purity and, eventually, maturity.

The Crucible of Disappointment

How you handle your disappointments
define you as a person;
either you get up after a fall,
or just lay there in defeat.
Author unknown

I find it interesting that in a search for the word, "disappointment" in my Bible Soft program, any reference for that word is only found in one modern translation, the New Living Translation. However, it is very obvious as I study Scripture that many of God's people did in fact experience great disappointments. Actually, opportunity for disappointment seems to be a common thread for many of God's people, called according to His purpose.

Recently the Lord lovingly warned me with a very interesting insight. I heard this phrase in my spirit. "Do not fall prey to the allurement of disappointment." As I sought the Lord about this phrase, He showed me that disappointment is often used by the devil to lead us into a downward progression of inner reactions. From normal everyday disappointment we can become discouraged in heart, then potentially disgruntled and irritated, eventually allowing an offense to enter our hearts. When an offense enters our hearts, we take on a victim mentality whereby we blame others, hold grudges, and become very bitter in our attitude. An offense in the heart is a seed-bed for demonic influence toward bitterness of spirit. This is all very likely due to a spirit of pride in our hearts when we feel that we are well within our rights about our attitude toward the source of disappointment.

Before I heard this word from the Lord, I had a very disappointing experience, which came while working at the steel mill when I had voluntarily taken a different position for far less pay.

The benefit was the schedule of a straight-day shift with weekends off. On the higher paying job, I worked a rotating swing shift, including weekends. Each week my shift rotated from midnights, to afternoons to days. I took this new position believing God, that since I was now off on weekends, He would provide an opportunity for me to enter the ministry, which is precisely what took place, and I could ease into full-time ministry when the time came. I was not sure exactly where God would lead, but I was willing to go through as an act of faith, trusting He would provide. I did not know it would eventually involve learning to accept disappointment by being faithful and trusting God in spite of seemingly unfair circumstances that developed.

Several years after taking this job the Lord indeed called me to minister in that small Baptist church. With the straight-day-shift schedule I was able to minister on Sundays and Wednesdays at the church as well as do all the normal duties of a pastor in the evenings. Because it was a small church the salary was not near what was needed to support my family. I was going to be eligible to retire early at age 48, four years from that time. My plans were to then go into full-time ministry receiving a modest retirement pension to supplement a small church pastor's salary. It seemed like a reasonable plan to me, but I was leaning upon my own understanding, and that proposition wasn't God's plan for my life.

Have you, like me, ever had preconceived ideas about something, but were totally wrong? Of course when the wrong perceptions are realized, frustrations come into play, usually leading to disappointment. Because of God's call on my life, I thought everything would fall into place the way I felt it should. I naively thought I was standing on the verse in Psalm 37:4, "Delight yourself also in the LORD, and He will give you the desires of your heart." But I was not truly delighting myself in Him; I was delighting in myself due to God's call, a subtle, but very immature difference.

However, God was teaching me a lesson. I have learned He will give us the desires of our heart—when they are in line with His desires. Actually, His work in our hearts will shift our desires to line up to His will. He knows what is best; we have limited understanding. God works on our heart as we delight ourselves in Him, thus transforming our desires. To delight truly means yieldedness and surrender of heart with a willingness to bend to His perfect will. Then we are thrilled in His will.

I had to learn that in the process of God's will He allows controversies, struggles, and conflicts, and He will work all these out for our good (Romans 8:28). But we must trust Him in these experiences. I was naive regarding God's process in those controversies and His methods of transformation. As I look back, I realize I had limited trust in God and even worse, I was full of myself. While thinking I was truly relying on God's plan, I was really leaning on my own understanding and not delighting in God. I would tell God what I thought was His will with thoughts of noble aspirations. I desired to grow, but only in the ways I thought I needed to grow. However, I had some major blind spots regarding my life, my motives, and my prideful attitude.

I served as pastor of that particular small church for those three years with these blind spots. Even with blinds spots, one can have a pure heart with pure motives. This was my first pastorate, and understood some that I really needed to grow. As is the case with every church, there were problems, and I had to grow as their pastor with on-the-job training. I had to learn church policies and traditions, and problems came when I stepped outside of those ambiguous boundaries. I felt the Lord's lead in attempting to bring small changes in order for the church to grow. This can be a very difficult task, especially when one was as green and immature as I was at the time. But God's purpose in this process was also to shift and transform me, not just in being their pastor, but as a disciple of Jesus Christ. His plans involved a deeper work in my soul for ongoing maturity and development. He was working on my character, and it was indeed a "going through" experience.

I liked being their pastor, even with all the challenges. I loved the people. I especially enjoyed preaching and teaching. God's call was to serve others and to equip the saints for the work of the ministry. However, although being a pastor had been God's will for that season in my life, I seemed to be naive as to God's ways. He wanted me to learn to wait upon Him, to grow in fellowship and intimacy, and to learn deeper dependency upon His Spirit. I also realized He placed the desire in me to serve, but not through my immature plans. I was going through, but not in trusting faith. I thought I was doing God's will and I was to some extent: I would pray; I would study and prepare to preach the Word; I would minister to the people, visiting them in their homes—as I was attempting to lead the church. But things were changing. I found myself in a place of frustration. Even though I had an inner need to be effective for God, I did not realize the price of the anointing to serve effectively. I was the one in need of change, but did not realize it; I needed to grow up, and God humbled me to experience necessary growth.

I began to sense the Lord's lead to resign as pastor. I was not in trouble; there were no blatant sins or indiscretions, only a knowing in my heart that this was God's will. During this time, the Lord privately and graciously exposed the pride I had allowed to enter my heart. I had permitted my ego to inflate. I needed to learn what author and pastor Francis Frangipane teaches. "God will lead you to become more humble than you plan." Learning the hard way, I was humbled and had to choose to become more humble, which is better than being humbled by circumstances, or so I learned.

A year after I had resigned from being a pastor, the steel mill where I worked filed for bankruptcy, and a larger steel corporation purchased our facility. Fortunately we retained our employment, but the disappointment I experienced only increased because I had twenty nine years of service, and the possibility for retirement with thirty years of service was taken away due to the bankruptcy. Because of the new contract I would have to wait 12 years to be eligible for retirement. My original plan was to retire at age 48 was no longer available. Additionally, more disappointment came as the straight day job was taken away and given to someone with more seniority. I was put back onto rotating shift work, not on the previously held higher paying job, but on the same lower pay grade. This became another blow to my heart, so circumstances had humbled me again. I was deeply dissatisfied. This was when I started to complain and grumble to the Lord, of which I have previously written. God was testing my trust in Him, because I needed to learn to reestablish submissive communion with Him. I was prideful and in great need to learn humility, which is not pleasant to the flesh, but it is a vital part of God's process of maturity.

Blind Spots Revealed

Why does God, who already knows everything need to test our hearts? The tests reveal to us what God knows, as David said in Psalm 139:1-2, "O LORD, You have searched me and known me. You know my sitting down and my rising up; You understand my thought afar off." We must be open to God's searches of our heart because we have blind spots.

We all have areas of which we are oblivious. These blind spots could include, self-deception, wrong attitudes, wrong perceptions, hidden pride, religious spirits, selfishness, wrong doctrine, being judgmental, a lustful heart, ungodly attitudes, lack of forgiveness, wrong assumptions, or misunderstanding God's process of maturing us, to name only a few. I list these because I have been guilty of all of them. Perhaps you can add to the list. Holy Spirit will expose these areas of our hearts, because we need them brought out into the open to be set free from them. He will allow and use tests, trials, and temptations—whatever it takes—to bring to light those areas that hold us back from transformation into the image of Jesus Christ.

After many such tests, I have come to acknowledge my heart needs testing regularly. I have not always had this attitude. I have actually said to the Lord in prayer, "I am sick and tired of being tested!" Yes, I was insolent with my precious Lord, but He was, and is, always gracious. He opened my mind by exposing these hidden areas of sin in my heart. I realize now that tests are a vital part of the crucible of trust while growing and maturing as His son.

However, I have also learned that God's ways are not always the crucible. He is gracious, generous, tender, and loving, as David would attest in Psalm 63:3: "Because Thy loving kindness is better than life, my lips shall praise You." Even as we pass through trying times and take up our crosses in our lives, we are encouraged by God's grace. His goodness, mercy, love, trustworthiness, and kindness give us hope, assurance, and confidence in Him. The songwriter and singer, John Michael Talbot writes in agreement in his book, *The Jesus Prayer*: "The Christian life is not all testing, trials, and crosses" (2013, 31). He expounds that God will also bring us to places of gladness in our lives as we learn to enjoy our journey, walking with Him every step of the way. Many of us have this particular blind spot of God's earnest desire for us, that we enjoy our journey of life, delighting in Him while abiding with Him, finding joy in just being His child.

God truly will bring His joy to overshadow our not-so-pleasant experiences. Consider how David understood this process from Psalm 30:5, 11: "For His anger is but for a moment, His favor is for life; Weeping may endure for a night, but joy comes in the morning…You have turned for me my mourning into dancing; You have put off my sackcloth and clothed me with gladness."

David acknowledged and embraced God's searching. Instead of waiting for the Lord to search him, he learned to ask God to do so, going from "You have searched me" (Psalm 139:1) to "Search me, O God, and know my heart; try me, and know my anxieties; and see if there is any wicked way in me, and lead me in the way everlasting" (Psalm 139:23-24). David's willingness for God to search his heart inspires us to follow his example in what it means to be a man after God's own heart. He knew personally of God's tender loving kindness. David loved God wholeheartedly and was open to His Fatherly guidance and correction as he pursued God passionately. 1 and 2 Samuel tell of many times he was on the "hot seat" of life. He also had blind spots going through his trials, struggles, and conflicts in life, yet David trusted God and experienced His faithfulness and trustworthiness, writing, "Surely goodness and mercy shall follow me all the days of my life" (Psalm 23:6). As with David, who learned— even with his blind spots—to abide under the Shadow of the wings of the Almighty, "trust is our gift back to God" (Manning, 2000, 2), and our crucible of trust can truly become the Secret Place of the Most High.

Is God's Silence Due to Sin?

If I regard iniquity in my heart, The Lord will not hear.
But certainly God has heard me; He has
attended to the voice of my prayer.
Blessed be God, Who has not turned away my prayer,
Nor His mercy from me!
Psalms 66:18-20

Have you ever experienced the silent treatment from someone you love? Most likely an issue needed to be resolved. Perhaps they were hurt or offended. Jesus taught that if we approach God with an offering of worship, which includes our prayers, and we know of an offense in the heart of someone toward us, then we must first go to the person seeking reconciliation before we may approach God with our offering or prayer. (Matthew 5:23-25). Reaching out to someone like this is a crucible experience. We generally don't want to go to an offended person, because it can be very humbling, but it is very necessary, for us and for the person we need to approach.

God expects us to have clear consciences in our relationships. "If it is possible, as much as depends on you, live peaceably with all men" (Romans 12:18). When we are not willing to reconcile or settle conflicts with others, then there are areas of our hearts that really need to be submitted to God, whether it is pride, laziness, indifference, or embarrassment. Within this tension we are faced with a dilemma, which is truly a testing of our hearts. If there is an offense in someone toward us, we actually have a problem with God, because He expects us to go to the other person in humility, resolving any conflicts with them before our prayers or offerings are acceptable. We need to choose the path of deference, respect, and honor in order to advance in our spiritual progress by taking initiative in doing what God asks of us. When attempts are made to reconcile with a person who is offended, and the offer is rejected, we are free in our hearts. I experienced this very thing in approaching a man who totally rejected my offer of apology. This hurt my heart a little, but I had done the right thing.

God desires truth to be in the inmost part of our hearts (Psalm 51:6). We are to be totally honest within our own souls regarding our inner thoughts of ourselves, our inner thoughts regarding others, and our approach to God. That requires being at peace in our own hearts and our relationships with others as much as it does with God. Jesus blessed the peacemakers, calling them the sons of God (Matthew 5:9). Paul admonishes us to pursue the things that make for peace and that which edifies others (Romans 14:19). When there is no attempt to address unresolved issues it negates our peace. If we think otherwise we are deceived. God is serious in His desire that we live at peace with others, growing in grace. If we are not careful to live at peace, we callous our heart little by little. In this hardened state of mind, one has difficulty hearing God, and it stifles any spiritual growth or advancement.

Does God give the silent treatment? I do not think He does in the way we do. His love is everlasting and His grace knows no bounds. However, we can grieve Him if we continue in sin, but thank God he offers us grace so we can confess our sins and repent for forgiveness based on the blood of Jesus (1 John 1:7-9). God always desires to commune with us. When we humble ourselves before God, having done all we can to reconcile with others, He will hear our prayers and will speak to us. If there is a perceived silence from God, perhaps He is lovingly wooing us, trying to get our attention. His silence actually communicates to us.

However, there are other reasons for the perception of God's silence. Did we totally obey Him, or only partially obey? If that is the case we have quenched His Spirit and this hinders our ability to hear from Him. God has wired our hearts so when we approach Him in humility, we receive His Grace, and something takes place within so we can hear His voice. Yet when we do not obey Him our conscience speaks to us. If we harden our conscience to God we actually stifle our ability to hear His voice. His instructions are always for our good, and He will patiently wait for us to do His bidding, because He desires our willing obedience.

There are other reasons we might miss His voice, like stepping into areas where God has not called us, or if we grieve, quench, or resist His Spirit. We can grieve the Spirit with backbiting, gossiping, and by allowing "bitterness, wrath, anger, clamor, and evil speaking…with malice" to manifest in our lives (Ephesians 4:30). We quench the Spirit by ignoring or compromising His initiatives and instructions, focusing on other things, even though we recognize His voice (1 Thessalonians 5:19). We resist the Spirit by blatant refusal of His influence when the conviction comes to the heart (Acts 7:51). Do Christians act in this manner? Sadly, yes, for I certainly recognize my own failings in this area. The Scriptures regarding these things were to the churches for instruction, admonition, and exhortation, then and now.

Could the perception of God's silence possibly be attributed to just not listening or an unclear conscience? What about harboring ill will or resentment toward someone, even God? Do we have sin in our lives? Maybe we do not want to hear God's voice because we do not want to be confronted with our own sinfulness. All God asks of us is to come to Him in honesty of heart, in willingness to repent, because He delights in mercy and is always ready to forgive and restore. He knows what is best for us. When we have a good conscience our communion with Him is pure and good, our health is better. "The softest pillow is a clear conscience" (source unknown).

God created us to live in tune with Him, and He truly wants us to abide with Him, because it is only in abiding we are able to live righteously. He wants us to hear His voice and obey His initiatives, which are always for our good. Jesus emphasized this truth when He quoted Deuteronomy 8:3 to the devil, "It is written, 'Man shall not live by bread alone, but by every word that proceeds from the mouth of God.'" We grow in our desire to tune our hearts to hear God's voice so we may keep them clean and pure, thereby hearing and knowing God personally and intimately.

However, when God seems quiet due to our unresponsiveness to His Spirit it is for chastening, not to hold out on us. When God is quiet in this way, it is because we have not sought His face. His ways are redemptive in nature, to get us to a place where we realize He is not silent, but we have missed Him due to our own hard-hearted condition. We are to be in an open and constant flow of abiding. If not, we will start leaning upon our own understanding, leading us to deception. He is the Vine; we are the branches. We need Him, His Word, and His Voice for our life's support. His purpose is for us to enjoy continual fellowship with Him; even in silence, God speaks.

THE CRUCIBLE OF REJECTION

When my father and my mother forsake me,
Then the LORD will take care of me.
Psalm 27:10

I have become a stranger to my brothers,
and an alien to my mother's children.
Psalm 69:8

I n the above psalms we see that David experienced rejection from his parents and his brothers, but he learned to trust the Lord in all areas of life, including family relationships. One day as I sought the Lord regarding why I struggled with relationships, He revealed to me that a spirit of rejection often attacks my heart seeking to destroy me, to make me feel unworthy and to get me to feel isolated and alone. This had very often led to the temptation to self-medicate with alcohol and sensual behavior. God further revealed that evil spirits are always trying get us to sin, or to get us where we have an offense in our heart and blame others or even God. Another truth God showed me was that different evil spirits work in conjunction with one another in whatever way they can to kill, steal, or destroy our lives. The spirit of rejection is what led me to a spirit of lust. Yes these are spirits, but they only can tempt or allure in influencing us into sinful behavior. We are the ones who choose, and we are responsible for our actions.

The attacks of rejection started very early in my life at age 4 as a result of my birth mother leaving my dad in divorce (as I expressed before). My dad actually confided in me years later that my mother said, in effect, "I do not want to be married and I do not want kids." This experience of abandonment from my mother affected me deeply and painfully, but at that age I did not understand these things. The sense of rejection was not what I felt at the time. Honestly, as I think back, I am not sure what I felt, but only remember that I was often sad, melancholy, and I craved attention. Dad remarried and my step mother was helpful, but those deep wounds were never really addressed, which carried over into adolescence, then adulthood.

As I reflect back, even though I did not understand it or even recognize it then, I seemed to have always felt rejected. With the wounds of abandonment not completely dealt with, during these early years of my life, the spirit of rejection began its work regarding all my relationships. My early teen years were very difficult with rebellion, acting out, trying to fit in, and trying to get attention. I did not realize it at the time but these behaviors were my attempt to feel accepted; my heart was crying out for approval. I started drinking alcohol at age 12, smoking pot and taking drugs at age 15, and continued in the habit of self-gratification. I learned years later that in my curiosity to experiment with drugs and alcohol, I was subconsciously attempting to medicate my pain of feeling rejected. The spirit of rejection does everything it can to lead to ungodly behaviors to entrap us in the bondages of sin. This happened to me before being born again, and it crept into my life after accepting Christ as Savior and Lord, through sinful behaviors with pornography.

I thank God He revealed this to me and set me free from its deception and influence. Yet even today, that spirit of rejection often attempts to reenter my life. This is an ongoing trial of trust, and I have to stay vigilant by casting down every lofty thing and imagination that exalts itself against the knowledge of Christ (2 Corinthians 10:4-5). With God's grace, I avoid the pull of going back to sinful behaviors. In all my experiences I have learned to not take things personally. I am not rejected. I am accepted by my precious Lord Jesus Christ. I want to encourage all who read this: God accepts every one of us with unconditional love. He continually draws us to Himself, asking for our repentance from sinful behavior. His love conquers everything so we may become victorious over sin.

My birth mother, at the early age of twenty three made a very selfish decision to leave and abandon her children. During my childhood there we no visits with her; she had not been a part of my life. However, some years after I was born again the Lord put grace in my heart to forgive and reconcile with her.

In 1981 when I was 26 years old, I asked for my mother's phone number from her mother, my Grandma Lucy. Remember, she and Papa Bud were prayer warriors on my behalf. They had been part of my childhood with many visits to their home. I recall only seeing my birth mother once after the divorce, and that was during my early teens when she happened to be at the store where my Grandma Lucy had worked. That was a very awkward moment for me, not really knowing what to say or how to respond to her. My brother and I had been dropped off there and were waiting for Grandma to get off work so we could go to her house to stay with her and Papa for a few days during the summer.

When God asked me to reconcile with my birth mother, I called in faith. That phone conversation was the very first time we had actually spoken together in a meaningful conversation and it was rather awkward at first, but God led me. I told her she had a grandson and that I wanted him to know his Granny. She was quiet. I know she was crying. I was crying. God's Spirit was leading me to forgive and accept my mother so He could bring healing to both our hearts. As the conversation progressed it became easier to talk with her. We made arrangements for me and my family to visit her home hundreds of miles from us. From that visit we established a relationship that lasted and grew until she died in 2005. In His grace and goodness, God gave back some of those years of relationship with my mother. I met her husband, Howard, during that time, and we became friends as well. During this process of reconciliation, God built within me a deeper trust in Him, while at the same time restored the love between mother and son even after I'd experienced the pain of rejection for all those years. God is so good!

Rejection: Real or Perceived

> But first He [Jesus] must suffer many things
> and be *rejected* by this generation.
> Luke 17:25

I realize almost everyone has experienced rejection in some shape or form. It is real. Pride, sin, betrayal, arrogance, and many other things all enter into the picture where rejection is concerned. Jesus Himself experienced rejection with His own people. The above verse is only one of many that record how Jesus was not accepted. Other Scriptures record that the Elders, the Scribes of the Law, the Pharisees, and the Sadducees were all conspiring to have him killed.

They despised and rejected Him, particularly rejecting His claims to be Messiah. Several of the Psalms and the Prophets, depicted prophetically and metaphorically the rejection that Messiah would experience.

The prophet Isaiah foresaw this in his day many centuries before Jesus was born. He wrote, "He is despised and *rejected by men*, a Man of sorrows and acquainted with grief. And we hid, as it were, our faces from Him; He was despised, and we did not esteem Him" (Isaiah 53:3). The fulfillment of that prophecy is found, among several other places, in John 1:11, "He came unto His own, and His own did not receive Him."

Our Lord Jesus experienced rejection so He can identify with everyone else who experiences it. Whether it is actual rejection, or only perceived, it affects the heart the same. Have you ever sensed (whether correctly or wrongly) a seeming disinterest in you when you are around others? I have experienced this perception numerous times wrongly attributing it to rejection. As stated before, there are evil spirits who are assigned to individuals to kill, steal, and destroy them; the spirit of rejection, among many others, deceives us and speaks lies into our hearts. These spirits attempt to stir an inner sense of not measuring up, self-doubt, despair, despondency, or numerous other negative thoughts and emotions, with a fear of being left out, or overlooked. I know this first-hand. Their task is to influence us toward invoking a feeling of isolation from God and others, intending to deceive our hearts, eventually leading us to think that God Himself is rejecting us. However, God never rejects anyone who truly calls upon His Name. He always draws near to those who draw near to Him (James 4:8).

Evil spirits know that God hates sin and that He will eventually reject all unrepentant sinners. Their agenda is to keep anyone and everyone from repentance in attempt to stir up numerous other things, like strife, betrayal, deceit, and division among brothers and sisters in Christ. But thank God there are also angels on assignment over individuals us as well (Matthew 18:10; Hebrews 1:13-14). Indeed, there are more for us as children of God than there are against us. Moreover, among many other psalms, Psalm 46:1 says, "God is our refuge and strength, a very present help in trouble." This is where prayer, trust, and submission will empower us as we cry out to our Heavenly Father, believing that He will help. The Lord hears our cries. He releases answers and delivers us, sending out His angels as ministers to the heirs of salvation—keeping our feet from dashing against the stones— as ministers of flame and fire for God's people (Psalm 91:11-12; 103:20; 104:4). Our Father never rejects our cries to Him for help, even when others seem to reject us. God is absolutely trustworthy; even when we are in these types of crucibles of experience, we can trust God who is our shield.

Rejection Often Leads to Withdrawal

Being under submission to God-ordained authority is part of the process of most everyone's spiritual progress as a disciple of Jesus Christ. In that process, God often places us under the tutelage of a mentor. Over the years, in my relationships with various spiritual mentors, perceived rejection has led to feelings of inadequacy or not measuring up. Because I was immature I was overly sensitive, which caused me to desire to withdraw. The spirit of rejection always attempts to usher in a spirit of offense and other more oppressive spirits to cause us to feel isolated and then to pull away from others. Offense can became very enticing to the soul, but I thank God this did not take place. As mentioned before, I have heard these words from the Lord "Do not fall prey to the allurement of disappointment." Disappointments can come from rejection, and if not dealt with, disappointment leads to discouragement, to disgruntlement, and then to offense. These emotions can also cause us to bury deeply those wounds of rejection, offense or whatever, that take years to come out in all sorts of dysfunctional manifestations, particularly a spirit of offense with pride.

I have learned that once a spirit of offense enters the heart, it begins to become adversarial, accusatory, and blame shifting. Then it leads to withdrawal. Two people can be living together in marriage with one or both living in withdrawal from the other. In withdrawal, the imagination becomes negatively influenced by very unhealthy emotions. An offense generally fosters a victim mindset that festers in the heart and breeds discontentment, doubt and unbelief, and especially pride. This can all start with rejection which can be real or perceived. In my case I was not necessarily offended, thank the Lord, but I had a deep wound of rejection which led me to be melancholy, somber, and depressed. I became good at putting on a false face, but inwardly I was miserable.

The Lord helped realize that when this was taking place I was actually in a crucible, falling into a lack of faith and trust. God was exposing wrong attitudes, perceptions, and perspectives that had developed in my heart. A spirit of rejection is a stronghold of the mind and works on the imagination. God taught me that even when feelings of rejection attempt to attack, I absolutely need to trust Him, to put off the old self of feeling abandoned in order to expose the stronghold of rejection and eradicate it from my life before a root of offense can take place. This can be done with putting on the new man by faith in the power of the Holy Spirit, quoting the Word standing on God's promises. The focus should be on the new man in Christ, not on the old self.

At the time, the problem was that my feelings were not in line with my faith in the Word of God. When I felt rejected I only wanted to remove myself from others. This is a dangerous place in spiritual development. I needed to realize that perhaps the person whom I thought was rejecting me was only distracted. Perhaps the Lord was leading this person to be cautious with me. Or even if the person (without really rejecting me) misunderstood me and was insensitive to my needs, God was using this to test my heart and to make me more reliant upon Him. We all need acceptance and understanding, but when these appear to not be offered by those with whom we would like, we must avoid feeling rejected. When I sense rejection or attribute certain demeanors as rejection, I have learned to present my heart and the situation to the Lord. He will never reject me. He always fills my heart with love and acceptance.

I recommend an article written by Dr. Mark Virkler called, "Perfect Peace When your Imagination is…" Virkler uses the ellipsis in the title to indicate the ongoing aspect of one's imagination, and how it affects outcomes. He expounds on the understanding that the imagination is very powerful in its effect on the heart: "If I enter a situation seeing myself being rejected, I send out a message to all saying, *Reject me,* and I act in such a way as to promote being rejected. If I imagine I will be accepted, I send out a message saying, *Accept me.* I act according to what I am imagining, and acceptance is what I create." Notice that whether I see myself as being rejected or accepted, I create an atmosphere reflective of whatever I imagine. This article really encouraged me to be more at peace with myself regarding my self-image in respect to relationships with others. Trust in God is an unsaid aspect in all human relationships. To present the mind to Holy Spirit, using imagination in a holy and pure manner is the way God would have us relate to others, whether sensing real rejection from others or sensing true acceptance. God wants us to rely upon Him in trust and faith.

Trust in Submission

God uses our submission to the spiritual authority of a mentor in our lives to help us grow and mature spiritually. God also uses mentors to train and raise up individuals for ministry. A true mentor will be a spiritual father or mother who accepts and lovingly encourages us in our spiritual progress. That is exactly what happened when I went to my mentor, as I previously wrote. God uses these relationships in all their ups and downs to form Christ in each of us, to train and to prepare us for His plans for our lives. We are in a crucible of trust all through life. Submission to, and learning from, the right mentor is very important in guiding us through the minefields of temptation and spiritual dysfunction that are lurking, ready to bring us down. Each of us is responsible for our own actions and behaviors, but with the loving influence of a mentor we will be better equipped and prepared.

I know God is pleased with our submission to those in whom He desires to be authority over our lives. All through Scripture there are patterns and examples of this very important, powerful dynamic in spiritual life and development. When in relationship with a spiritual mentor, they model truths and principles. These are more often "caught" by us, over being taught. Watching our mentors live, choose, relate to others, resolve conflicts, solve problems, and exhibit the Fruit of the Holy Spirit is very powerful in the influence and shaping of our own behaviors and attitudes (Hebrews 6:12b).

Everyone needs to seek the Lord for the right spiritual authority and mentor(s) to submit to and learn from them. Sometimes God will place a person in our lives for a season or for a reason in our spiritual progress. But if you are truly blessed God will place a lifetime mentor in your life. I personally have one in particular with two or three others who have been very instrumental in my spiritual progress as a disciple of Jesus Christ. God uses people in our lives to influence us and to stir us up for love and good deeds. He also uses mentors to impart anointing, to train, and to encourage us during our development. This is a Kingdom principle found in both Old and New Testaments. God will use our relationship with a mentor in the process for our transformation, an integral part of the crucible of trust.

For example, years ago I had a disagreement with my mentor. I was not happy with something he wanted me to do, and was resistant to his request. But in seeking counsel from other, godly and wise, individuals and also in deep prayer, I did it anyway. The request was very reasonable, only it was my own stubborn will that was in question. The advice of the other mentors was that I should follow through with what I was asked to do. This episode became a crucible of trust as I had to submit my will. When I submitted, I grew tremendously afterward. When I agreed and accepted in my heart to follow the mentor's request, a peace I cannot explain entered my heart.

God is so very gracious in our development, but He will take us places in our lives where we absolutely have to yield our wills and trust Him, while rejecting our own, limited perceptions—our blind spots. He knows best and we must submit to His will, even when we disagree out of a lack of understanding. Usually in these cases our heart is being tested by the Lord.

In Scripture there are numerous examples of truth being caught from a mentor. The one under the tutelage of a mentor will experience many trials and tests in their development. God will prove a person in the refining fires of the crucible of trust before he will move them into their assignment in ministry. The following two sections are offered as examples of this process and refinement.

Elijah and Elisha

Elijah, the mighty prophet was instructed by God to place his mantle upon Elisha as the one who would succeed him as prophet (1 Kings 19:19-21). Elisha must have been ready, anticipating something from God, because he immediately left his own life as a farmer and burned the yoke of the oxen with which he was plowing and sacrificed the oxen. He then went with Elijah. Scripture does not disclose exactly how long, but I believe it was several years, because in the next four chapters of the Bible, Elisha's name is not mentioned, but he is with Elijah, watching and learning through all of his experiences. Then in 2 Kings 2:1-6 it is recorded that Elijah was to pass on his mantle as prophet to Elisha. Three times Elijah told Elisha that God had summoned him away, and each time Elijah told Elisha to stay back and not come with him. Yet Elisha would not stay back. He pursued and followed Elijah each time, because he truly desired the mantle of anointing befitting a prophet of God. Elijah followed God's unique commands all during his life as a prophet (1 Kings 19—2 Kings 2). Elisha would also be used by God to bring unique commands for miraculous manifestations (2 Kings 2—2 Kings 13).

Each of the places to which Elijah was summoned had deep spiritual implications, having been a crucible of trust for some of God's people. The first was Bethel, the place where Jacob had the prophetic dream of a connection between heaven and earth with the angels of God ascending and descending (Genesis 28:10-22). Jacob began to trust God from his experience there, calling it the gate of heaven, and renaming it from Luz to Bethel (House of God). Now Elijah, who had operated in the power of the Spirit of God with an open heaven of angelic activity prevalent during his ministry, was summoned there by God. Elisha committed to go with Elijah, even though Elijah told him to stay behind. Elisha would later operate with an open heaven of angelic activity in his ministry (2 Kings 6:14-18).

The second place was Jericho, a place of absolute victory as the Lord gave it into Joshua's and the Israelites' hands because of their obedience (Joshua 6). Joshua submitted, obeyed, and trusted God's unique strategy of having the Israelites walk around the city once a day for six days in total silence. Then they were to walk around it seven times on the seventh day. The final time around they were to shout and the walls of Jericho would come down. The Israelites took the city because of Joshua's obedience to God's unique instructions, which was truly a crucible of trust to obey God in this manner.

The third place was the Jordan River, which represents crossing over into new territory and experiencing God's anointing and provision from the obedience of His commands and instructions. In order for the Israelites to enter the Promised Land, they had to cross the Jordan River at the height of flood stage. Joshua instructed the Levites and priests to take the Ark of the Covenant and march down into the Jordan. As they obeyed the waters parted and gave way for them to walk across on dry ground. All Israel followed, passing over into the Promised Land. Joshua trusted God's instructions, and the Levites and priests trusted that Joshua had heard God.

Elijah, also in trust and faith, took his mantle and struck the waters of the Jordan, causing them to part. He and Elisha crossed to the east side. Elisha, in answer to Elijah's question as to just what he wanted, asked for a double portion of the Spirit that was upon Elijah. Elisha was told that if he saw Elijah as he was taken away he would receive what he asked. Just as Elijah was taken up to heaven by the whirlwind with the fiery chariot, Elisha looked and saw him taken up; Elijah's mantle fell to the ground and Elisha picked it up. He received the double portion of the Spirit. Elisha then also struck the waters of the Jordan with the mantle he had received. The waters parted for him to cross back to the west side.

Elisha was persistent in staying with Elijah each time it was suggested for him to stay back. He did not allow any spirit of rejection to come forth. He pursued and pressed in with his mentor prophet as he caught the Spirit and his mantle of prophetic anointing. Scripture reveals that Elisha administered twice as many miracles as Elijah.

To be honest, I am not so sure I would have been so mature. This lesson shows that true submission to God-ordained authority is very important in order to be effective in our God-ordained assignments. However, hunger and desire, along with sensitivity to the Holy Spirit influenced Elisha to understand the older prophet's tactic. By staying with Elijah, Elisha was tested. He was in the crucible of trust, yet passing with results of receiving the double portion of Elijah's anointing.

Persevering through our own crucible of trust with commitment, dedication, and tenacity is vitally important. God has a deeper blessing He wants to bring forth while we are going through what seems like rejection. He will not reject; He will anoint us as we stay in faith as Elisha modeled.

Jesus and Simon Peter

Several occasions during the time Simon Peter spent with Jesus he experienced what could have been perceived as rejection. The first time came as Jesus asked the disciples, "Who do men say that I, the Son of man, am?" Some of the other disciples answered with, John the Baptist, Elijah, Jeremiah, or one of the prophets, but Simon Peter said, "You are the Christ, the Son of living God." Jesus answered and said to him,

Blessed are you, Simon Bar-Jonah, for flesh and blood has not revealed this to you, but My Father who is in heaven. And I also say to you that you are Peter, and on this rock I will build My church, and the gates of Hades shall not prevail against it. And I will give you the keys of the kingdom of heaven, and whatever you bind on earth will be bound in heaven, and whatever you loose on earth will be loosed in heaven" (Matthew 16:13-19).

Jesus renamed Simon, His outspoken disciple, to Peter, who had caught the Father's revelation that Jesus was the Christ. Just after this, Jesus began to tell the disciples of His imminent suffering at the hands of the elders, chief priests, and the scribes. He told them He was going to be arrested and killed. Peter took Jesus to the side and rebuked Him saying that this shall not happen to Him. Jesus sharply said, "Get behind me, Satan! You are an offense to Me, for you are not mindful of the things of God, but the things of men." Peter had just been approved for confessing that Jesus was the Christ, the Son of God, and could have allowed the rebuke to sting his heart as rejection. Jesus' reproof was out of love and sternness that portrayed the seriousness and gravity of His need to go to the cross.

The second time Peter might have felt rejected was recorded in Matthew 17:1-9 when Jesus took Peter, James, and John up onto a high mountain to witness the revelation of Jesus as the Eternal Son of God. While on the mountain Jesus was transfigured before their very eyes revealing His true glory. His face shone like the sun. His cloths became as white as light. Then Moses and Elijah appeared with Jesus. Peter was beside himself and asked Jesus if he should build three tabernacles. Jesus was silent, but a voice came out of the cloud, "This is my beloved Son in Whom I am well pleased. Hear

Him!" Again Peter was lovingly admonished, but he did not allow a sense of rejection to enter his heart. This truly impacted Peter as he wrote about this experience years later (2 Peter 1:16-18).

The third time was when Jesus told Peter, in the presence of the other disciples that he would deny Him three times before the cock crowed. Jesus said He had prayed that when Peter turned back from this denial in repentance he was to strengthen his brothers. Peter denied Jesus three times, as Jesus had said, and was deeply distressed over it. He deeply repented with bitter tears. However, after Jesus was raised from the dead, He appeared to Peter personally to reassure him, to reveal more of Himself to him, establishing the call upon his life as an apostle.

Both Elisha and Peter went through the crucible of trust in their relationships with their spiritual leaders. Both passed tests of experiencing what could have been considered rejection (but was correction and guidance in love); both were richer from their lessons. Their experiences were recorded in Scripture as examples. The Lord leads us through many types of crucibles like these so we will stand in faith and trust, catching His vision, knowing experientially that God is trustworthy. He will never reject us, even in chastening us, and He will always take us to victory, just like these two mighty men of God.

LOVE AND TRUST OVERRIDE FEAR

Love has been perfected among us in this,
that we may have boldness
in the Day of Judgment; because as He is,
so are we in this world.
There is no fear in love; but perfect love casts out fear, because
fear involves torment.
But he who fears has not been made perfect in love.
1 John 4:17, 18

Before I was born again I had several experiences where fear totally gripped me. One time in particular when I was around 17 years old, some friends came over to our house when my parents were out for the evening. That night we were just hanging around smoking pot, when we heard a strange noise outside and went to investigate. There was an object in the sky that was not a plane or a helicopter. It was creepy, with lights shining all around. We could not identify it as anything we could recognize. This object seemed to just hover in the sky. My friends laughed at it. For some reason it struck deep fear in my heart like I had never felt before, but I pretended that I was not afraid to my friends.

I was in great fear that night. The object was obviously an aircraft of some type, but my fear reminded me of something I had heard about in the book of Revelation. Even though I was not born again at the time, I knew of Judgment Day and actually thought something along those lines was happening. I had heard the Gospel of salvation as a child, yet I knew deep down in my heart that I was not ready. I was intensely afraid. I am not sure if it was the fear of the Lord, or if it was a spiritual attack of fear to torment, or both. At the time I had no knowledge of the true, healthy fear of the Lord, but was often fearful of punishment and judgment. I did not know of the love of God either, and the Lord used this incident to prepare me and, to lead me to Himself and His love for me when I was open to receiving Him.

Thanks to God, His kindness led me to repentance and to be born again a few years later. I have since learned that God's perfect love can indeed cast out all fear, which is an ongoing process for me. I had to let God's wonderful and perfect love work in my heart in order for this to take place. As trust developed in my heart I learned to distinguish the fear of the Lord from the fear of other things, and especially the—evil-spirit oriented—fear that torments the soul.

We all have experiences where fear grips our hearts. Fear seems to be a natural occurrence, and comes in many varieties. Babies experience fear when left alone, which comes from the need to feel secure. My own experience of being afraid of the dark as a child was due to the unknown which generated wild imaginations that flared and was quite upsetting to my young, innocent heart. Even in adulthood, our imaginations can cause fears and trepidations. Fear is also a faith killer because our focus in not on God, but on the thing that brings fear.

Origin of Fear

Then the LORD God called to Adam and said to him,
"Where are you?"
So he said, "I heard Your voice in the garden, and
I was afraid because I was naked; and I hid myself."
Genesis 3:9-10

Where does fear come from? Fear seems to have started in the
Garden of Eden when Adam and Eve disobeyed God by eating of
the Tree of Knowledge of Good and Evil (Genesis 3:1-10). This
began with the lie from the serpent (Satan), who enticed them to
doubt God. Satan and his minion demons have continued doing
this in the hearts of people down through the ages. Jesus warned
us while He was here that the thief (Satan) comes to steal, kill, and
destroy (John 10:10). Satan does this through whatever means,
including fear and intimidation, by allurement to sin, and initiating division between people. Disconnecting hearts from God is
his goal, but he often uses the torment of fear to isolate us from
our Heavenly Father.

However, God is love, and His love, which is perfect, casts
out all fear. Jesus came that we might have life in Him and to
have it more abundantly (John 10:10b). In providing abundant
life, He also came to heal all those oppressed by the devil (Acts
10:38) and to reveal and model the Father's love, which never fails.
Indeed, God demonstrated His love toward us in that while we
were still sinners, Christ died for us (Romans 5:8). He loved the
world so much that He gave us His only begotten Son (John 3:16).
By trusting and believing in Jesus Christ we no longer need to be
afraid; we have abundant life and eternal life with Him. However,
apart from trusting God and experiencing His love we will continue to suffer the torment of fear.

Where there is a lack of trust in God, natural and spiritual fear is the result. Adam and Eve clearly did not totally understand their need to trust God regarding the command to not eat from the Tree of Knowledge. God had provided so many other trees to enjoy, particularly the Tree of Life, but they were drawn to the one restriction God had imposed. Their disobedience led to their being afraid of God. I believe if it had been anyone of us, we too would have been allured by that tree, falling victim to sin and fear as well.

Is there a distinction between being afraid of God and the fear of the Lord? Being afraid brings discomfort, inner uneasiness, torment, even terror. However, the fear of the LORD is the beginning of understanding and of wisdom, and it also leads us to worship Him.

That night my friends and I witnessed that strange object in the sky, I was inwardly terrified in my young and foolish heart, thinking God was beginning judgment. Being afraid of God is a natural response when we do not know Him and He reveals Himself to our unclean heart. Adam experienced being afraid of God and so did many others recorded in Scripture.

The Israelites were also in great fear of God's voice, but Moses told them not to fear in the sense of being horrified, but allow the healthy fear of the Lord to be activated so they would not sin (Exodus 20:20). In this verse, two different words —*yare'* and *yirah*—are used in the Hebrew for fear (Strong). When Adam said he was afraid (yare') it was the same word in the Hebrew that Moses used when telling the Israelites not to fear. However, the other word infers our proper fear (yirah) of the Lord, a reverential awe and respect of God, which has more to do with love, veneration, worship, and honor than with being afraid or terrified.

Adam and Eve had been in God's presence often and had not been afraid of Him until after eating from the Tree of Knowledge, but that does not mean they did not have a healthy respect for

God. They had enjoyed His presence until then. Why were they afraid now? Scripture says they realized they were naked before God and were afraid. They obviously did not know why they felt naked, but somehow eating from the Tree of Knowledge opened their understanding to their nakedness. Until then they had lived in innocence, but this new understanding seemed to open their minds to the difference between good and evil. The fact that this knowledge came to them apart from their relationship with God had been a result of Satan's subtle lie. He told them their eyes would be opened, but he also told Eve, with Adam right there with her, that in eating of the tree they would be like God. Satan's allurement seemed to make them forget and negate the fact they were already made in the image of God. (Genesis 1:26; 3:5).

God's original intent was for them to rule and to *discern* good over evil with His guidance, not to personally be familiar with good and evil apart from Him (Genesis 1:28; Hebrews 5:12-14). But now they felt naked before God and covering themselves with fig leaves was their futile effort to cover their sin, done out of ignorance. We do similarly in covering our lives in business, possessions, and distractions. God had wanted them covered in His righteousness and glory, which He wanted for all their descendants for all time. One can only speculate, but it looks like God intended them to choose to eat from the Tree of Life without eating from the Tree of knowledge of Good and Evil.

The Tree of Life is now Christ. He is the Life giving Spirit, for them and for us (1 Corinthians 15:45). Adam and Eve's assignment before their disobedience was to rule over all the earth, subduing all under God's authority and obviously it would have been their great enjoyment with Him, perpetuated forever had they first eaten from the Tree of Life. Instead, because of their disobedience, they had to deal with the knowledge of good and evil from their own natural perspective, something God offered for them to avoid, but

He knew all along they would disobey. God gave them a choice, and He gives all of us a similar choice in our free will to choose His Life, which is only found in His Son, Jesus Christ, dwelling within our hearts as the Tree of Life.

Only after eating from the forbidden tree did God's presence make Adam and Eve aware of their nakedness. God is holy, pure, and righteous. Up to this point in their relationship with God they had been innocent, made and existing in the image and likeness of God. Now due to disobedience, their innocence was contaminated, bringing upon them the curse of sin. In God's presence, they were exposed. In a way, fear of anything causes a feeling of nakedness, of exposure, and of helplessness regarding what is feared or not understood.

I felt exposed in my heart as I observed that unidentified thing in the sky that night. I did not know what it was and I felt bare in my mind due to the fear that was in my heart. I did not know the Lord to be able to trust Him in the midst of fear. Adam and Eve felt uncovered as well. Their lack of trust was exposed in realizing their nakedness before God and trying to cover themselves with fig leaves. They felt naked before their Righteous and Holy Creator God, which was caused by their sin of disobedience. I know now that sin was why I was afraid that night. I wanted to run and hide. Isn't that the way many of us respond to God at times? We try to cover ourselves with many things, like pride, possessions, work, relationships, business, compromise, or whatever distractions to hide from or not think of God.

Jesus Conquers Fear

I am He who lives, and was dead, and behold,
I am alive forevermore. Amen.
And I have the keys of Hades and of Death
Revelation 1:18

God is a God of order, sovereign in all His ways, while Satan is the author of confusion, the accuser of the saints, the disrupter of faith, and the father of all lies. Jesus Christ conquered every area of Satan's domain by what He accomplished on the cross and subsequent resurrection. He overcomes our fears because He is the Author and Finisher of our faith (Hebrews 12:2). And fear and faith cannot truly exist together. When we are confused, fears attempt to come into our minds to undermine what Christ is doing in our hearts. When fears come, we can potentially be in bondage to those fears, but Jesus' perfect love in our hearts conquers all fear.

Satan attempts to use the power of fear that is outside the Fear of the Lord to torment our hearts. Before Jesus went to the cross, Satan had the power of death; however, in His resurrection Jesus conquered death, hell, and the grave. It has been said that all fear originates from the natural fear of death. Jesus identifies with us in this fear, but He did not submit to it. He faced and experienced the fear of death. He not only refused to succumb to it, He in fact, overcame it! He knew He could trust the Father to raise Him from the dead by Holy Spirit. By His death and resurrection He conquered fear and He liberates all who trust Him. Hebrews 2:14-18 says, "Inasmuch then as the children have partaken of flesh and blood, He Himself likewise shared in the same, that through death He might destroy him who had the power of death, that is, the devil, and release those who through fear of death were all their lifetime subject to bondage." Jesus conquered all fear so that since we are in Him, we are no longer subject to its bondage.

Because of our trust in what Jesus did on the cross and the power of His resurrection, we are free from the fear of death. This freedom from fear is ours only because we are now God's children. "For you did not receive the spirit of bondage *again to fear*, but you received the Spirit of adoption by whom we cry out, 'Abba, Father.' The Spirit Himself bears witness with our spirit that we are children of God, and if children, then heirs—heirs of God and joint heirs with Christ, if indeed we suffer with Him, that we may also be glorified together" (Romans 8:15-17). We are totally at liberty to cry out to God as our Abba, which is an endearing term for Daddy. Father God absolutely accepts us as His children and gives us free access to Himself. Our Father embraces each of us individually as His own dear child, giving us great freedom, authority, and power over fear.

When fear attempts to attack (and it will) we should present it to God. If potential fears are not presented to our Lord, Satan will endeavor to fill our hearts with more tormenting fear. "Whatever is not presented to God, Satan will attempt to fill," (Virkler).

Scripture says, "And they overcame him [Satan] by the blood of the Lamb and by the word of their testimony, and they did not love their lives to the death." (Revelation 12:11). We are over-comers by the blood of Jesus Christ. How we overcome is determined by what we believe, who we trust, and what we say. Our testimony is to be active faith with trust in our hearts and our confession is to be the promises of God found in the Scriptures. We declare Scriptural promises based on our specific situations because the Word of God has provided light and help in its promises and power. By speaking out regarding our faith and trust in God, it becomes the word of our testimony. By taking up our crosses (death to self) we follow Him into His resurrection life; we overcome because He overcame!

Death and life are indeed in the power of the tongue through our confessions (Proverbs 18:21). We choose life, and that life is in Jesus Christ, the Son of the Living God! We believe, therefore we speak. Jesus holds the keys of authority and He conquers all fear with His perfect love.

When we are faced with something that could elicit fear, we must resist by entrusting our lives to God, by declaring His Word, and by trusting what Jesus accomplished on Calvary. Apostle Paul wrote, "And since we have the same spirit of faith, according to what is written, 'I believed and therefore I spoke,' we also believe and therefore speak, knowing that He who raised up the Lord Jesus will also raise us up with Jesus, and will present us with you" (2 Corinthians 4:13, 14). The context regards facing death, believing in the power of Jesus' resurrection.

There is a spirit of faith and there is a spirit of fear. The spirit of faith is our human spirit influenced by Holy Spirit in our hearts to believe and trust God. Faith is a gift from God's Spirit (Ephesians 2:8). As we will discuss in the next section, a spirit of fear does not come from God.

The Spirit of Fear

For God has not given us a spirit of fear,
but of power and of love and of a sound mind.
2 Timothy 1:7

Because of Adam's and Eve's disobedience, the torment of fear was birthed in the human heart, which was orchestrated by Satan's scheme to discredit God. This type of fear opened them, and the entire human race, to the evil of tormenting fear. Fear of this type invites demonic attacks, because God does not give the spirit of fear—it is from Satan and his minion spirits.

The spirit of fear is actually an evil spirit, influencing a strong, negative, and terrifying mindset, with emotion, caused by expectation or awareness of danger (perceived or real). The strategy of Satan is to establish anxious concerns, worries, and attacks in the heart to attempt to undermine trust in God. Paul, the apostle, wrote his protégé, Timothy, "For God has not given us a spirit of fear, but of power and of love and of a sound mind" (2 Timothy 1:7). Notice Paul referred to fear as a spirit. Timothy was facing many challenges as a young pastor of the large church in Ephesus; he seemed to be fraught with timidity and fear which were affecting his effectiveness in ministry. His mentor lovingly encouraged him to trust God's Spirit within him for power, love, and a sound mind. Holy Spirit gives empowerment for ministry; He provides us with a capacity to love God and others. The Spirit of God also gives us power, delegated to us in the authority of the Name of Jesus, and He gives us the sound, disciplined mind of Christ.

This Scripture is written for our encouragement today just as much as it was for Timothy. This Word from God encourages us to realize His power is in our lives, and that the love of God (which never fails) has been poured into our hearts by Holy Spirit (1 Corinthians 13:8; Romans 5:5). We are able to trust God because He infuses His love in our hearts by His Spirit (Romans 5:5). This love of God casts out all fear, instilling hope, providing everything needed when we face any and all challenges that could cause fear. Great hope is ours in the love of God in conquering the spirit of fear.

Overcoming Fear

"Fear is the mind killer."
Frank Herbert

Love never fails.
1 Corinthians 13:8a

Fear has a debilitating effect on the mind and heart if it is not checked by God's love. Without perfect love fear causes torment, generates inward weakness, stifles encouragement, drains creativity, and disheartens. Fear starts as a thought in the mind and attempts to become a stronghold. We must take every thought captive, whether of fear or anything else, into subjection to the obedience of Christ, because fear exalts itself against the knowledge of God (2 Corinthians 10:4-6). Fear can be faced and dealt with by faith in God and by His love, which is generated by trust in His Word and trust in His Spirit—His love is in us and our love is perfected in Him.

Proverbs 4:23 says to keep, or guard our hearts with all diligence, for out of it flows the issues of life. Jesus said that out the abundance of the heart, the mouth speaks (Luke 6:45). So we must deposit good things of the Word of God in our hearts so they can influence a positive paradigm of living and frame of reference in our thinking. If we are not cautious, we might speak of fears that are attempting to enter our hearts, but what really needs to come from our mouths are words of faith and trust in what God has said in His Word. We can avoid allowing worry to enter our hearts if we simply confess God's Word while believing in our hearts, being anxious for nothing, but with thanksgiving making our request to God (Philippians 4:6). We are given the privilege and opportunity to obey the Word, that says over and over again,

"Fear not…" (Isaiah 41:10, 13, 14; 43:1, 5; 44:2; Joel 2:21; Luke 12:32 and many more).

When God speaks through His Word, He provides grace for us to act on that Word. We are to be in Christ, in faith, and in trust. All fear must be dealt with in His love and in our trust of Him. Because we are in Christ, out of our hearts should flow the issues of His life in us as we experience the renewal in our minds, not the issues of natural or secular life. The abundance that is in our hearts is to be the Word of Christ richly dwelling there (Colossians 3:16). Jesus Christ is the Greater One who dwells in us, and He is greater than any and all of our fears.

Faith, hope, and love lead to a strong trust in God that overcomes fear. Faith comes by hearing the Word of God (Romans 10:17). Trust develops from love for and submission to God. "There is no fear in love; but perfect love casts out fear, because fear involves torment" (1 John 4:18). The love of God in Christ Jesus overrides fear, and nothing can separate us from this love (Romans 8:35-39). Yet in His Fatherly love, God allows and uses natural experiences that cause us to face fear so we will overcome it as we learn to trust Him, perfecting our hearts in His love. Jesus offers His victory over fear to be ours as well and He provides us with His Spirit so that we are overcomers, encouraging us to exercise faith by telling us in His Word that we are more than conquerors (Romans 8:37).

Addressing the fears we face by faith is a very important aspect of our experience in the crucible of trust, so that we truly rely upon God, focusing on Him, His Word, and His love. We are in the world, but not of it. Existing in this world is God's plan for teaching us to have reliance upon and trust in Him. We are in His Kingdom as sons, and we are growing to become like Him while in this world and in crucibles of trust—truly the place of training for reigning under the Sovereignty of Almighty God as He prepares us to be regents in His Kingdom as kings and priests for God's eternal realm (Revelation 1:6; 5:10).

As overcomers we have faith and trust Him, and by His love in our hearts we rise above fear that tries to manifest. Indeed, in our spirits we are seated with Him in heavenly places. If our hearts are not grounded in the love of God and trust in Christ, fear will come upon us when we least expect it. If we are not careful, fear becomes a faith killer undermining our trust in the Lord and our identity as His sons and His ambassadors. Faith works through love (Galatians 5:6b), the foundation of trust.

Fear also manifests as worry, which means to be overly anxious in our hearts regarding something we face in life or something that we assume we do not have the power to change. But we do have the power to change by having the opportunity to trust and believe by prayer, in speaking life with our confessions. We are not to lean on our own limited understanding when facing fear, but acknowledge Him in trust (Proverbs 3:5-6). The antidote of fear is God's love. This manifests in the inner action of trust with the prayer of thanksgiving leading to peace: "Be anxious for nothing, but in everything by prayer and supplication, with thanksgiving, let your requests be made known to God; and the peace of God, which surpasses all understanding, will guard your hearts and minds through Christ Jesus" (Philippians 4:6-7). When we believe and trust God by praying to Him with thanksgiving, He will guard our hearts with His peace, overriding anxious perceptions and fear. This belief leads to deeper trust, which is founded in love that casts out all fear.

What's to Fear About the Fear of the Lord?

In this discussion about fear, there is one fear that is good. The Fear of the Lord is the spiritual, respectful, and reverential awe of God in the realization that He is All Powerful, All Present, All Knowing, and Immutable. Even with all of these supernatural attributes of God, the one that draws us to Him, more than any other is His great love, which is revealed in the fact that He is always good, faithful, trustworthy, merciful, and kind. There is nothing to fear about the Fear of the Lord; it is healthy, wholesome, and necessary. Indeed, proper fear of the Lord produces many blessings. To fear the Lord in this manner is to reveal love and trust in Him. The book of Proverbs mentions many benefits of the Fear of the Lord. Listed below are only a few:

- It is the beginning of wisdom and of knowledge.
- It leads one to depart from evil.
- It brings blessings of honor and riches.
- There is abhorrence to evil with the fear of the Lord.
- It brings strong confidence.
- It leads to life and brings one to the personal knowledge of God.

When we have a healthy and proper fear of the Lord it always leads to overcoming any natural or supernatural fear. When we have this healthy fear of God, a purity of heart is revealed. As disciples of Jesus Christ our growth in holiness is primarily due to our abiding in Him along with our healthy fear of the Lord: "Therefore, having these promises, beloved, let us cleanse ourselves from all filthiness of the flesh and spirit, perfecting holiness in the fear of God" (2 Corinthians 7:1).

A healthy, spiritual fear of God leads us to become like Him, to be holy. Our Lord Jesus fulfilled the prophecy found in Isaiah 11:1-3a, which is also to become our paradigm in life: "The Spirit of the LORD shall rest upon Him; The Spirit of wisdom and understanding; The Spirit of counsel and might; The Spirit of knowledge and of the fear of the LORD. His delight is in the fear of the LORD." Jesus satisfied and modeled the fear of the Lord as He walked this earth. Hebrews 5:7-10, says of Him, "Who, in the days of His flesh, when He had offered up prayers and supplications, with vehement cries and tears to Him who was able to save Him from death, and was heard because of *His godly fear,* though He was a Son, yet He learned obedience by the things which He suffered. And having been perfected, He became the author of eternal salvation to all who obey Him."

I do not fully understand why the sinless Son of God needed to be perfected in godly fear and learn obedience through the things He suffered. Perhaps as He was also called the Son of Man, He was modeling godly fear through His crucible of trust so we also can follow His lead in our being perfected through ours. I only know and believe that in His life on earth, as a man, He was absolutely obedient to the Father's will, exhibiting His reverence, holy fear, and submission to the Father.

Learning from David and Others

David, the king of Israel, addressed fear in his life as he wrote of being in the Secret Place of the Most High, of being hidden under the shadow of the wings of the Almighty. We have access to this same Secret Place in our walk with the Spirit of God. Like David, we can trust God and be assured of His faithfulness, no matter what we face. Several of David's Psalms reveal he faced many challenges, including death, betrayal, abandonment, and rejection. His confidence and trust in God were very real and instrumental in overcoming his fears. Consider a few of David's Psalms in light of facing fear:

- Psalm 23:4, "Yea, though I walk through the valley of the shadow of death, I will fear no evil, for You are with me; Your rod and Your staff, they comfort me."
- Psalm 34:4, "I sought the LORD, and He heard me, and delivered me from all my fears."
- Psalm 56:3-4, "Whenever I am afraid, I will trust in You. In God I will praise His word. In God I have put my trust; I will not fear."
- Psalm 57:7, "My heart is steadfast, O God, my heart is steadfast; I will sing and give praise" (written while David hid in a cave as a fugitive).

Every fear in life must be faced with trust in our hearts that we are God's children. In other words, we must resist fear; we must be fearless. It is our inheritance to trust the Lord and to be under the protection of Almighty God. Notice David resolved not to fear. He mentions being afraid, and whenever he was tempted to fear his trust in God was activated.

David had learned through experience that God was trustworthy. When David needed courage, provisions were available because he trusted God. As with David, our perspective must be one of trusting God, not our own abilities or personal courage in facing fears or worries. God does provide courage when life brings challenges potentially leading to fear; during these challenges we are to worship God with our whole hearts, because when we worship God, which is an expression of love and adoration, we can conquer fear.

Fears are potential inner responses to daunting, frightening situations (real or perceived). Response to fear is at the heart level, revealing either trust or showing the lack of trust. The "flight or fight" reactions are natural when it comes to facing fear, but there is a third response for those of us in Christ: faith which transforms into absolute trust. To the disciple of Jesus, trusting Him should be the only response. In trusting we will praise Him regardless of potential fear. He is with us and inside us in the Person of His Spirit providing courage within our hearts.

John Brunner, a career officer in the Marine Corp tells his story of facing the challenges and fears that accompanied life in the Corp in his inspirational devotional booklet he wrote for soldiers, called, *Battlefield Verses*. From his own multiple experiences he puts together many Scriptures applicable to various challenging situations he faced. These Scriptures helped him to stir and sustain faith and trust in his heart toward his Lord Jesus. He also tells of becoming friends with Captain Red McDaniel, USN, who had been a POW for seven years in Vietnam. McDaniel had a depth of understanding regarding fear, saying, "Courage is not the absence of fear; courage is simply the presence of faith" (2015, 20).

Faith overrides fear because with true, spiritual faith Jesus Christ is present with us; His trust is also present within us. Having faith in Jesus is to trust His promise to never leave nor forsake us. His presence is a very real place of courage within our hearts; as we face any fear Jesus' Spirit is within us manifesting His strength.

GOING THROUGH IN TRUST–
THE IMPORTANCE
OF OUR WORDS

"Yea, though I walk through the
valley of the shadow of death,
I will fear no evil; For You are with me;
Your rod and Your staff, they comfort me."
Psalm 23:4

D avid sang Psalm 23 and all his psalms to the Lord as his
praise, his testimony, his prayers, and his confession.
During his life he faced death, turmoil, betrayal, and deceit. Yet
he would say, "But as for me, I will trust in the Lord." He believed
God would be with him to lead, guide, and comfort him through
every situation. The trials we face are no different. The truth is
that God is with us to comfort, edify, and exhort in and through
every trial or adversity. We have this awesome promise found in
Isaiah 43:2: "When you pass through the waters, I will be with you;
And through the rivers, they shall not overflow you. When you
walk through the fire, you shall not be burned, nor shall the flame

scorch you." What valley are you facing? What evil is attempting to bring you down, to squelch your faith and trust in God? Whatever we face, God not only gets us through as we trust Him, but He will establish something of value within us in our character and as over-comers living in victory.

Consider the story of Shadrack, Meshach, and Abednego found in Daniel 3:1-17. They would not bow to the image of gold made by King Nebuchadnezzar, and for their refusal they faced being thrown into a fiery furnace to be burned alive. Their faith, resolve, and trust level were so high, they were not daunted; they were resolute to not bow whether God rescued them or not. Perhaps, like me you wonder if they had heard Isaiah's prophetic promise written many years earlier regarding walking through the fire. Irrespective, they would bow to no one other than Jehovah, the God of Abraham, Isaac, and Jacob. They willingly went into that furnace in their trust of and honor for Jehovah. These three literally entered a crucible trusting their very lives to God.

The Lord did indeed come through by being present with them in that crucible. When Nebuchadnezzar looked into the furnace he observed a fourth Man with the three men, seeing one like the Son of God. The four were walking around together, unaffected by the intense heat. God was with them. These three men totally trusted God and walked out unscathed, unburned, and didn't even smell like smoke. Nebuchadnezzar was so astounded that he blessed and honored the God of Shadrack, Meshach, and Abednego.

God stands with His faithful ones as they go through overwhelming challenges. He is no respecter of persons, because He is faithful to everyone who calls upon Him in faith and trust. "For the eyes of the LORD run to and fro throughout the whole earth, to show Himself strong on behalf of those whose heart is loyal to Him" (2 Chronicles 16:9a). He is therefore a respecter of loyalty, which truly is founded in faith, trust, reliance, and importunity in prayer.

He revealed Himself strong on behalf to these three Hebrew men who willingly risked their lives for their faith in God and the honor of His Name. The Lord will do the same in our lives. He is drawn to the one who stands loyal and who calls upon His Name while facing trials. God does not promise to take us out of trouble. He promises to take us through and get us beyond in order to experience His victory and His trustworthiness (2 Corinthians 2:14). For us, however, the encounter becomes a refining fire in testing our hearts as we walk toward maturity and purity in His sight.

Our experiences in this life are to be about our relationship with our Heavenly Father and the journey with His Spirit while going through them. While the destination is everlasting life with Him in His eternal Kingdom, the Kingdom of God is not just for eternity. It is also for today, as we live in righteousness, peace, and joy in the Holy Spirit (Romans 14:17). Our journey involves walking with God's Spirit and living our lives from the spiritual realities of faith, hope, and love in our intimate relationship with our Lord. From this bond we are privileged to pray in faith to our Heavenly Father, "Thy Kingdom come, Thy will be done, on earth as it is in heaven." Our journey involves praying with Him and believing His Word so intently that we actually are used by our Father to implement His Kingdom and His will on earth throughout our lives for His glory. In other words, God chooses to use and to lead us in our prayers to bring about His will.

As we live through occurrences and incidents in life, He is with us. Whether we face trials, tests, or temptations, our devoted Heavenly Father is right there loving us, our faithful Lord Jesus ever lives to intercede for us, and Holy Spirit is ever present providing the way of escape and the grace in order that we may bear any experience (1 Corinthians 10:13). God desires to lead us forth in triumph over sin, the pulls of the flesh, and any spiritual attacks. In doing this He establishes His Kingdom within our hearts over anything that exalts itself against the knowledge of the glory of God. The blessing during this process is an ongoing intimacy with the Father, our Lord Jesus, and Holy Spirit. From our relationship with them there is the strengthening of our inner man with power resulting in growth, maturity, patience, victory, and character, which come as we learn to trust and rely upon the Holy Spirit (Ephesians. 3:16).

There have been times when I thought I was relying upon God, but realized I did not completely trust Him. Unfortunately, I learned the hard way that it was only in His strength that I am able to overcome. Holy Spirit opened my understanding that I had lived in the cycle of regret, and He led, and continually leads, me to live out of my intimate relationship with Him into the cycle of trust. I had to get over my preconceived notion that spiritual maturity was all about me plodding through whatever I face. Learning to persevere in *His strength* was something that was foreign to me, and only came after failing in my own mental effort and emotional zeal. Leaning on my own resolve and hard work resulted in frustration and disappointment. This became a crucible of trust as the Lord revealed through this trial that I was able to go through in victory only as I trusted and relied upon Him. "Therefore let him who thinks he stands take heed lest he fall" (1Corinthians 10:12). I came to realize the only efforts on my part are to trust, rely upon Holy Spirit, stand upon the Word, and believe, so the results of going through whatever I face are of God's strength and His loving guidance.

Confession

Let us hold fast the confession of our hope
without wavering, for He who promised is faithful.
Hebrews 10:23

Our confessions are more important than we realize and will help us in going through life's challenges. What we say sets the tone of our lives and actually creates atmospheres in our mind. Most of us have heard the adage, "Confession is good for the soul." Certainly we are to confess our sins to God and to one another, but confession should also include daily positive affirmations and declarations regarding what God says in His Word. Even secular business people use confessions to stir their hearts toward success, therefore, should not God's children confess His Word and His Promises?

God told Joshua to not let the word depart from his mouth, but to meditate upon it day and night. To meditate includes muttering, pondering, envisioning, and also confession (Strong). As we confess God's Word out loud through prayer and declarations, we are obedient. Hebrews 4:14 records: since we have such a great High Priest in Jesus Christ, "let us hold fast our confession." The word for confession in the Greek is *homologia,* meaning to say the same thing (Strong). We are to profess what is written in Scripture, to verbally repeat promises from Scripture. For example: "The greater One dwells within me." "I am always being led forth in triumph." "I am more than a conqueror." "No weapon formed against me will prosper." The truth of Scripture will generate faith and trust in our hearts as we confess them.

Hebrews 10:23 also tells us to hold fast to the confession of our hope, without wavering. Proper confession is to be done consistently, declaring what we believe and what we hope based on Scripture. Jesus said that if we confess Him before others, He will acknowledge us before the Father (Matthew 10:32). Confessing Jesus as Lord helps establish our hope in Him and confirms what we believe in our hearts. No one can confess Jesus as Lord except by the Holy Spirit (1 Corinthians 12:3).

Apostle Paul also wrote of confession in 2 Corinthians 4:13-15:

> And since we have the same spirit of faith, according
> to what is written, 'I believed and therefore I spoke,'
> we also believe and therefore speak, knowing that
> He who raised up the Lord Jesus will also raise us
> up with Jesus, and will present us with you. For
> all things are for your sakes, that grace, having
> spread through the many, may cause thanksgiving
> to abound to the glory of God.

Paul writes not only as one who is sent to preach good news, but also as one who personally believes, who has thanksgiving in his heart, and who expresses what he believes with words.

Death and Life are in the power of the tongue or confession (Proverbs 18:21). We will enjoy the fruit of our lips (Proverbs 12:14). Our confessions should be from the voice of truth and promises from God not from the voice of doubt and unbelief— the difference between being in the cycle of trust over the cycle of regret. "For then you will have your delight in the Almighty, and lift up your face to God. You will make your prayer to Him, He will hear you, and you will pay your vows. *You will also declare a thing, and it will be established for you; so light will shine on your ways*" (Job 22:26-28). What are we declaring with our words? What are we establishing as light to shine on our ways? We are declaring God's manifold wisdom, His promises, and His plans (Ephesians 3:10). We must desire to establish what the Word of God says for our lives, not in the limits of what we think or understand.

Our understanding needs guidance and renewal, and our confessions should be spoken from what generates faith, or what is good, pure, hopeful, encouraging, faithful, trustful, or respectful. Paul, the apostle was often heard speaking and confessing the truth and manifold wisdom of God, and he admonishes us in Philippians 4:8, 9:

> Finally, brethren, whatever things are true, whatever things are noble, whatever things are just, whatever things are pure, whatever things are lovely, whatever things are of good report, if there is any virtue and if there is anything praiseworthy — meditate on these things. The things which you learned and received and *heard* and saw in me, these do, and the God of peace will be with you.

The things we meditate upon fill our hearts, as Jesus said, "Out the abundance of the heart, the mouth speaks" (Matthew 12:34). Following and imitating godly behavior of mature saints who watch their words and speak only what encourages and uplifts leads us to do the same. We must be careful with our words and avoid corrupt speaking (Ephesians 4:29). Our tongues and our confessions are to be transformed by the renewing of our minds into fountains of life (Proverbs 10:11; 13:14).

King David understood this principle and modeled discipline in His speaking. He wrote in Psalm 141:3. "Set a guard, O LORD, over my mouth; Keep watch over the door of my lips." Jesus also emphasized proper speaking in guarding our words. In His rebuke to the Pharisees there is applicable truth for our understanding found in Matthew 12:34-37:

> Brood of vipers! How can you, being evil, speak good things? For out of the abundance of the heart the mouth speaks. A good man out of the good treasure of his heart brings forth good things, and an evil man out of the evil treasure brings forth evil things. But I say to you that for every idle word men may speak, they will give account of it in the

Day of Judgment. *For by your words you will be justified, and by your words you will be condemned.*

Our confessions originate from the heart's meditations or what Jesus referred to as treasure, good or evil. That is why David said, "Let the words of my mouth and the meditation of my heart be acceptable in Your sight, O LORD, my strength and my Redeemer" (Psalm 19:14).

Truly our words set the tone of how we face our crucibles of what we go through and experience. The problems we face are not the true problem. The perspective of our problems all too often is our problem and our words about them come from our hearts' condition. Words from our mouths very often create crucibles of our own making, so let us make a good confession of Jesus, of His Word, and of declaring the manifold wisdom of God, not the problems.

TRUSTING GOD HIS WAY

Enter by the narrow gate;
for wide is the gate and broad is the way
that leads to destruction,
and there are many who go in by it.
Because narrow is the gate and difficult is the way which
leads to life, and there are few who find it.
Matthew 7:13-14

My friend, Liz Ridlon, wrote a wonderful little book entitled, *God Meets all our Needs*. She and her husband have been dear friends of ours for many years. I really appreciate her simple, yet profound message as she expounds from her own mature, childlike faith that God is indeed trustworthy. Her subtitle, *Finding Contentment by Trusting God to Meet all our Needs*, speaks much truth. In the book Liz writes, "Even though God knows our thoughts, it is good for us to talk to Him in prayer. It shows we depend on Him and want to enjoy fellowship with our creator" (2005, 42). Her words speak volumes and I have learned much from them.

In my experience, I desired to fellowship and talk with God, to depend upon Him, but I was doing all the talking, telling Him what I wanted. I believe what Liz means in talking to God involves listening to Him as well. Through Liz's insights, I learned why I had experienced such frustration, which was the result of a lack of trust. God was doing a deep work in my heart through my life's circumstances, because I needed to recognize this, so I would yield and cooperate with Him.

God desires wholehearted trust, but I trusted God my own way and with my own limited perception. Because of this I had expectations—that were not of God and—that did not always work out the way I thought they should. Part of how God works is by patiently allowing us to go through times when things just do not work out the way we expect due to our incorrect assumptions.

However, God is not capricious, overbearing, or mean. He has given us free will and His desire is that we recognize the need for the renewal of the mind within that free will. I experienced this when I lost that straight-day position. Instead of trusting I grew impatient with God, thinking He was not fulfilling His promise. The trouble was that I did not truly know, or trust God for who He is in all His goodness and ultimate trustworthiness. Instead I was full of childishness, pride, and selfishness. Doubt had crept in with wrong thinking that God would not fulfill His promise to me in the call He had given me. I was blinded by my circumstances, because they were the constant object of my focus. I needed to be fixing my eyes on Jesus. Nevertheless, God was (and is) always patient, faithful, and trustworthy with me. The need to readjust myself to God's ways became very evident. He heard me grumble and complain, yet in His grace He was working things out for my good, leading me to His much more superior way.

The Crisis of Belief

"Lord, I believe, help my unbelief."
Mark 9:24b

God's ways are not our ways, but He always leads us in a way that gives us opportunities to learn His ways as we yield to Him. As disciples of Jesus we learn to adjust from our own, natural way of thinking and doing, and entrust our lives to His ways. He draws us to Himself by His Spirit, who takes us by the hand as our Guide and Navigator along the narrow road of life in Christ. He always provides us with direction and help as we travel on the slender highway of righteous living. By His Spirit's leading, aid comes to us through His Word and His providence.

Additionally, our submission to Him and our obedience to His Word will not only provide a wonderful path of experiential knowledge, they will also bring to us many challenges in which we must rely upon His Word, totally trusting His heart. When this road gets more difficult at times we find ourselves in sort of a conflict of trust. That was my experience in having wrong expectations. We must entrust our lives to His will to stabilize our walk, thus He becomes our steadfastness, our constancy. He is our Rock and our Shelter in our journey.

One of the main challenges of belief is in being doers of the Word, particularly to love others as God loves us. Jesus said in John 14:21, "He who has My commandments and keeps them, it is he who loves Me. And he who loves Me will be loved by My Father, and I will love him and manifest Myself to him." The greatest commandment, according to Jesus, was to love the Lord your God with all your heart, with all your soul, with your entire mind and with all your strength, and the second was to love your neighbor as yourself.

We truly love others only through the strength of Holy Spirit with His love preeminent within our hearts. Jesus modeled this kind of love by loving the Father and extending that love toward others. The level of love between the Father and the Son was Jesus' most powerful motivator to obey the Father's will, particularly in going to the cross, which modeled ultimate love. This same love also motivates us to obey, and truly helps us walk the narrow path. By grace the Lord strengthens us in His will to love others by empowering our hearts with His Spirit, thus experiencing more of God, who is the Personification of Love.

In the book, *Experiencing God*, Dr. Henry Blackaby describes principles he observed in his personal occurrences as a man of God and a leader of pastors (2008). He speaks of seven realities in experiencing God when growing into knowing Him intimately in living out His will.

1. God is always at work around you.
2. God pursues a continuing love relationship with you that is real and personal.
3. God invites you to become involved with Him in His work.
4. God speaks by the Holy Spirit through the Bible, prayer, circumstances, and the church to reveal Himself, His purposes, and His ways.
5. God's invitation for you to work with Him always leads you to a *crisis of belief* that requires faith and action.
6. You must make major adjustments in your life to join God in what He is doing.
7. You come to know God by experience as you obey Him and He accomplishes His work through you.

To illustrate experiencing God, and particularly the crisis of belief dynamic, Blackaby uses the journey of Abram's life as told in Genesis, chapters 12-25. God's call to Abram was to totally trust through obedience, even when not knowing what was required. Abram revealed himself to be a man of prayer and trust when God told him to leave his country and, "Go to a land that I will show you" (Genesis 12:1). Abram departed in obedience not knowing where God was leading him. God did not say where to go; He just told him to go and in going the path would be revealed. Consequently, in obeying these instructions, while adjusting his life to God's plans, Abram was given some very amazing promises. God would make of him a great nation; would bless him, and make his name great; would make him a blessing; would bless those who bless him and curse those who curse him; and in him all the nations of the world would be blessed. Abram believed God and obeyed; in believing it was accounted to him as righteousness (Genesis 15:6). Abram modeled the paradigm of trusting God—as he revealed his relationship of faith and belief in the Lord—by his worship, prayer life, and his obedience.

God's promises to Abram were wonderful, even though they came with the command to go to an unknown land. During his journeys Abram had many trials, tests, and tribulations. God had promised him a son. How could God make of him a great nation when he was 75 years old, had no children, and his wife was past child bearing years? Abram prayed to God about this, and he steadfastly believed and trusted God.

Even though God blessed Abram with material blessings, it took twenty-five years for the promise of a son through his wife Sarah to be realized. Abram's name means *exalted father*, and God eventually changed his name to Abraham, which means *father of a multitude*. With this name change, God established a covenant with him with promises.

One of the promises to Abraham was that within his seed the nations of the world would be blessed. The promised seed was his son, Isaac. However, the ultimate fulfillment of that promised seed was Christ, who down through the generations from Isaac's seed came forth in the person of Jesus of Nazareth, the Christ and Son of the Living God (Galatians 3:16). Jesus became the definitive Blessing to all mankind, as He came to reveal the Father, to establish the Kingdom of God, to destroy the works of the devil, and to restore us to having access and relationship with the Father. He gave His life as a blessing on the cross as payment for the sins of the world so we could have eternal life in Him, becoming the Mediator between God and man.

Jesus Christ is the Seed of Abraham and fulfills multiple other prophecies found in the Old Testament, including that He would be the Desire of all nations (Haggai 2:7). Christ is what this world needs. Christ not only provides salvation, but He will righteously rule and reign as King of kings and Prince of Peace in the Eternal Kingdom of God. Those who trust in Him receive salvation and much more.

Through Christ we have been made to be partakers of the Divine nature of God. In Christ we become co-laborers with Him to bring redemption to others. Scripture says that those in Christ receive all the promises to Abraham (Galatians 3:7-14). When we believe and receive Jesus Christ as Savior and Lord, then Christ Himself dwells within our hearts by the power of the Holy Spirit (Ephesians 3:14-19). We become rooted and grounded in His love, thus becoming His testimony to the world. From our willingness to be used by Him, we are witnesses to those with whom we come into contact. All the nations will eventually be blessed through His presence in our lives as we declare the Gospel and lead others to Christ.

God told Abram to go to a land He would show him. He trusted and obeyed. In similitude Jesus tells His disciples, to go into the entire world. This mandate to His disciples back then is also for us today. "Peace to you. As the Father has sent Me, I also send you" (John 20:21). After He said that He breathed on them saying, "Receive you the Holy Spirit." Because we are born again believers in Jesus Christ, we are empowered by the Holy Spirit and we are given an assignment of trust in that power, to go into all the world and make disciples, teaching them what we have been taught (Matthew 28:18-20; 2 Timothy 2:2).

Our Father truly desires for us to experience Him as He does His work through us. Blackaby emphasizes that as we trust the Lord in accepting His invitation to join Him, we become coworkers together with Him. At God's invitation to join in with Him, we will experience a crisis of belief that necessitates faith and action on our part. This place of action causes us to experience a challenge to our belief in God. In order for us to join God in His work, and truly experience Him the way He desires, we will have to adjust ourselves to His ways. The Lord has set forth our works to be done through willing obedience—and yieldedness—with our participation in His work of redemption (2 Corinthians 6:1).

Scripture teaches we truly are blessed with Abraham when we have faith in Jesus Christ (Galatians 5:9). Following Abraham's example, we believe and obey God. Abraham experienced another crucible of trust when he was asked to present his son, Isaac, to the Lord as a sacrifice. God's intent was to test Abraham's willingness to obey, but God provided a ram as the sacrifice in place of Isaac (Genesis 22:1-18). This was a type and a shadow, a picture of the Father offering Christ Jesus to become the sacrifice for our sin.

God then asks us, as His children, to present our own bodies as living sacrifices by faith (Romans 12:1-2). Because we are in Christ, our sacrifice is to give up our lives and become ministers of reconciliation for others (2 Corinthians 5:18-19). As we live for Jesus, allowing His life to manifest through us, we become the administration of His grace as stewards of that same blessing promised to

Abraham. Because of Christ in us, all the nations of the world will be blessed through our obedience to present the Gospel of Jesus Christ, the only true hope for blessing from God.

God invites us into His labors, but because of our flesh (and the devil's attacks against God's work) this invitation will lead us to experience crises which challenge our trust. As we seek the Lord, He opens our minds to recognize our need to change due to these challenges. This crisis of belief (what I call the crucible of trust) then requires life adjustments to God's ways in order for us to experience Him and all He has planned. His Spirit lovingly stretches and challenges us during our crises, leading us to regularly and consistently adjust from our natural ways into His divine ways, which is a purifying process like a refining fire.

The Blank Contract of Trust

Several years ago I was sitting quietly with the Lord in prayer and meditation pondering His will and intention for my life, not exactly certain where He was leading. I was willingly seeking Him with what I considered legitimate questions. Was I to pursue becoming a pastor again? Was I to wait till retirement several years into the future? Was I to retire early? I knew of the call on my life to minister in His Name, but felt the need to know and experience more in training before launching out into ministry. So I asked the Lord to reveal His will and purpose. I had experienced several crises of belief and finally perceived what it meant to be in God's process of preparation.

As I presented my petition before Him in prayer I had my eyes closed, and I began to see a blank contract in my imagination. I sensed this question in my heart. "Are you willing to sign this blank contract in following my will?" As strange as it seemed to do this, yet realizing that this was similar to Abram's challenge, I said yes to the Lord, and in my imagination I signed the bottom of what appeared to be a blank sheet of paper. As I said to the Lord that I trusted Him, a sense of entering a new period in my life of learning deeper trust became very real. Yet there was this naïve thought that I was so noble and trusting in signing this imaginary contract. Perhaps I was, but I was actually entering a new phase of taking the crucible of my trust, to another level.

Signing a blank contract seems ludicrous to the natural mind, but with God, this is often the case for those whom He calls. He desires to be believed and trusted. As my spiritual mentor says, "God does not always make sense; He makes faith." When God makes faith rise up in us, He is building trust in Him for our good, which is for our growth and our maturity toward perfection. His approach to each of us is unique to our relationship with Him. His desire is our transformation into the image of His Son, Jesus Christ. He leads us into the unknown so we will learn absolute reliance upon His Spirit. His purpose is to keep us connected to Him, abiding in prayer and trust, relationally, lovingly, and intimately.

Signing a blank contract only illustrates the truth that Jesus is the Vine. We are His branches and must stay in a place of abiding, not only in order to survive but to bear fruit for His glory. God leads us to so much more than just survival. He is leading us to thrive, flourish, and live above our circumstances. And as we trust Him, abiding in Him, He will lead us to produce fruit in our lives that will be worthy for the Father.

God often leads us in ambiguity so we will grow to trust Him and rely upon Him in our journey. In the mystery of the unknown, God reveals His goodness and His desire in our hearts, which is for us to know Him as Father, and from our relationship with Him comes our fulfillment and maturity as His sons. He will open our hearts to His knowledge, wisdom, and understanding. The blank contract, for me, was God's way of teaching me to not lean upon my own understanding, but to trust and acknowledge Him in all my ways.

Born of the Spirit

"The wind blows where it wishes,
and you hear the sound of it,
but cannot tell where it comes from and where it goes.
So is everyone who is born of the Spirit."
John 3:8

All who are born of the Spirit are to be led by the Spirit. We do not necessarily know where that will take us, which can often be realized as a crucible of trust. Being led by the Spirit involves prayer and trust seeking the Father, which also means communion and obedience while not always knowing exactly where He is leading. Being unsure means we must trust as He leads believing He knows best. His purpose is that as we go, we experience Him in our journey, and the beauty of His purposes is that He desires to incrementally reveal more of Himself to us along the way. Knowing He is with us through every trial and every victory builds precious intimacy with Him, and that connection of love with Him becomes better than knowing our destination. "Because your loving kindness is better than life, my lips shall praise you" (Psalm 63:3).

That day I imaginatively signed a blank contract I did not know where God was taking me. I was then, and am desirous today to be led into whatever His assignment is upon my life. I honestly believed He would quickly fill in the blanks, but this was not His will at that time. I am glad now. He wanted me to enter into a deeper relationship of prayer, trust, and abiding with Him. At that time, not only was my prayer life weak, anemic, and ineffective, God also revealed to me that I had blind spots in my heart and faith; He began to lovingly and graciously open my understanding to what I needed.

Our Father opened my eyes to show me that my trust in Him is a direct result of my prayer life in His Spirit. The more I pray in the Spirit in faith and trust—which includes listening more than speaking—the more I get to know Him, the more I delight myself in Him, and the more I grow in joy and willingness to obey His will. "Delight yourself also in the LORD, and He shall give you the desires of your heart," says Psalm 37:4. To delight oneself in this context means to willingly yield to God's leading in cheerful obedience. God's guidance to us comes from prayer and His Word, as His Spirit leads, which as we submit to Him, always progresses to deeper trust. Prayer and trust go hand in hand as we walk with the Lord.

God places His desires in our hearts as we yield our personal desires. My desires to minister and to write are examples, and He has shown me these are part of that blank contract. I know He will provide the fulfillment of those desires according to His will. Being led by the Spirit will change our hearts little by little as He interposes His desires into us, which are always best. The best part of that blank contract He asked me to sign, even in not knowing the outcome, is walking and abiding with Jesus, being led intimately by His Spirit, growing in trust and reliance upon Holy Spirit, and expecting the best outcome according to His perfect will.

FOCUSED PRAYER
THROUGH TRUST

One day while in prayer, I asked the Lord to help me to avoid distractions and keep my focus upon Him. I heard these words. "The more you grow in ability to stay focused in the moment with Me in private, the more you will grow to be able to stay focused on Me in public." The Father is drawing us to Himself by teaching us that we must grow to keep our eyes on Jesus in every circumstance and each situation.

Our focus is to be on Jesus Christ—abiding in Him—growing in our awareness of His very presence in our hearts. We have the privilege to commune in a constant attitude and atmosphere of prayer. Our minds are to be centered upon Him, not our circumstances. In order to accomplish this we are to be reading and meditating upon God's Word daily, remembering and praying God's promises, and being led by and communing with Holy Spirit.

To only have our sight on the circumstances of our trials or on the crisis of belief is the strategy of the enemy, a tactic of distraction. We do not ignore them; we trust the Lord, always presenting them to Him as we experience them. This is why Jesus instructed us to always pray and not faint, and why Paul instructed us to pray without ceasing (Luke 18:1; 1 Thessalonians 5:17). Praying without ceasing may seem impracticable, but our prayer life is really our lifestyle and our lifeline as we abide in Christ and His Word abides in us. We are to be in a spirit of prayer all day. Even during mundane duties and responsibilities we bring Christ into every aspect of our daily routines. Prayer is our connection to God as we keep our minds on Him throughout the day, thus He will bring us perfect peace (Isaiah 26:3). Meditation and prayer go hand in hand.

Paul the apostle writes in 2 Corinthians 10:4-5 that the weapons of our warfare are mighty through God for the pulling down of strongholds. He cautions us to cast down imaginations and every lofty thing that exalts itself against the knowledge of God, to bring every thought captive to the obedience of Christ. If not, we become distracted by the cares of this world, choking the Word and our faith, draining our spiritual energy, sapping, and compromising our trust. Therefore, our disciplined thought life is indeed integral to our prayer life and is a mighty weapon—way more than we may realize.

Some years ago the Lord opened my understanding about prayer. Most of my prayers had been focused on the problems. I was always praying the problems, crying out to God to fix them. Then Holy Spirit taught me that prayer must be from faith, believing for the answers as I focus upon the Word of God. He told me to pray and speak the answers, not the problems (Mark 11:23-24). Prayers are to be *from* victory, not *toward* victory. We are seated with Christ in the heavenly place, so our prayers are actually from the perspective of His presence.

In a statement by Dr. Mark Virkler this truth is considered from a different perspective: "What you focus upon grows within you; what grows within you, you become." Virkler teaches that if we pray with our attentions on the problems and challenges, it is essentially praying with an idol in our hearts. Our focus is not on the Lord, but on the issues, which become bigger the more we focus upon them. In prayer, our attention should be on the Awesome God of our faith as we acknowledge He is greater than any problem. He will answer according to His will and purpose. Therefore, we keep our eyes on Jesus when we pray and believe God for answers.

When our true spiritual focus is on Jesus during prayer, or during any trial or temptation, we grow in transformation toward Christ likeness. We keep our hearts focused on Him and in doing so we are in the Spirit. The more we are in the Spirit, the more we become like Jesus. "But we all, with unveiled face, beholding as in a mirror the glory of the Lord, are being transformed into the same image from glory to glory, just as by the Spirit of the Lord" (2 Corinthians 3:18).

The Still Small Voice

Elijah, the great prophet of God experienced the fire of God falling on the altar on Mount Carmel (1 Kings 18:20-40). This was his paradigm of God's communications. Then 1 Kings 19:9-12 records Elijah's experience with God in a different way. The Lord led him to go to Mount Horeb. While there the Lord passed by him in an interesting encounter. There was the experience of strong winds that broke rocks. He also witnessed an earthquake and finally, fire, but Scripture says God was not in any those things. Then Elijah heard a still small voice. The word *still* in Hebrew means calm, quiet, and silence (Strong). When Elijah perceived the calm and quiet of God's voice, he understood God speaks in many different ways, and he understood what God was saying and obeyed.

God had spoken years earlier on that same Mount Horeb to the Children of Israel in thunderous ways. The Israelites were so terrified they begged Moses to have God only speak to him as their mediator (Exodus 20:18-20), which is heartbreaking because God truly wanted intimate communication with all His children. He still does. The good news is that He now speaks through, Jesus Christ the Mediator of the New Covenant:

> God, who at various times and in various ways spoke in time past to the fathers by the prophets, has in these last days spoken to us by *His* Son, whom He has appointed heir of all things, through whom also He made the worlds; who being the brightness of His glory and the express image of His person, and upholding all things by the word of His power, when He had by Himself purged our sins, sat down at the right hand of the Majesty on high (Hebrews 1:1-3).

Interestingly, where it reads His Son, the word *His* is not in the original Greek manuscripts, but was added by the translators for clarification, or so they thought. God seems to be speaking in the language of *Son* who heard the Father constantly. Scripture records that Jesus often spent time with the Father, in prayer and in quietude. The Lord wants all His children to acquire this ability that Jesus modeled. He is leading us to use the spiritual sense of listening to hear, of hearing to perceive, of perceiving to commune and of communing to be in fellowship, and in fellowship be intimate with the Father. Perhaps like me, your times with Jesus in the Spirit and of intimacy with the Father are very often in silence and quietude.

Ability to hear the Spirit of God leads to spiritual enlightenment, not necessarily mental awareness. Cognitive perceptions do come from God; He gives understanding, but that is not always what takes place during spiritual communion with God. There comes an intimacy with the Lord not experienced outside of silence with Him. Quiet transformations take place as He works in us to will and to do according to His good pleasure (Philippians 2:13). Many things from God work deeper than the mind. They go into our spirits, and as a result of our involvement our minds are renewed by the Spirit of God. He does a deep work in our hearts, revealed in how we live, how we treat others, and how we make decisions. From this deep abiding relationship we are imputed with the Mind of Christ—which comes to us by being one with Jesus through Holy Spirit. "But he who is joined to the Lord is one spirit with Him" (1 Corinthians 6:17).

One with Holy Spirit

As born again disciples of Jesus Christ, we are in fellowship with Holy Spirit (2 Corinthians 13:7). He is communing with us at all times, especially during times of silence overseeing the growth in our souls and leading us toward spiritual transformation. Holy Spirit works inside our hearts, revealing Christ in us as we are being transformed, training us to trust God's Word. He is always ready to open our understanding to deeper revelations of Christ. Learning to quiet ourselves with the Spirit of God opens our hearts and souls to the solace of His tranquility; in oneness with Him, His calmness and confidence are imparted into our spirits. This is where the Fruit of the Spirit originates, which are actually attributes of the Divine Nature. When we grow in our ability to model His nature, He knows He can trust us; He opens our hearts through our contemplation and reliance upon Him and in our obedience to embrace His ability within our hearts to confidently steward His grace as ambassadors of the King.

Through this type of deep contemplative prayer, we grow in consciously being present with the indwelling Christ. By recognizing the inner witness of the Spirit we become more aware of and more sensitive to His presence. I truly believe the depth of personal communion with the Spirit of God is more often experienced in silence and solitude, but can and should be developed in our hearts when we are in public. This in part is what David referred to as the Secret Place of the Most High (Psalm 91). Focusing upon and communing with the Spirit of God is imperative at all times, whether in private or in public.

Sadly, many Christians who know and love the Lord do not experience this level of praying or communing. Charles H. Spurgeon, the prince of preachers during the Victorian England era, wrote in his daily devotional, *Morning and Evening.* "There are the common frames and feelings of repentance, and faith, and joy, and hope, which are enjoyed by the entire family; but there is an upper realm of rapture, of communion, and conscious union with Christ, which is far from being the common dwelling-place of believers." The same is true today, as most Christians seem to just go about their lives as though God is to be approached only as He is needed or just on Sunday. But God desires and constantly invites all of His children to commune with Him in every area of life. I believe Spurgeon would agree that it takes spending quality time in quietude and contemplation, being alone in His presence drawn to Him by His great love to enter the inner chambers of God in the "upper realm...of conscious union with Christ."

Consider what Jesus mentions in Matthew 6:6 about prayer: "But you, when you pray, go into your room, and when you have shut your door, pray to your Father who is in the secret place; and your Father who sees in secret will reward you openly." The Lord desires our private, intimate times with Him, and in doing so we will tangibly sense His reward from our prayer life, which is true intimacy with the Father along with open rewards in answered prayers.

For me personally, I silently, humbly, and lovingly present myself to God. I call it "quiet abiding." Quieting myself with the Lord is very often the only way I am able to sense and hear His voice imparted into my spirit by His Spirit. Jesus taught us that abiding in Him, His Word abiding within us, and abiding in the Father's love will yield much fruit (John 15:1-10).

The different nuances of the Greek word *meno,* translated to *abide,* brings a richer understanding for us in experiencing true fellowship with the Lord. It means to stay, abide, continue, dwell, remain, endure, and *to be present* (Strong). In prayer and abiding we must be *present* with the Lord. What does this mean for you personally?

Praying is communing with God. Whether with words or in silence it is to be there, present with Him. The Lord spoke to me recently saying, "I like your presence, My son." Friends, God likes our presence, our attention upon Him; He compels us to come boldly unto His throne of grace (Hebrews 4:16). Even though He invites and compels us to come, we really don't have to say a word, but only abide in His presence by faith. Certainly, He encourages us to pray and ask Him things, but silence is golden with the Lord as He allows His precious Spirit to wash over our minds and our souls, restoring and renewing, so we learn to truly hear His voice while enjoying His presence.

Conscious effort must be made to still our minds and hearts so we can be present with God in this manner. We must work through, avoiding the various distractions like, the phone, television, radio, random thoughts, things to do, food, and many other normal draws on our attentions. May I offer a simple, practical suggestion? If distractions come to mind while in prayer or reading the Word, have a pad of paper ready to jot down whatever thoughts that may be of importance for later reference, but stay in the moment with God.

Satan definitely does not want us to dwell in this Secret Place of abiding. He uses whatever it takes to distract us from God's presence and our relationship with Him. But the neat thing about the Secret Place is that it does not matter where we are, or what we are doing. As we quiet ourselves before Him, at work or doing normal everyday things, God will speak to our hearts with words of life, peace, joy, comfort, encouragement, edification, ideas, enlightenment, and whatever else He knows we need.

God's voice is more often silent, released as impressions, unction, intuitions, insights, or thoughts. It makes no sense to the rational mind; nonetheless, it is truth. God speaks in the still, quiet, small voice—Holy Spirit to our spirits. We know He speaks through His Word, and anything we hear from God intuitively will always be in line with His Word. Interestingly, God also speaks through normal circumstances, through our parents, our spiritual leaders, through authorities, through whatever means He decides. He has spoken to my heart through many means, including dreams, my pastors, my dad, my granddaughter, and even my boss. And God is always speaking silently, through nature, the heavens, and through quietude in His Spirit. "The heavens declare the glory of God; and the firmament show His handiwork" (Psalm 19:1).

What if we are not hearing God speak or we do recognize His voice, thinking He is silent? God's silence is really not silence in the Spirit, though it may seem like it to our intellects. Holy Spirit is always with us ever ready to commune with our hearts. Does communing always involve perceivable words of understanding? I have learned (well, I am still learning) to just sit with God, trusting Him to interpose through the silence. We need to train our souls in the ability to get quiet and commune from our spirits with Holy Spirit.

The Lord says to, "Be still and know that I am God…" (Psalm 46:10). It takes great faith and confidence to quiet ourselves in order to be still before the Lord, giving up our sense of control, yielding over to Him. This is true submission and surrender, and getting quiet with Him from this perspective leads to knowing Him through a sense of childlike wonder. Let us always be astonished and amazed by our Heavenly Father.

From our Western Culture training and paradigm, with its rationalistic, intellectual, and reasoning perspectives, God speaking through silence may seem difficult to grasp, even ludicrous. This is because most of our schooling, our instruction, even in Christian education, are from this reasoned and rationalistic approach, whether to life, to God, or to His Word. The Scientific Method must be adhered to, or so we think. Even in Systematic Theology, which I personally like and have studied, we have categorized God by placing Him in a neat, organized construct. We think that, from this logical, rationalistic perspective, our time spent with God must be filled with understandable thoughts and experiences. However, we must not lean on understandable experience, but always acknowledge and trust the Lord wholeheartedly. God will bring understanding as we need it, but our perception that God is silent is wrong. We must be cautious not to neglect the Mystery of God, His Wonder, His Majesty, and His Sovereignty. God most assuredly speaks through silence to our hearts and our spirits.

Trusting God's Work of Cleansing

I have experienced wonderful peace in silence before the LORD, but I also have been broken and undone in His presence. Has the Spirit of God ever "wrecked" you? He has me. By that I mean God's presence shook me to the very core of my being. Let us make no mistake: God is Holy! In His presence I have been humbled and my heart greatly disheveled. God's holiness and purity exposes our inner hearts' attitudes, but praise God, the blood of Jesus cleanses us and gives us access into His presence. This wrecking takes place because of our physical, natural existence. The purpose is always in leading us into godly sorrow of heart in order to reveal any areas in our lives needing repentance, adjustment, or removal and always leads into restoration and renewal.

When we experience God's wrecking, however, it is simply because of His pure and sovereign holiness; His purity of love has this effect on our hearts as we stand amazed in His glorious presence. The prophet Isaiah had an encounter in God's presence that very few have been given the opportunity to experience. He found himself in the very throne room of God. Whether in a vision, or a sovereign act of God, he saw the Lord high and exalted (Isaiah 6:1-8). He was broken, undone, and awestruck by God's presence, totally humbled, perhaps falling to his knees immediately in the realization of his heart condition before God.

However, God brought Isaiah to His Presence because He was looking for a humble, willing heart to speak and write words of prophecy, truth, and trust. Isaiah was such a man who spoke and wrote words from God. The Lord reveled even more of Himself to Isaiah in order for him to realize and to establish that he was chosen as one to be sent. The Lord cleansed Isaiah in preparation for the adjustment in his assignment by sending forth an angel with a coal from the altar of incense to touch his mouth.

God will wreck any of us in preparation or adjustment for our assignment. That is part of the crucible of trust. He cleanses us by the blood of Jesus and the washing of the water of the Word. Then His Spirit will begin to deal with our hearts with loving conviction in those areas that need adjustment, which will lead us to humble ourselves before Him. God could humble us at any time, but He desires we yield in our own volition. This is most important as we must embrace Him and participate in this cleansing by faith, confession, and repentance, so we can commune with Him. We must go through this cleansing and purification in order to be prepared, like Isaiah, for our assignment.

When we submit to God He draws us into intimacy and communion with Himself. He loves us just the way we are, but His purpose is to restore and sanctify us, to make us holy. He knows our frame and condition and is working patiently in the process of transforming us progressively back into His image. He is the Potter; we are the clay. He is doing a work in us, but we must yield to His hand as He shapes us and fashions us into the vessel of His making. His hands are firm, yet gentle and loving, always tenderly at work on our hearts and characters, transforming us into the image of His Son, Jesus Christ.

His compassions for us are unlimited, particularly when we are humble before Him. When we yield to Him in this humble spirit of vulnerability, the Lord is drawn to us: "For thus says the High and Lofty One Who inhabits eternity, whose name is Holy: 'I dwell in the high and holy place, with him who has a contrite and humble spirit, to revive the spirit of the humble, and to revive the heart of the contrite ones'" (Isaiah 57:15). The exalted Most High God dwells in splendor and majesty upon His throne, existing as the Everlasting I AM. Yet He is drawn to and dwells with the contrite and the humble soul to restore and to revive. Humbling ourselves before the Lord causes His great compassions and mercies to be activated on our behalf. He is drawn to the one who is of a poor and contrite spirit, who trembles at His Word (Isaiah 66:1-2).

While in times of silence with the Lord Jesus, as we realize who He really is, when we truly humble ourselves before Him, we are given the revelation that He is God, the Son, and Lord of lords and King of kings. And as our hearts are drawn to His love He reveals Himself to us in whatever capacity we need for that moment or season. Knowing Jesus always leads to deeper intimacy with Him, and with the Father, and a deeper life in His Spirit. The anointing oils of transformation are at work in this place of silence, birthing within us only what comes from God: revival of our spirit, oneness with His Spirit, and becoming just like Jesus as a son of the Father.

DAVID'S SECRET PLACE OF TRUST

He who dwells in the secret place of the Most High
Shall abide under the shadow of the Almighty.
I will say of the LORD, "He is my refuge and my fortress;
My God, in Him I will trust.
Psalm 91:1-2

D avid trusted the Lord *almost* completely, entrusting his life into God's hands. As we examine his life, his trust wavered at times through certain trials and struggles, compromises, and sin, but he always came back to a place in his heart where he cried out to God. In his relationship with the Almighty, he learned to enter God's presence with a repentant heart, with trust toward God. His relationship with God was one of love and intimacy, one of which he seemed to know God initiated. He knew God's love was good, and he was always drawn to Him.

David poetically named his place of trust in God as The Secret Place of the Most High. David was truly a man after God's heart. He wholeheartedly pursued God through most of his life, spending much time in quiet with Him. This started on the quiet hills of Judea when he was a shepherd boy for his father. Imagine the countless hours in solitude with the sheep where he began to realize that the God of the universe was His own Shepherd. As he matured into manhood, David had already learned to wait in quietude before God with a trusting heart, continually seeking His face. His trust in God worked in very practical ways. God had been with him, had been his strength for him against a lion and a bear when these had attacked the sheep. Throughout his life, he was always drawn back to abiding in that Secret Place with God, whether in good times or bad, in times of falling short of the glory of God or in times of faithfully serving Him. David modeled a life-style of what I earlier described as the cycle of trust.

Like David, we are given the opportunity to get to the place where we can live this truth he learned: "My soul, wait silently for God alone, for my expectation is from Him. He only is my rock and my salvation; He is my defense; I shall not be moved. In God is my salvation and my glory; the rock of my strength, and my refuge, is in God" (Psalm 62:5-7).

God not only is, but He must be our refuge, whether during every trial as we are in the crucible of trust, or in times of peace and contentment, or in times of great exuberance and celebration. In the beloved Psalm 23, David speaks of the Lord as his Shepherd who causes him to lie down in green pastures of rest and quiet, who leads him beside the still waters—images of peace and tranquility. God restored his soul and will restore the souls of all who seek Him. Whether in these pastoral places, or in the valley of the shadow of death, or at a prepared table in the presence of enemies, the Lord was his Shepherd and his Secret Place. Just like David, all of us who are after God's heart are drawn into this astonishing Place. As we abide with Him in this Secret Place, God does His brilliant and loving work of transforming our souls in all circumstances, whether in the quiet and peaceful or not so peaceful settings, where we are actually drawn into His heart, to learn of Him and to grow like Him.

David learned to be still in God's presence as Psalm 131:2 illustrates: "Surely I have calmed and quieted my soul, like a weaned child with his mother. Like a weaned child is my soul within me." A weaned child with his mother portrays trust, reliance, relationship, and intimacy. Wherever we find ourselves, whatever we face, we can live in this Secret Place of abiding with God's Spirit as we walk out our every-day experiences in this mortal body.

When we quiet ourselves with God, He responds with His love, His peace, His inner joy, and His acceptance of us. We enjoy His approval of our lives in Him, which causes us to grow in confidence in Him and trusting His plan for our lives. Only as we live in His presence are we truly able to mature as His dear children. God is very fond of us—perhaps beyond what we can realize. We became *His children* when we were born again. We learn experientially of God's fondness, particularly due to being quiet with our Abba, Father. We love our Lord Jesus because of all He did for us in going to the cross; we love Holy Spirit because He is our Comforter, Guide, and constant Companion; and we love our Father because His goodness and mercy surely follow us all the days of our lives.

Jesus' love for us surpasses understanding, and just the hint of knowing we are loved in this way is very powerful. Growing in the knowledge of His love leads us to be overcomers, victors, and conquerors. This is why Satan despises God's love and will attempt anything to get us to doubt or question Jesus' love. So, we abide in God's love, acknowledging by faith we are loved and accepted into the beloved. We know experientially that we dwell in the quietude of His Secret Place where He releases peace, even when we are uncertain or when we go through any crucible of trust.

However, when we try to figure things out from our own limited perspective it only leads to problems or discouragement. Trust in the Lord must be with our whole heart without leaning on our own understanding. We acknowledge our Father in everything, trusting even when we are not certain. The word translated to acknowledge is *yada'* in Hebrew, meaning to know, to get to know, to perceive, to find out, or to ascertain (Strong). We acknowledge God to get to know Him more personally. This same word is expressed as *know* in Psalm 46:10 which says, "Be still and know that I am God."

Satisfaction in our souls and assurance in our hearts come as we trust the Lord wholeheartedly and become more experienced in the Secret Place. When life tries to disquiet us, we must learn to be quiet before the Lord within our hearts, and the activation of the Secret Place will take effect. When we rest in His presence, He gives more *revelation* of Himself while *impartation* from His Spirit changes us little by little. Revelation implies knowledge with understanding. Impartation implies influence with empowerment. We need both to know and experience the knowledge of Him and His influence upon our hearts. In silence and solitude with Him we learn to be vulnerable, growing to be totally reliant upon God's Spirit, thus empowered to live as He desires, while abiding in the absolute trustworthiness of the Secret Place of the Most High God.

God Is Absolutely Trustworthy

Fear not, for I am with you;
Be not dismayed, for I am your God.
I will strengthen you. Yes, I will help you,
I will uphold you with My righteous right hand.
Isaiah 41:10

My good friend, Jim was a Navy SEAL during the Vietnam War and had enlisted in the Navy under the "buddy plan" with his best friend, Fred. They had been buddies from grade school and all through high school, and were on the football team together and learned to rely upon each other on and off the field. I did not meet or become friends with Jim until after he had been discharged from the Navy. We had many conversations over the years about his rigorous and demanding training, of his designation in Nam on a gunboat patrolling the Mai Kong River, of his missions, and of his various other experiences in the Navy.

SEALs are trained in such a way that stretches them to the limits of their capabilities mentally and physically, and they are taught to keep their emotions in check during the most demanding and conflicting situations. While in training, a bell is available to ring if a trainee gets to the point of breaking. Only one in one hundred candidates make it all the way through. During training, Jim almost rang that bell on several occasions, but Fred would encourage him to stick it out, to stay the course. This also happened to Fred and Jim would do the same with him. From these experiences they learned to rely upon one another (and their comrades) in a far deeper way than during high school football games.

Reliance upon team members was an integral part of the strength in these elite warriors. As SEALs they absolutely had to trust their brothers-in-arms before, during, and after their missions. There is a code of honor and loyalty, an esprit de corps that most people do not have the privilege of experiencing. Helping or supporting their team members was ingrained in them during their rigorous training, so that in a fight and in dire need they always had someone to rely upon. During one of their patrols a fierce battle took place. Jim was shot and also ended up with his neck broken from being catapulted backwards. He was still able to get up to get to Fred, who had been fatally wounded, dying in his arms. This affected him deeply.

Jim was a survivor, but not without a fight and conflict. He came home and needed close to a full year of healing and rehabilitation, but even as his body healed he had much trouble adjusting after Vietnam. Post Traumatic Stress Disorder became something very real to him. As he attempted to adapt back to civilian life, regrets, and struggles attacked him. He had continuous nightmares about what he had done in battle; there was an inner rage in his heart which resulted in many fights. He had been trained well to defend himself, and he used it very effectively. However, all the training that held his emotions in check began to unravel. What is repressed will eventually manifest.

He got married and had a son, and several years later Jim was born again. He really tried to make a go of being a Christian. But after several years, because of his past rage and many other factors, his marriage ended in divorce which he did not want. On top of all this, he was also betrayed by supposed friends. He went through many years of trying to experience peace. But even through all his dysfunction God was working to show Jim of His trustworthiness. In the course of all his trials, and there were many, he eventually grew to learn that just as he trusted his comrades in battle, he could absolutely trust and rely upon God even more.

However, reliance upon another is not always easy. Hopefully we all have friends who will come through in a pinch. That is the kind of relationship Jim and I had. After I had been Jim's friend for many years, he finally told me that I reminded him of his buddy, Fred, which was what drew him to me as a friend. I had not known this, and it touched my heart, because he had told me all the stories and I had grown to respect Jim's honoring of his good friend.

As I write this, my heart grieves because just last night Jim passed and has gone on to be with the Lord. His health had been failing for quite some time, and life had taken its toll. Agent Orange from Vietnam had caused cancer. He ended up spending the last several months of his life under Hospice care in a VA hospital. Even as my heart grieves, my heart also soars, because during one of my last visits, when I entered his room, I could sense God's presence. Jim's countenance was beaming, which was not always the case with his pain and discomfort from the cancer. He told me of the awesome encounter He had just had with the Lord right before I entered the room. In tears of joy and awe, he told me of the Father revealing His great love for him. God revealed Himself to Jim in His trustworthiness by visiting him in a very tangible way. With tears he said, "Tom, I did not know. I did not realize how much God loves me." He asked me to pray and as I did the presence of Holy Spirit was very strong. I was able to visit Jim one more time, and we spoke of the Lord. Jim was very confident of his readiness to go on to be with the Jesus. He died that next week. Jim was a very dear, loyal, and faithful friend. I miss him.

Certainly many of us have experienced the opposite. Betrayals take place. Supposed friends do not stick it out with us, or they do not stand with us when we need them. This is very often our experience when sinful, fallen people are involved. Even God's people can exhibit lack of faithfulness, toward God and toward others. All too often, people get caught up in deceit, gossip, backbiting, wrong desire, and sin, which lead to disloyalty, accusations, and lack of trust in relationships, both human and toward God.

However, our Father can absolutely be trusted. He draws and influences His children to trust Him and in turn become trustworthy to Him and others. God is entirely and completely good. His goodness is always available to anyone who cries out to Him in faith, and sometimes when we do not cry out. He desires to reveal His trustworthiness by giving abundant life through His Son, Jesus Christ, to all who seek Him (John 10:10). Among other things, like having all needs met, abundant life is all about knowing and trusting God intimately; having peace with Him and with others; experiencing and walking in His joy; having personal inner peace; and having a purpose and a destiny. Abundant life is His gift to us, and truly is the result of constant abiding with Him. We are given everlasting life which is in us now, and when we pass from this life we will live eternally in His presence. Jesus declares in John 17:3-4, "And this is eternal life, that they may know You, the only true God, and Jesus Christ whom You have sent."

God upheld Jim even through all the struggles and attacks he went through, revealing His great love to him leading Jim into a deeper and final trust. God will uphold any of us as we trust Him, because we all will go through spiritual, mental, and physical attacks as part of our experiences in the Crucible of Trust. But God is Faithful to us in all of life's struggles.

God's Integrity

No temptation has overtaken you except
such as is common to man;
but God is faithful, who will not allow you to
be tempted beyond what you are able,
but with the temptation will also make the way
of escape, that you may be able to bear it.
1 Corinthians 10:13

The greatest blessing in life is to know Father God through a relationship with Jesus Christ immersed in the fellowship with His Holy Spirit. From our bond with Him, God's purpose is to transform each of us into mature sons. Because of His blessing and purpose our lives become open to mental, physical, and spiritual attacks. But God knows what He is doing in our lives and has purpose in every eventuality. As we stand in faith, abiding with and trusting Holy Spirit, who will intervene on our behalf as we call out to Him, He gives us grace to handle and to overcome. No matter what the enemy attempts to do against us, the Father makes sure it will not be overbearing. Even though the devil, with all his minion evil spirits, hates relentlessly, the Father's love supersedes. Isaiah 59:19 speaks of an aspect of God's love as He protects us and deals with our enemy: "So shall they fear the name of the LORD from the west, and His glory from the rising of the sun; when the enemy comes in like a flood, the Spirit of the LORD will lift up a standard against him."

There are no punctuations marks in the original Hebrew text, so the emphasis of a flood is more likely the Lord's standard, which is more powerful than the enemy. Either way, the Lord raises Himself as our banner to thwart the devil's attacks.

The devil is a liar and the father of all lies. In his deception, among myriads of other ways, his strategy is twofold: to get us to at least think of the idea that God holds out on His people; and to doubt our identity as sons. He started that with Adam and Eve who actually were in God's presence daily. Satan's tactics haven't changed as he continually allures people into the bondage of sin, getting them to doubt God's integrity.

God is merciful and kind to everyone who acknowledges their sin and seeks Him wholeheartedly. He resists the proud of heart, but He gives grace to the humble of heart (James 4:6). His love is generously extended and offered to every human being in the world (John 3:16; Titus 2:11). He yearns for all to accept His Son and His love so they may know Him, personally. Even with His hatred of sinfulness and wickedness, God provides ways against sin and accepts all people with unconditional love to draw them away from their sin.

God is love, but He is also holy. Because of sin, humankind is in need of salvation in order to be able to withstand His sovereign glory and holiness when we eventually face Him, as each one of us will individually be presented to Him to give account for our lives. In His integrity He gives us free choice and wants us to respond to His offer of love and forgiveness, to repent from sin and turn to Him, believing in and trusting Jesus as Savior, making Him Lord. He is always faithful in this offer as long as we live.

Romans 3:23 says, "All have sinned and fallen short of the glory of God." The result of sin is death, but God's gift is eternal life in Jesus Christ, our Lord (Romans 6:23). He demonstrated His love and willingness to rescue sinners from God's judgment of sin by laying down His life when He went to the cross—taking our judgment upon Himself. To be rescued from sin requires admittance of the need to be rescued. God provides a way for us to be clean from sin by the shed blood of Jesus on the cross. As we believe this, He asks us to repent by turning away from our sin and selfishness. Then we trust Him accepting His offer of grace and mercy, confessing Him as Lord. When we do this, He gives us His precious Spirit. Jesus said the Spirit of God will lead us into all truth and into intimacy with the Father.

God delights in mercy and is compassionate with limitless love. While many do not grasp the love, mercy, and integrity of God, we can embrace His love by placing our trust and faith in His Son, and we will grow to realize His trustworthiness. As we approach God through the Son, He reveals to our hearts that He wants to be loved, believed, and trusted, which is what brings Him great pleasure. He created us for His good pleasure and to enjoy His love, fellowship, and intimacy. He is a good Father desiring to see us become His mature children. Holy Spirit inspired John, the beloved apostle of Jesus to write in 1 John 3:1, "Behold what manner of love the Father has bestowed on us, that we should be called children of God!"

Just as with natural children, God's child must be taught, trained, and disciplined; the Father's plans are to raise His sons and daughters to be mature and perfect in Him. This life is a precursor for eternity. From His awesome work of sanctification in our lives, which is the ongoing maturity toward holiness, we will carry over all we have learned in the Spirit, along with our character development, into God's eternal Kingdom. We are trained by what we experience in this life for our place to rule and reign with Him in the future Kingdom. And God gives us the opportunity to begin to walk in our inheritance now.

Additionally, in our training, Scripture encourages us to follow spiritual leaders who model godly, mature behavior. Following them as they follow Jesus is God's pattern and purpose for us. We are admonished to "not be sluggish, but imitate those who through faith and patience inherit the promises" (Hebrews 6:12). We need true spiritual fathers or mothers to help in our training.

Yet God's intent even goes deeper. We face a fierce enemy, but the Greater One dwells in our hearts (1 John 4:4). And God's Spirit is personally working a great work to prepare us, using ministry gifts and functions of apostles, prophets, evangelists, pastors, and teachers "till we all come to the unity of the faith and of the knowledge of the Son of God, to a perfect man, to the measure of the stature of the fullness of Christ; that we should no longer be children, tossed to and fro and carried about with every wind of doctrine, by the trickery of men, in the cunning craftiness of deceitful plotting, but, speaking the truth in love, may grow up in all things into Him who is the head — Christ — from whom the whole body, joined and knit together by what every joint supplies, according to the effective working by which every part does its share, causes growth of the body for the edifying of itself in love" (Ephesians 4:11-16).

As His maturing children we are being trained to be just like Jesus was when here on earth, learning to hear and obey the voice of the Father, modeling holiness. We have been given His own divine nature with the potential to grow in and to exhibit holiness (Acts 17:29; 2 Peter 1:3-4). The divine nature is developed in our heart by the presence of Holy Spirit's influence and revealed in our behavior and demeanor. Time spent with God reveals His integrity and is needed to grow in relationship with Him, thus becoming more like Him as a son of the Father.

God's Trust in Us

Love is the key in the Kingdom of God, love for the Lord God Almighty, and love for each other. In any spiritual training, in every aspect of life, trusting God is to be the focus, based on our love and intimate relationship with Him. God's intent is to train up faith-filled children who are just like Jesus, living a lifestyle of love and trust in the Father. The integral aspect of our faith in pleasing God is to love Him first and foremost, because faith works through love, or as a result of love (Galatians 5:6b). From our love for God, we grow to the place where the Lord can trust us with His delegated authority—empowered in the anointing, demonstrating Holy Spirit power.

The Father's good pleasure is to give us the Kingdom, which implies an entrusted authority (Luke 12:32). We become administrators of His authority and stewards of the mysteries of God and His grace (1 Corinthians 4:1-2; Ephesians 3:2). His intent during our entire discipleship journey is to train us to reign with Him in His eternal Kingdom (Revelation 5:10; 20:6; 22:5). However, to reign with Christ, we must first be tested, having passed through the crucible of trust, thus refining and perfecting the divine nature with which we have been entrusted. An anonymous author has said, "God proves you before He moves you."

God is omniscient and already knows of our need for proving. He wants us to know, experientially, that we can trust Him in all things and that we can be confident that He trusts us with His Kingdom authority. When He trusts us, He will release demonstration of His power, which comes to those who recognize their own weakness and know that any power released from us originates from God (1 Corinthians 2:3-5). The Father is leading us into a spiritually delegated reigning under His divine authority.

In His Fatherly love for us He allows certain experiences to test our faith and trust in Him. He allows us to go through what is necessary to teach and train in accordance with His purposes and will for our lives, which is to live from His presence in total dependence upon Him. Often in these tests we could feel (in our flesh and soul) afflicted, crushed, and exposed. Sometimes it feels like we are abandoned, but we are not. He is right there with us.

God promises to not put us through more than we can handle. He knows just what is needed to test us and just how far to go in order to stretch us toward maturity. God shakes whatever can be shaken to be exposed and removed, so that whatever cannot be shaken will remain (Hebrews 12:25-29). What cannot be shaken? The Kingdom of God is unshakable and is on the inside of every born-again child of God. Jesus said the Kingdom of God is within you (Luke 17:20-21). Paul writes in Romans 14:17 of the inner realities of the heart and spirit regarding our citizenship in this wonderful Kingdom, which are righteousness, peace and joy in the Holy Spirit.

Jesus taught us the following parable to illustrate shaking:

> Therefore whoever hears these sayings of Mine, and
> does them, I will liken him to a wise man who built

his house on the rock: and the rain descended, the floods came, and the winds blew and beat on that house; and it did not fall, for it was founded on the rock. But everyone who hears these sayings of Mine, and does not do them, will be like a foolish man who built his house on the sand: and the rain descended, the floods came, and the winds blew and beat on that house; and it fell. And great was its fall (Matthew 7:24-27).

When this shaking of rain, storms, and floods takes place and we apply Jesus' teachings as our lifestyle, we are equipped with an ability to stand firm in faith and trust upon the Rock of our Salvation. If we are not standing upon Jesus as our Rock, obeying His teachings, then our lack of trust in the Word of God and in Holy Spirit is revealed in our experience resulting in disaster.

Trust in the Father will draw Him to show Himself strong on behalf of all whose hearts are perfect toward Him (2 Chronicles 16:9). Being perfect toward Him means completeness and friendliness toward God (Strong). It also involves total dependency upon Him, so His strength comes into our lives through our trusting and waiting upon Him, and standing in faith. Scripture says the joy of the Lord is our strength, and I've found when I sense His joy in my heart that my trust level increases. We must activate joy by rejoicing and trust while truly allowing Christ, who is our strength, to live through our lives. Trust involves love, reliance, vulnerability, and dependence with expectation and confidence in the One in whom we trust, the Lord Jesus Christ.

Scripture reveals Jesus was obviously trusted by the Father, because He honored Him by only doing and saying what He heard from the Father (John 5:19-23). Reliance upon His Father revealed His trust in the Father as Jesus went through the tests, trials, and temptations in all the aspects of humanity (Hebrews 4:15). The Father always showed Himself strong on Jesus' behalf, even when He was on the cross, because resurrection power was about to be released through Jesus' trust in the Father. By following Jesus' example of trust in going through every life circumstance, we will experience the Father showing Himself strong on our behalf as well. God, in turn, entrusts us with His Kingdom authority and anointing.

Into Your Hands

Into Your hand I commit my spirit;
You have redeemed me, O LORD God of truth.
Psalm 31:5

And when Jesus had cried out with a loud voice,
He said, "Father, into Your hands I commit My spirit."
Having said this, He breathed His last.
Luke 23:46

A leak developed in the plumbing behind the wall near our washing machine. I am able to do simple plumbing around the house, but this particular leak involved multiple pipes converging together, a labyrinth of water lines going to several places in the house. It was way beyond my ability, so I called a licensed plumber who was able to fix the leak in a short time. His fee was well worth it, because he knew exactly what to do and how to accomplish the task.

When anything in our lives involves more than we can handle we must rely upon someone else saying, "I leave this in your capable hands," and we rely upon and trust in this person's skills. This is the perspective we must have toward God as He guides every area of our lives. Jesus is our Good Shepherd in Whom we absolutely commit our spirits. We entrust our very lives into His infinitely capable Hands.

Because God is absolutely good, He is absolutely trustworthy. Jesus trusted the Father implicitly, though He knew it was the Father's will for Him to die on the cross. With His own life He willingly paid the price for the sins of all humanity. From the cross He cried, "Father, into your hands I commit my spirit." As I meditated upon this verse I sensed the Lord lead me to reverse the order as an application for my life as He trusts me: "Lord, into your Spirit I commit my hands." Holy Spirit activates and establishes the works of our hands as we commit them to Him (Psalm 90:17). He will bless our efforts in our stewardship, trusting us to commit the fruit of our labors back to Him in trust.

Jesus absolutely trusted the Father's will, even while facing death on the cross, entrusting His life to the Father in the hope of resurrection. He knew it was written of His death in many places in the Old Testament. David wrote Psalm 16:9-10, which prophetically refers to Jesus' resurrection, saying, "Therefore my heart is glad, and my glory rejoices. My flesh also will rest in hope. For You will not leave my soul in Sheol, nor will You allow Your Holy One to see corruption." David also wrote prophetically regarding much of what Jesus actually experienced on the cross in Psalm 22. Jesus knew and trusted these prophetic Words, and many others.

Just as Jesus totally relied upon and trusted the Father, we also trust our lives into the Father's purposes while we abide in and rely upon Him. We also should seek to only say and do what we hear and see from the Father. Because Jesus presented His body as a dying sacrifice, relying upon Holy Spirit to go through crucifixion, we can rely upon His Spirit to help us deny ourselves and take up our crosses as we present our bodies as living sacrifices, which is our reasonable service of worship (Romans 12:1).

Jesus committed His Spirit into the Father's hand, and that same Holy Spirit was sent back by the Father to raise Him from the dead three days later. Then after Jesus ascended back to heaven, Holy Spirit was sent on the day of Pentecost coming upon the 120 disciples of Jesus who were in the upper room. They were baptized with Holy Spirit and fire. The same Spirit that raised Christ from the dead, the same Spirit that baptized those 120 disciples is available for us today giving the LIFE of God into our mortal bodies (Romans 8:11). He empowers our everyday lives so we can walk in victory, and be Christ's witnesses to extend the Kingdom of God. He is in us forever and will be with us as we face our time to die. Eventually, those of us in Christ will also experience His actual resurrection life, but the life we now live, we live by faith in the Son of God as we are empowered by the same Holy Spirit as Jesus and His disciples.

God began that good work in our lives by releasing His Spirit's indwelling presence within when we were born again. As children of God, born of His Spirit, we need the ongoing infilling of Holy Spirit (Ephesians 5:18). Being filled with Holy Spirit really means to be under His control (Strong). Daily we are to choose, allow, and reaffirm Holy Spirit's control over our lives. On our own, in our own strength we are not capable of accomplishing what God requires or what we were designed to do or to become. But because we are in Him now and the transforming work of His Spirit is active, we are His children, growing and maturing to fullness and into the image of Jesus Christ.

As His children we are commissioned to make disciples of all nations, representing the Father in the Name of Jesus to the world in which we live. As mature sons and daughters, we extend the Father's heart to all with whom we come into contact. We need to willingly and trustingly put our lives into the hands of our

Heavenly Father in order to accomplish His plans and good plea
sure. Lord, we give our lives into your capable hands.

Even though we entrusted our lives to the Lord, God continues to give us free will and we are the ones who must make
the everyday decisions. Since we are disciples of Jesus Christ and
children of God, His grace—which is His Divine influence—will
help us make those decisions. We do so in obedience to His daily
initiatives and as acts of faith and trust in accordance with His
written Word with reliance upon His Spirit. Our objective must be
to be led by and to yield to Holy Spirit in every choice. We desire
His direction; He is our life and the Path of Life. Because we seek
His Kingdom and righteousness first, all the things necessary for
our lives will be added (Matthew 6:33).

David said in Psalm 23:1, "The LORD is my shepherd I shall
not want." Jesus said in John 10:11 that He is the Good Shepherd
who gives His life for His sheep. The wolf (the devil or evil spirits)
comes to try to snatch the sheep out of the Father's hands, but Jesus
declared no one is able to snatch His sheep out of His hand or the
Father's hands. He also said, "I and the Father are one" (John 10:30).
We can trust Him to take care of all our affairs because He is the
Good Shepherd who takes care of His sheep.

The devil comes to steal, kill, and destroy, to tear down our
lives, wreaking havoc any way he can, but Jesus comes to give
life and that more abundantly, empowering us to overcome. We
must choose the abundant life of Christ, however. Our choices in
life affect how we appropriate this rich life in His Spirit. The wolf
cannot necessarily snatch us out of the Father's hand, but he can
allure us away from abiding with the Good Shepherd. Satan will
lie, partially lie, deceive, allure, entice, tempt, and use any other
means to keep us from trusting the Lord. But we trust and submit
to Jesus, and into His hands we commit our bodies, our souls, and
our spirits. He is absolutely trustworthy as our Good Shepherd.

SECTION III

WAITING IN TRUST

Fear not, O tempted and tried believer,
Jesus will come, if patience be exercised,
and faith held fast. His delay will serve to make
His coming the more richly blessed.
Pray on. Wait on. Thou canst not fail.
If Christ delay, wait for Him.
In His own good time, He will come,
and will not tarry.

E.M. Bounds

PATIENCE IN GOD'S CALL

But let patience have its perfect work,
that you may be perfect and complete,
lacking nothing.
James 1:4

G od had called me His chosen vessel. At the time I expected that in the near future I would be called upon to minister or preach, which eventually happened. Yet before any ministry took place He led me to start college at 37 years old while I was working at the steel mill. This meant instead of immediately launching a ministry, God worked on my patience and began to equip me through formal education. One does not necessarily need an education to be an effective minister, only Holy Spirit-anointing, which comes through much prayer, spending time in God's presence, spending time under the anointed ministry of others, and a well-rounded knowledge of the Word of God. But an education was God's will for me in the process of my training. The making of the man before the ministry was in effect.

God began to work on my heart; because of wrong thinking I had mistaken expectations regarding His plans and purposes. Due to my lack of allowing the Lord to bring needed adjustments to my heart attitude, difficulty in trusting Him developed within me. God wanted to bring the source of that lack of trust out into the light and renew my trust in Him. My lack of trust was primarily due to impatience and misunderstanding regarding the process one has to go through in order for His call to being fully realized. He was working on my character and this continues to this day.

The words of E.M. Bounds written under the Section III heading really encouraged me when I discovered them; they still uplift my soul. Those words remind me of 1 Thessalonians 5:24 (NASB), "Faithful is He who calls you, and He also will bring it to pass." Would you agree that adding the thought "eventually" with "He will bring it to pass" is not necessarily violating the truth of this Scripture? When God makes a promise He stands over His Word and it will come to pass sooner or later (Jeremiah 1:12 NASB). His Word will not return to Him void or empty (Isaiah 55:11). God will at a time in our near future bring to pass all that He spoke and has called us to do, if we obey Him and wait patiently for His timing. Scripture truly says that God is faithful to us, with His timing always in our best interest. He knows *what* is best and *when* is best. He will lead us into all that He has planned, and it is His will to bring it to pass. Our patient obedience is the catalyst for God's will and for His call to manifest.

God gently and progressively —sometimes a little more assertively—brings and fulfills His call to all of us. I had been ordained into the Gospel ministry, becoming a bi-vocational pastor ministering for three years as I continued my current job as a steelworker.

God then led me to resign in 2002. There were no issues, scandal or controversy, only a leading from the Lord to step away from that particular ministry. I needed a break from ministry and, more importantly, I needed adjustments in my character. From there my wife and I sensed the leading to join a non-denominational church. After a few months I was asked to be an usher. Through that, God worked on my character and my willingness to serve. A year or so later I was asked to preach and minister on occasion. Being patient always brings about God's blessings and purpose, so six years from the time we joined that church I was ordained as an elder and became the pastor's assistant. If he went out of town, I would minister as pastor in his stead. In 2009 he felt the Lord leading him to start a church in Texas, and he sensed I was to be the pastor to serve in his stead, which lasted 18 months.

Our lead pastor, through various circumstances, was then led to come back to us. He did not ask me to do so, but as I prayed and sought the will of God, I felt the pull of the Spirit to step down, to allow him to take his rightful place. As difficult as that was for me, I made the commitment to obey. When I informed him that I was stepping down so he could resume as pastor he was deeply touched. He graciously said that in the Kingdom of God, one does not necessarily step down in situations like this, they step aside. When I did so, grace came into me as I trusted the Lord. God was pleased as I resumed the role of assistant pastor.

I have learned that the call of God and our walk as disciples requires a journey of patience, trust, and obedience. There is an inward work of patience which involves waiting with God. Patience works deep in the soul, and waiting on God creates endurance and reliance upon Him. The fruit of these ongoing lessons in patience might be unknown or unrealized in the moment, yet are evident in their results, thus revealed as character qualities of love, patience, kindness, gentleness, and deference of spirit toward others. We continually learn to trust the Lord as we grow in patience as disciples of Jesus.

Brennan Manning says, "It seems to me that learning to trust God defines the meaning of Christian living" (1986, 28). For our discipleship of Jesus to truly be realized, we must rely on His process in patience, learning to trust, waiting with His Spirit. Only from patient reliance upon Him can we truly grow as His disciples. Then our ministry will be much more effective. The disciple's lifestyle is to be one of trust, abiding dependence, and endurance, which involve the need for obedience and submission. This is true "Christian living" for all of us.

Trusting Patience's Perfect Work

Has someone ever said to you, "Just be patient" when simply trying to encourage you? Or how about, "Patience is a virtue"? Why do these words seem to discourage more than encourage? What was meant as well-meaning can become a source of pain, a jab at the heart. Perhaps you have been patient, but your patience seems to be wearing thin. This inward struggle while trying to be patient through circumstances very often leads to frustration. I know, because this is what happened to me. I had to learn and relearn to trust the Lord while He worked on my heart during the process of patience doing its perfect work—the purpose of which is to produce endurance of soul, to build inward character, and to build Christ-likeness into my heart. I am still growing.

However, at one point I came to the realization I was not really cooperating with God's process, nor relying upon His Spirit. So instead of endurance I was producing disappointment because of my frustrated heart condition. The reason was due to a lack of trust. I failed to realize that in the delay of experiencing God's promises to me, He was working on my heart. I believed in His promises to me, but was naïve regarding God's ways in bringing them about. I knew intellectually that God is faithful in fulfillment of His promises, but I had to learn experiential dependence and reliance upon God. I needed to continually lean upon Him, acknowledging Him in everything, and realize that I needed to stop leaning upon my own very limited perceptions. I also had to learn the principle that delay is not denial. Delay is God's way of revealing my own true character, and more of Himself through the process.

If we have a promise from the Lord that has not yet come to pass, we must choose our response to patiently wait and stand on God's promises. God will provide fulfillment at the right time. In the waiting we draw near to Him. Isaiah 40:31 encourages, "But those who wait on the LORD shall renew their strength; they shall mount up with wings like eagles, they shall run and not be weary, they shall walk and not faint." Waiting on God is not passive, but serving Him in His Kingdom and abiding and communing with Him while believing for His promises to come to pass. Waiting patiently on God causes our spirit man to expand and it enlarges our heart's capacity to receive from Him. While waiting *on* God we pray and believe; while waiting *for* God we trust Him and stand on His promises; while waiting *with* God we grow in abiding intimacy with Him and become more like Him in character and love.

Another very important aspect in patience is that we obey the last understood command God gave us. When we postpone obedience—which is actually disobedience—God patiently waits for our willingness to comply, and He will provide many opportunities for us to comply with His requests. Yet many of God's well-meaning people have gone to their grave in disobedience regarding something that God wanted them to do. I have been guilty of disobedience. When I realized that I was not obeying what God had previously spoken, which was to be patient while waiting and to let the work of patience build my character, I repented and sought restoration, because disobedience is sin.

Father God loves to commune with the heart of His child who willingly waits with Him. Waiting not only renews strength, it builds trust; it establishes the ongoing and loving relationship that pleases our Father. We learn the power of patience as we wait, which is manifested with our spirit man activating ascendancy over our soul. In fact, it is in that trusting reliance upon God that strength in our spirits is established. After all, the end result of God's purposes in patience is fulfillment in Him and transformation into full Christlikeness. Philippians 1:6 refers to this as "being confident of this very thing that He who has begun a good work in you will complete it until the day of Jesus Christ."

According to Strong's Exhaustive Concordance, the word for "complete" in the Greek language is *epiteleo*, a combination of two words. *Epi* is the prepositional dynamic of an ongoing process, such as upon or toward, usually involving time, place, and order. *Teleo* means to end, to conclude, to complete, to mature, or to execute. This combination of words truly indicates an ongoing progression toward a conclusion: fullness of maturity in Christ.

While going through this process of patience having its perfect work, we find ourselves in a crucible of trust. Ephesians 4:13 conveys the continuing aspect of this inevitability: "*Till* we all come to the unity of the faith and of the knowledge of the Son of God, to a perfect man, to the measure of the stature of the fullness of Christ." God's Spirit progressively activates us toward that fullness in Christ. The key is abiding with Christ in patience, which means trusting Him in the relationship of intimacy, love, reliance, vulnerability, and communion.

Out of our relationship with Holy Spirit we are called into a ministry function in the Body of Christ: "As each one has received a gift, minister it to one another, as good stewards of the manifold grace of God" (1 Peter 4:10). Every disciple of Jesus Christ is gifted by Holy Spirit in diverse manifestations of the Spirit (Romans 12:4-7; 1 Corinthians 12:4-11). We are in the process of development of these gifts as we step out in faith into and toward their full operation.

God works in our lives to bring us to maturity. As part of our inward growth there is a call for us to use our gifts and extend ministry to others. During the work of patience, we must learn to deny ourselves, putting other people first as we use our gifts for the glory of God and the building up of others. This was a lesson I had to learn.

The Self-Denial of Patience

Jesus asks us and then empowers us with grace to deny ourselves, to take up our crosses, and to follow Him. Self-denial is related to true spiritual patience, because, while going through life's issues we must stop trying to always figure out everything for ourselves, which is more of self-awareness than self-denial. Leaning on and trusting God, His Word, and His Spirit are integral aspects of patience as well. We must let go of the control of our lives and rely on God's strength, not our own strength and ability. We grow in trust and dependence upon God, which leads us to the deeper elements of true spiritual patience: steadfastness, perseverance, and endurance with joy (Colossians 1:11).

We all desire the sure outcome of success and provision. True spiritual patience will eventually produce fruit and have rewards, which can only come to us by putting our lives and futures into God's hands, believing He will work things out in the manner that will bring glory to Him and blessings for us. However, this only comes to us as we learn to delight ourselves in the Lord, which means to willingly and cheerfully submit to Him and obey His voice (Psalm 37:4). Then we experience the fulfillment of our dreams and desires according to His purposes.

When we deny ourselves we admit our weakness, and His strength becomes perfect in us, for when we are weak we are strong (2 Corinthians 12:9-10). What is impossible for us in the natural becomes possible through Christ. We walk in an increasing measure of ability each day as we grow in God's grace from strength to strength (Psalm 84:7). The increase of that strength manifests itself in the proportion of our faith, patience, and trust in God and to the degree of our surrendered weaknesses. We are growing in faith, believing patiently that as we rely upon God, we can do all things through Christ who strengthens us. To let go of the control of our lives for His sake, leads us to the finding of our lives in the abundant life of His Spirit. Our walk with Him builds trust as patience does its perfect work within our hearts, leading us to maturity and into the fullness of the measure of Christ.

Spiritual Patience

Patience, like all of the Fruit of the Spirit, is developed by walking in the Spirit through life's experiences as He infuses us with His own character qualities. Patience, which I define as a deep characteristic in the heart influenced by the Holy Spirit to persevere, to endure, to withstand whatever comes with equanimity (poise or calm temperament under pressure or duress). True spiritual patience also involves joy because it has to do with being in His presence while living out our lives in the flesh. Patience has been defined as "joyful expectation without irritability." Patience involves another deeper characteristic as well: an attitude of the heart that affects the words that come out of our mouths. Noah Webster defines patience as "a calm temper which bears evil *without murmuring* or discontent" (1828). When I am exercising godly patience, my words will be of faith and trust, not of complaining, murmuring, or dissatisfaction.

Patience always reverts to the capacity to wait on God, for God and with God, while it instills in the heart the ongoing development of trust in Him. Patience, by definition, involves timing and waiting, which establish expectation and believing in God's trustworthiness. Our trust is deepened from the heart because God is faithful to the uttermost. From both God's perspective and ours, waiting upon Him means time spent with Him in personal intimacy.

What does it mean to be in God's presence? In Brennan Manning's book, *The Signature of Jesus*, he teaches on this dynamic of discipleship by encouraging the practice of what is called contemplative prayer: "Take a few minutes to relax your body and quiet your spirit. Then, in simple faith, be present to God dwelling in the depths of your being" (1996, 204). To be present with God is to experience Holy Spirit being present with us, in other words, communion.

As I was praying in this manner one day, the Spirit whispered in my heart, "I like your presence." I truly sensed He liked being with me as I spent time with Him and this really touched my heart. Jesus said He would never leave or forsake us. He makes a very interesting statement in John 17:21 that we are in Him and He is in us as He is in the Father and the Father is in Him. God has chosen, as we love and are in relationship with Jesus, to place us within His relationship with His Son, Jesus. Truly our fellowship is with the Father and His Son, Jesus (1 John 1:3).

As we spend time with the Lord we become more cognizant of being present with God, and we really should be attentive to what we sense in the experience. God will speak to us by bringing to our mind a thought, an idea, a Scripture, or an insight heard from someone else (Manning, 1996). Jesus said in John 10:27 that His sheep hear His voice. Whenever God speaks it will bring encouragement, comfort, and edification, and it could also bring loving correction with reproof, but never condemnation. Just knowing He is with us and will speak to us gives us consolation.

We truly need to be aware of the truth that we are in the presence of God every minute of every day. This is a discipline that takes some time to develop as we grow in patience. We will experience distractions. We also have responsibilities. But God is always with us.

There was a 17th century Catholic monk from France, named Brother Lawrence who developed the simple habit of practicing God's presence in the ordinary situations of life, whether doing menial chores or routine work. He said he experienced more awareness of God's presence during commonplace, daily life, than in chapel or the required time of prayer.

He was not a leader, but worked in the kitchen and also repaired sandals. His superiors in the monastery recognized something about him, though. He was always patient, humble, wise, steadfast, and constantly cheerful; he never complained. They were compelled to visit him, drawn to his simple yet profound wisdom and serenity. Gleaned from their conversations, his thoughts and insights were written down. These eventually were compiled and then published years later into a little booklet called *The Practice of the Presence of God.* This booklet can be downloaded as a PDF for free. Reading these conversations is very encouraging and edifying. Brother Lawrence's influence was truly inspirational for all who spent time with him and to many who have read this booklet, including myself.

To practice the presence of God is the privilege and the blessing of every disciple of Jesus. What it means to be truly attentive to the Spirit of God in our hearts. We learn to sense His precious presence by being sensitive to Him, through trust, patience, and personally abiding with Him. He is with us helping and comforting us in any difficult task or simple assignment we face as we practice being in His presence, developing perseverance within our hearts as we abide with Him. We truly rely upon and submit to Him, even though we cannot make sense of what is happening at times. Let us all come to that the place of spiritual patience where we believe and trust that God knows what He is doing in our lives, especially when we are uncertain or do not understand what we experiencing.

TRUSTING THROUGH QUIETUDE AND SILENCE– LEARNING TO LISTEN TO GOD'S VOICE

Be still, and know that I am God.
Psalm 46:10a

When I was a preteen the song "The Sounds of Silence" by Paul Simon and Art Garfunkel was very popular. A couple of years later our ninth grade literature teacher used that song as an illustration of creative expression. Our assignment was to write a short essay on what we thought the lyrics meant. We were all astounded with this song; we had heard it on the radio, but really never considered the meaning of the words. How can silence have sounds? We had little clue at that early age regarding the depth of the philosophical meaning in Simon's words. We had some fun in our discussions and the teacher was very helpful to bring out the nuances of those lyrics in ways we could understand. As I look back on that experience, I now realize that silence indeed has merit and particularly, meaning can arise from quietude.

Years later, when I was in my early forties, and a deacon in a Baptist church I was asked to volunteer as a chaperon for a youth camp called Super Summer. This was a five-day retreat for high school students from all across southern Illinois, held at Greenville College (now University), a small Free Methodist institution. My assignment was to be the "papa" for one of the small groups of high school juniors and seniors. I was accompanied by a sister in the Lord from another church who was "mama" for our group. I was to oversee the boys and she the girls. And we coordinated together all the activities for the entire group.

Super Summer events are very organized with specific schedules for large group activities, small group interactions, free time, and meals. This brought some order to an exciting and sometimes chaotic time with teenagers. It was truly a challenge to my faith, not to mention my patience. I learned to rely upon the Lord, and I had a great experience. To be part of what God was doing in the lives of those teenagers was a wonderful blessing, not to mention what He did in my own heart by my involvement.

During small group we had a great time of laughter and fun as we followed the curriculum for the discipleship theme. Even though working with teenagers can be awkward, we had very lively and edifying discussions. Some opened up within the group; others were quieter. During our sessions the Spirit led me to ask very deep questions regarding personal faith, trust in God, commitment, and true-life applications in being a disciple of Jesus Christ in their generation. This would often cause times of silent reflection, definitely slowing things down a bit. The looks on their faces revealed they were really pondering; something was happening within them. It was a little bit uncomfortable, yet no one broke this silence.

As the leader, it was difficult not to speak because it seems as leaders we always need to be doing or saying something when we gather together, or so I thought. What God was doing in the quiet at the time was unclear to me. I only allowed the awkward silence because I did not know what else to do with it, but God was at work in this quietude. He was speaking to all our hearts in the silence, and introducing to my heart how He speaks in times of silence. I did not realize, then, the depths to which God was speaking to those kids or to me for that matter.

Many years later, Robin, my wife received a friend request on Facebook from a young lady she recognized as being part of the youth group from our church. As it turns out, she had been one of the students from my Super Summer experience. She reached out to Robin in order to connect with me because I did not have a Facebook account at that time. In her note to me, through Robin's Facebook, she emphasized how that week at Super Summer influenced her greatly and truly helped her grow as a disciple. Particularly, she mentioned that those times of silence during group sessions were the most meaningful and inspirational to her. She expressed gratitude to me for being patient through those awkward moments. She also indicated that other students felt the same way. I had not fully grasped how those times of silence had been truly used by the Lord.

This young woman had grown up to become a strong disciple of Jesus Christ, a Bible teacher, and a discipleship leader for young ladies in her church. When my wife showed me the note I was moved to tears. I began to reflect back on those students. I saw them in the silence, and I realized how, in my ignorance, I had been obedient not breaking those times of quietude. God used silence to speak to those kids, and to me.

How do we hear God speak in silence? We hear God's voice when we learn to quiet ourselves, tuning into His Spirit while keeping our spiritual eyes fixed upon Jesus. We have spiritual senses, and we can tune them to be sensitive to the Spirit of God as we learn to be still with Him. Through listening spiritually, we are given spiritual insight that would not have been realized otherwise. David expressed several times in the Psalms regarding this truth. Psalm 62:1 records, "Truly my soul silently waits for God; from Him comes my salvation." Recall the previously quoted Psalm 131:2: "Surely I have calmed and quieted my soul, like a weaned child with his mother; like a weaned child is my soul within me." Isaiah and Jeremiah also wrote of the benefits in of being quiet before the Lord in Isaiah 30:15 and Lamentations 3:26. Yet our rationalistic and reasoning minds sometimes have trouble with this concept.

Are we supposed to mentally understand God all the time? As disciples we are encouraged to walk by faith, not by sight, by trust and not by understanding (2 Corinthians 5:7; Proverbs 3:5-6). Sight in this context refers to not only what is seen with the eye, but what is understood in the mind. In Proverbs 2:6 God's Word says He gives wisdom and understanding, and these will enter our hearts. 1 Corinthians 1:10a tells us, "But of Him you are in Christ Jesus, who became for us, wisdom from God." Our wisdom is found in Jesus Christ.

Perhaps what we perceive as God's silence actually is our own lack of faith, simple neglect, or not knowing how to tune in to His Spirit. We are to trust the Lord with our whole heart and not lean on our own understanding (cognitive ability), but acknowledge Him in everything we experience (Proverbs 3:5-6). Do we know everything about God and all his ways? No one in this life is capable. What we can do is trust Him, acknowledging Him in all our ways, even in what we perceive as the silences of God.

Perhaps God's silence is often His pause before He speaks more clearly. However, even in these moments, He is speaking, for God truly desires to reveal Himself to His children. God continually draws us to get our attention upon His Spirit within, but sometimes we don't perceive His overtures toward our hearts. We have been trained to understand that God primarily speaks through His Word, and God absolutely speaks through His Word. He will bring *rhema*, meaning "utterance, narration or command" to our hearts through His precious Word (Strong). In other words, He speaks directly to our hearts in ways we understand. Jesus said, "My sheep hear My voice, and I know them and they follow Me" (John 10:27). We learn to quiet ourselves and listen in order to recognize, and hear, the Voice of our Shepherd.

Actually, it is in stillness and quiet where we really learn to hear God's voice, and in the silence of our souls we experience the healing forgiveness of God's grace, mercy, and love. It is the quieting of our hearts we experience the presence of the Holy Spirit. In silent prayer we quiet our thoughts and emotions, and are drawn into God's presence more easily, to embrace His love, and actually perceive what He is saying, not what we are trying to say to Him or ask of Him. Silence before God is true submission as we wait on Him. Denial of self starts with quieting the mind of all its concerns for self. Then we develop and gain the ability to truly hear His voice. Silence is golden in hearing God's voice when we spend time in quiet abiding and communing with Him. "God speaks in the silence of the heart, and we listen. And then we speak to God from the fullness of our heart, and God listens. And this listening and this speaking is what prayer is meant to be" (Mother Teresa).

Communing with God

One aspect of communing with God is waiting with Him. In our connection with the Spirit of God, love, trust, and companionship are the active dynamics in our hearts, whether in silence with God, in worship of Him, in service to Him, or in everyday experience. Transformation results from silent trust, because what is transpiring is deeper than cognitive thought. The deep of our spirits are in active response and interaction as we commune with the deep of God's Spirit. Being still with God, which is easier when in quietude, activates our spirits while heightening our awareness of Holy Spirit. We are thus influenced toward developing of the Fruit of the Holy Spirit. We trust Christ more, drawing toward deeper intimacy with Him, and activating reliance upon His Spirit.

The most wonderful thing that takes place during communion with God's Spirit is learning of Jesus, who is gentle and meek (Matthew 11:28-30). Holy Spirit will always point to Jesus. When we spend quiet interactive and intimate time with Holy Spirit, we learn about Jesus, taking His yoke and burden, which are light and easy, and thus we become more like Him. One of the beautiful benefits of knowing Jesus is finding rest and peace in our souls. Patience with peace becomes our paradigm as we truly delight ourselves in the Lord Jesus.

During communion with Him, He lovingly interposes and imparts His nature into ours: "Now the Lord is the Spirit; and where the Spirit of the Lord is, there is liberty. But we all, with unveiled face, beholding as in a mirror the glory of the Lord, are being transformed into the same image from glory to glory, just as by the Spirit of the Lord" (2 Corinthians 3:17-18).

Our Heavenly Father is revealed in the Person of Jesus Christ, who is the express image of God, the exact representation of His likeness (Hebrews 1:3; Colossians 1:15-16). Jesus was meek and humble, yet He also spoke as one with authority, because whoever has seen Jesus has seen the Father (John 14:9). With all His holiness, power, and dominion, God the Father is also tender in His mercy, loving in His kindness, and gracious in His love. All these attributes are revealed in Jesus. Coming to Him in response to His loving invitation not only gives rest to our souls, but transforms us with His righteousness, peace, and joy along with His gentleness and humility. He truly desires intimacy with His children.

We are in union with Holy Spirit as He touches our souls in transformation. We also receive truth from the Word of God from the presence of Holy Spirit through our spirits, which then enlightens our hearts—the bridge between our soul and our spirit—and is transferred into our souls, which is our mind, will, and emotions. The Word of God reads our hearts while it brings conviction, life, and transformation. "For the word of God is living and powerful, and sharper than any two-edged sword, piercing even to the division of soul and spirit, and of joints and marrow, and is a discerner of the thoughts and intents of the heart. And there is no creature hidden from His sight, but all things are naked and open to the eyes of Him to whom we must give account" (Hebrews 4:12-13). Words from the late Pastor Frans Du Plessis, one of my beloved mentors, comes to mind: "Read your Bible. It will read you."

The Word of God cuts and it heals, weighing the heart and allowing us to see ourselves as God sees us. We change from the inside out as we meditate upon the Word, through which we are given glimpses of His glory. We trust God as He divides soul and spirit by His Word since He is transforming us into the image of His Son (Romans 8:28-29; 2 Corinthians 3:17-18).

Trust is an action of the heart that effects change in the soul. Learning to sit in silence we grow in the ability to commune with Holy Spirit. "The spirit of man is as a candle to the Lord, searching all the inner depths of the heart" (Proverbs 20:27). Inner strength builds as we interact with God in this manner: "For thus says the Lord GOD, the Holy One of Israel: 'In returning and rest you shall be saved; in *quietness* and confidence (which means trust) shall be your strength. But you would not'" (Isaiah 30:15).

Spiritual power is released in us when we are quiet before the Lord if we seek Him in silence and trust, but first we must repent, turning to Him and resting in His quietness. Notice the Israelites rejected God's request instead of repenting. We have the same invitation to repent, but we are under the New Covenant as Christian disciples today. Can we fall victim to the same sin of rebellion as the Israelites in our walk with God? Absolutely, because God does not change; He offers His peace to all through resting, repenting, returning, and quieting themselves with our precious Lord. The Word of God says that strength is found in quietness and confidence, which come to us in our communion with the Lord.

Turn to Appendix A for a well-rounded, Scriptural instruction on learning how to hear God's voice. Drs. Mark and Patti Virkler have a wonderful teaching called "Communion With God." Their sound Biblical approach of four keys to learning to commune with God is especially helpful. I learned in a practical way how to hear from God in this simple, yet profound approach. I know this will help many others learn to trust that they can actually hear Him. God is always ready to speak to His children. Before I learned these simple but profound keys in hearing God's voice, my experience was more or less a hit or miss prospect in hearing God. I did hear His voice, but through these four keys, I have grown in my ability to hear the Spirit of God when I need a word, which is daily.

ENJOY THE JOURNEY

The steps of a good man are ordered by the LORD,
And He delights in his way.
Though he fall, he shall not be utterly cast down;
For the LORD upholds him with His hand.
Psalms 37:23-24

I used to own a Harley Davidson 1200 Sportster Low, metallic blue in color with just enough chrome accents—a really sharp looking motorcycle. I enjoyed riding, whether to work or to just run up to a store. On my days off from work, I would occasionally take a ride up the Great River Road, a very scenic highway along the Mississippi River. My precious wife does not enjoy wind in her face, so I did this alone. The scenery was beautiful as I rode along, with the river to the one side and the bluffs along the other side. Eagles live on those bluffs, and I would occasionally see one soaring overhead. I was not necessarily going anywhere, but just enjoying the ride. As I look back on my enjoyment of those rides I now realize how much God wants me to enjoy my life in Him as a journey of faith, trusting Jesus in each step or season of life.

Unfortunately I had a serious accident on New Year's Day, 2016, which fell on Friday, a day I was to meet my SEAL friend, Jim, for fellowship over a fish sandwich. That afternoon was a beautiful, very sunny, forty degree January day with no wind. So wearing a thick leather coat and gloves, I decided to ride my bike the six or seven miles to the restaurant. After all, I was a Harley rider.

As I was cruising along at about 40 mph in typical Friday evening traffic, all of a sudden, the driver of a pickup truck, who did not see me, pulled out into my path. I did not see him, nor do I remember anything about how the accident happened. All I remember is waking in excruciating pain and trying to get to my feet. But my body would not respond to what my mind was initiating. From my view of lying on the road I could see blood on the pavement, my bike as a pile of wreckage, and the front of a GMC pickup. I continued my attempts to get up. Then I heard a voice, "Don't move, sir; try not to move, sir." I passed out again. My life journey—my steps—took a turn.

The next thing I remember was realizing I was in a helicopter. With just a glimpse of the flight nurse looking down at me, I passed out again. They transported me to St. Louis University Hospital, the best trauma center in our region. As my consciousness regained, I realized a doctor and some nurses were attending to me. I was in shock, but recognized my injuries were very bad. Pain suffused my body, but my arms seemed to hurt worse than any other area, especially if someone touched them. I thought they were broken, but found out later that the pain was the result of severe nerve damage due to two broken neck vertebrate. My wife was there looking at me with love and deep concern. As she stood there I said, "I didn't do anything wrong. All I wanted was a fish sandwich." Even in that miserable condition, with all those injuries, Scriptures also came from my mouth: "Even though I walk through the valley of death, I will fear no evil." And "No weapon formed against me shall prosper." Then I lost consciousness. I don't remember much of the next day or two.

After experiencing a near-death accident, my journey was of a different kind now. There was the broken orbital (skull) bone above my right eye, with damage to that eye, two broken neck vertebrate, a broken hip, and a broken pelvis with multiple torn ligaments and tendons. My right-hand thumb ligaments were torn as well. I spent two weeks in that hospital and had two major surgeries: hip and pelvis repositioning, with a screw to realign them and a metal plate with pins; then a week later, neck surgery with the fusion of the C-4, 5 and 6 vertebrate.

I spent an additional week in another hospital for rehabilitation to learn the wheelchair, and all the other things that go with the limitations I was to live with for 12 more weeks. I had to follow instructions limiting any standing, with absolutely no weight bearing permitted on the left leg, and I was told I couldn't bend over at the waist at all. Outpatient thumb surgery was a couple of months later after release from the hospital.

The changes in my journey that started that day were not enjoyable. My trust in the Lord was being tested; I was in the crucible of trust. Relearning how to enjoy my journey with Christ Jesus became my immediate challenge, but during my time of recovery the Father revealed Himself to me several times, in my stay at the hospital and at home later. This is how I know the crucible of trust truly becomes the Secret Place of the Most High as we entrust our hearts and souls to Him, even when in the valley of the shadow of death.

However, if faith and trust are not activated, the crucible of life can lead us to discouragement and doubt, which attempted to overtake me, but God is near the broken-hearted. He is with the hurting and the damaged: spiritually, physically, mentally, and emotionally. We must learn to sense His presence through the pain of whatever crucible we face, and that takes focused effort, and crying out to Him asking what He wants to be for us during our trials.

I remember one, very specific experience in the hospital. I was really struggling in my heart that day. I was miserably in pain and began to fall into depression. I was not blaming God, but I was having a pity puppy moment. So, recognizing this, I began attempting to draw near to Him from my downcast heart. All of a sudden I sensed our Heavenly Father's presence. It was as if I felt His loving arms holding me, literally. As I closed my eyes I felt the warm tears of comfort and release on my face. I sensed His loving touch in a way that I shall never forget. Sometimes tears are the only response when God reveals Himself. He saw my need for encouragement and assurance that day, and He came through. He revealed His tender love, His compassion, His kindness, His comfort, and His trustworthiness, so I would realize that to trust Him was the best and only option, even through this very bad experience, or any other areas of discomfort in life for that matter. The Father will always provide times of intimacy, refreshment, and exhortation no matter what we go through. He loves to reveal Himself in the very thing we need Him to be for us. That day I needed Him to be Comforter and Encourager, and He was.

I did not understand why this disaster happened. Prior to the accident I had been walking with God in faith, pressing into Him, seeking Him for my life assignment. Just one week earlier I had been laid off from my job at the steel plant. Corporate leaders had decided to shut it down completely. I had worked there for 42 years, so with my seniority the Supplemental Unemployment Benefits that was provided (60% of my wage) for two years was modest, but adequate. Actually, I was looking forward to time off from work to seek the Lord and finish my doctorate. I loved God and believed Him for His provision.

Then this accident took place where I was almost killed. Even though the Lord showed His loving heart to me while I was in the hospital, many weeks later when I was home, I allowed myself to become confused. I found myself leaning on my own limited understanding—again. The need to relearn how to acknowledge Him in my new experiences became very pressing. God was directing my path to lead me toward the continuation of my life's voyage as one in the cycle of trust. That is what life's journey of faith is to be— one of always trusting God no matter what we encounter or experience.

I was limited to a wheelchair. I had to deal with limitations when using the restroom, grooming and hygiene, getting into and out of bed, or a car, etc. I had to learn how to give myself a sponge bath by using a grabber since I couldn't lean over. These necessities seemed so easy before the accident, but now they were a major challenge. I could not take a real shower or a bath for three months. I had daily physical therapy, which involved moving my legs while lying down and also some arm motions.

I was a runner before the accident, so I would close my eyes and imagine running as I exercised in therapy. In fact, my doctors said that had I not been in the physical shape I was in, my injuries would have been far greater, even fatal. Thank God for that.

I grew to sense the Lord as always with me during all the ups and downs, and He always has been, even though I had not always acknowledged or sensed His presence. Through it all I began to experience more and more of His initiation of intimacy with me, because now I had time to seek Him all the more. He showed me He was with me during this entire journey, that He had not left or forsaken me, because of which, I began to grow toward whole-hearted trust.

Trust and Hope

During my recovery, however, there were a couple of times I had to relearn how to stir hope for God's plans for my life. Learning to trust the Lord completely is ongoing. Perhaps like me you have some trust, but to have total trust all the time needs improvement. Learning how to stir faith and trust can become a challenge when facing life's ups and downs, but it is absolutely necessary. This is where having a vigilant hope can stir trust.

One day in particular I was feeling very down. Being in the wheel chair was starting to wear on my heart. My hope was weakening. Then Holy Spirit reminded me of a sermon I had preached several years back that I had called "That Hope of His." He stirred me to remember the revelation that it was Christ's hope in me in which I stand. I sensed the Spirit leading me to look up my sermon notes on my laptop. As I went over this sermon tears began to flow; I was convicted in my heart at my lack of hope, realizing it was due directly to my lack of trust. I started to recognize that having hope things will work out—one way or another—is truly what trusting God is all about, that hope and trust are related. Hope believes the promises of God while trust sees them by faith: "Faith is the evidence of things hoped for and the assurance of things not seen (Hebrews 11:1)."

Then the idea came to look up every Scripture in my Bible Soft program where the word "hope" is found. This took several hours. As I meditated on hope, encouragement began to rise up in me. One Scripture however, Romans 15:13, really spoke to my heart: "Now may the God of hope fill you with all joy and peace in believing, that *you may abound in hope by the power of the Holy Spirit*." The Lord graciously showed me it is only in the power of His Spirit, not in my own strength, that I am able to abound in hope continuously. Joy and peace, which are fruit of the Spirit, should accompany my hope as I believe and trust God during every season in the journey of life. By faith I must receive and allow Holy Spirit fruit to manifest in my heart. Meditating on God's Word regarding hope caused my inner man to stir; His grace was released so I would abound in His hope in joy and peace while believing (beyond the time in that wheelchair) by the power of Holy Spirit.

Because God had shown me how hope and trust are interrelated, He led me into the deeper ways of His inner gladness within my heart. All of us in Christ should know and trust that God is at work within us to will and to do according to His good pleasure (Philippians 2:13), in which all things work together for our good as He raises us up as His children to full maturity (Romans 8:28-29). Our goal is completeness in Him. It becomes our hope that in faith we continue to develop complete trust in God, for every area of life, maturity, and our future.

Running by Trust

But those who wait on the LORD
shall renew their strength;
They shall mount up with wings like eagles.
They shall run and not be weary,
They shall walk and not faint.
Isaiah 40:31

While in recovery from the accident, I believed and trusted the Lord for being able to run again, because running is a joy to me. I began to focus on my goal: by the first of May I would run again. My surgeon had told me he was not sure if I would ever be able to run, but I did not receive that report. By prayer and trust, running was to be in my future.

My wife had made our dining room into a make-shift hospital room for me, because our bedroom is upstairs. For three months, each morning I would wake up and begin my exercises while lying in the bed. My exercises took around 20 minutes. Then I would get into the wheelchair to go about my daily routines. I was to do the physical therapy with three specific exercises twice a day. My therapist told me I was too aggressive in doing the individual exercises, so I reduced my intensity and would do more repetitions, which she said was okay. I would do 150 repetitions instead of the recommended twenty. During my sessions I would envision myself running on the trail near our house. In my spirit I *was* running.

Finally, I was released from that wheel chair on March 23, 2016. I used to say I fired that wheelchair. Oh yes, there was some definite instability on my feet at first, but I started walking short distances, which was difficult and very painful. However, I worked through the pain and increased the distance a small amount each day. Additionally, I started going to the gym a couple times per week and doing light workouts, building strength in my legs and hips little by little on the treadmill and bike machine.

I progressed from strolls to power walks. I did not make the goal of running by May first. But on May sixth I ran two miles. Hallelujah! What a joy it was for me. The same is true in our journey in Christ: we grow from faith to faith, from strength to strength, from glory to glory in our trust as we focus on Christ (Romans 1:7; Psalm 84:7; 2 Corinthians 3:18). Just as my legs and hips were getting stronger each day, through faith, trust, and some determination, and most importantly, believing prayer, we also become stronger in spirit with a renewed mind and grow in the Mind of Christ:

> Therefore we do not lose heart. Even though our
> outward man is perishing, yet the inward man is

being renewed day by day. For our light affliction, which is but for a moment, is working for us a far more exceeding and eternal weight of glory, while we do not look at the things which are seen, but at the things which are not seen. For the things which are seen are temporary, but the things which are not seen are eternal (2 Corinthians 4:16-18).

When I went to a follow-up visit, I told my surgeon that I ran; he was astonished and delighted. That was my last visit. He laughingly said, "Get out of here; I don't want to see you again." I still run a couple of miles two or three times a week. I trust God for the ability to run for many years to come. Trusting Him, I will run my race of faith, with endurance and confidence as I enjoy my walk with Him. God is faithful and trustworthy. To Him goes all praise, adoration, and worship as I continue to grow in my journey of trust.

And all who are in Christ are to mature from faith to trust to deeper trust. In *Ruthless Trust*, Brennan Manning says, "Somewhere along the way, in the life of the maturing Christian, faith combined with hope grows into trust" (2000, 23). Growing from a deep faith in God to an absolute trust in Him and His ways is truly the pathway of intimacy with the Almighty.

FAITH LEADS TO TRUST

Trust in the LORD with all your heart,
And lean not on your own understanding;
In all your ways acknowledge Him,
And He shall direct your paths.
Proverbs 3:5-6

"For years I had faith in what God
was planning to do in our lives,
but as I got older I developed trust.
God will always take you from faith to trust
and faith and trust are on two completely different levels."
Pat Schatzline

There are experiences in our walk with the Lord that often befuddle the mind and the heart. They cause us to ask ourselves, "Do I really live by faith? Do I really trust the Lord?" I heard the Lord say to my heart one day, "Will you trust Me?" He asks this question of anyone who is seeking His will. Learning to deepen one's faith into complete trust is an ongoing development because sometimes what appears to be the will of God makes no sense. As my mentor, Dr. Andries Van Schalkwyk says, "God does not always make sense; He makes faith." This is where trust comes into play. We must have heartfelt faith to trust our Lord Jesus when we can make no sense of what we are experiencing. He makes a way when we do not understand, because He is the Way.

I worked in a steel mill for forty-three years, and then the Lord led me to retire. My pension was somewhat modest, however, and at that time I was still fairly young at 61. Knowing God had plans for me to be in ministry, I acknowledged that God's process of preparation for ministry takes time, at any age. So in waiting I decided to apply for a part time job at a funeral chapel to supplement my modest income until social security would be an option. I was employed as an assistant and was told there was a three-month trial period, but never felt there would be an issue. I was willing to learn and I knew I could grow from this experience.

As a funeral director's assistant, I had various duties in all aspects of funeral services. There was greeting people at the door; organizing parking for the processional to the cemetery; the orderly dismissal after the services; driving the coach to the cemetery; instructing pall bearers and assisting with the transfer of caskets. I learned very much from the directors and the other, more experienced assistants in ministering to grieving individuals. Particularly, the owner modeled dignity and honor in ways that continue to influence me greatly. I enjoyed the work, but I knew this was to be only a season of my life. When I would tell others that I was working at a funeral chapel they would respond, saying, "I can see you doing that. You are well suited for it." I felt the same way. While I was working there the Lord led me to begin writing this book.

After three months I was let go with no specific reason given, other than we were not a good fit. This sort of blindsided me and affected me emotionally at first. I admit to briefly reverting back to complaining and whining that day. I did not understand. Why did this happen? What did I do wrong? My reaction was more of a blow to my pride than anything else. As I reflected, I realized earlier that very morning I had thought the very same thing. I really did not fit here. God had spoken through my thoughts, but I had not listened. I was not ready for what transpired. I had never been fired before. I was a man of God. I was to be above reproach in all my ways. How could this happen?

My plan had been to continue serving there for a couple of years, finishing this book in my spare time. In my heart I knew I was doing a good thing while working there. I would silently pray during services for those in bereavement to be comforted by the Lord. Even in making some blunders, and I made some dandies, I had a heart to serve and bring comfort to those in mourning. This aspect of ministry was not very familiar to me, but I was adjusting, attempting my best effort. At least I thought so. In my subjective estimation it really did not make sense to be let go. Objectively, the release was gracious and respectful, but it still hurt.

That day I went home and did some real, deep soul searching. I took a seven-mile walk on the bike trail to pray, to cry, to seek the Lord's perspective, and His comfort—allowing Him to help me clear my mind and heart of negative thoughts and emotions. While I walked the Lord opened my understanding to the fact He had other plans. I was not a good fit for this position because it was not in the Father's plan for me to work there any longer. Even though others felt it was a good fit for me to work there, it was not God's will. My release most likely involved the mistakes that I made, so I accepted the responsibility. The truth of the matter was this: I was tempted to digress again to not trusting God's process, to digress back to the cycle of regret. This was another instance of having to resist leaning upon my own limited understanding, while staying in the cycle of trust. The Lord, in His graciousness drew me back to faith and trust.

Process of Trust

In our sometimes stubborn attempts to learn truth, we come to the realization that God knows what is best in the ongoing work of the transformation of our heart. God's desire is that we trust Him, even though we do not understand everything. He wants our trust to be based on our relationship of love and intimacy, not for us to try to make sense of everything. As we seek the Lord for wisdom, He will, of course, open our minds so we will gain necessary understanding from His perspective. Because of our devotion and closeness with the Lord our faith grows toward deeper trust. We might go through a season of not perceiving what He is doing, but with God's guiding hand leading by Holy Spirit, He will get us through and we will be better for it because we are relying upon Him. He is always there wooing us to get us to the place of being flexible in His Masterful Hands.

God is at work as the Master Potter. We are His clay on the wheel of life. He is making us into vessels for His use, vessels of honor (Jeremiah 18:1-6; Romans 9:20-21; 2 Timothy 2:20-21). Though there are lumps and areas in need of adjustment in our hearts, God loves us and ever draws us closer in shaping us into the image of His Son. As we walk through this life these imperfections are revealed to us in the crucible of life by Holy Spirit. Going through testing exposes what God already knows—where we need renewal and upgrading into the Mind of Christ. God's purpose is our maturity, and He allows us to go through whatever it takes to open our eyes so we will keep them on Him in order to transform us into Christlikeness.

God has removed numerous imperfections from me, with many more to go. At times these removals can feel very uncomfortable. It is not pleasant on the flesh to go through the refining fires of God that test the heart. But refining is necessary. Trials and tests expose what is inside us, whether of Christ or of the flesh, and they challenge our faith and trust in God. God uses trials and tests in order to get us to a place where our entire beings involve our trust of Him. No one who loves God and is called by Him is exempt from this process, which *should* always lead us to ever deepen our trust in our faithful Heavenly Father.

David's Example

You have tested my heart;
You have visited me in the night;
You have tried me and have found nothing;
I have purposed that my mouth shall not transgress.
Psalm 17:3

Consider David, the beloved king of Israel, who before he became king was tested when Saul was pursuing him to kill him. David loved and trusted God. He was intimate with the Almighty as his psalms reveal. He also understood submission to God's anointed king, Saul. He was willing to wait and trust God's timing, and said, "But as for me, I trust in you O LORD. I say, 'You are my God.' My times are in your hand. Deliver me from the hand of my enemies, And from those who persecute me" (Psalm 31:14-15).

David trusted God, even when King Saul became his enemy. The Lord had anointed David to become the future king, to succeed Saul, but his time had not yet come. David had to learn to willingly trust God as he went through the trials and testing of his heart before he became king. For fifteen years David's crucible of trust was to be as a fugitive from Saul's several attempts to kill him. However, God blessed David for his trust; he became king over the tribe of Judah at age 30. David yielded to God's process and timing for his own life's calling and assignment to be realized. After becoming king of Judah, David continued in his crucible of trust throughout his lifetime. Seven years passed before the remaining tribes of Israel submitted to him as their king, and throughout it all, David embraced and honored God's process.

God further made a covenant with David that a descendant of his would be on the throne forever (2 Samuel 7:1-17; Isaiah 9:6-7). We know from Scripture that God's plan was that through David and the tribe of Judah, Jesus of Nazareth would come forth as the Christ—called the Son of David—as the fulfillment of this promised covenant. Jesus will be King eternally upon the throne of David. David's trust was revealed through obedience, which God rewards.

Faith leads to Trust and Obedience

But without faith it is impossible to please Him,
for he who comes to God must believe that He is,
and that He is a rewarder of those who
diligently seek Him.
Hebrews 11:6

My mentor, Dr. Andries Van Schalkwyk teaches that radical obedience leads to radical results. God rewards our obedience. It takes great faith along with deep trust to thoroughly obey. To have faith is to believe and accept. To have trust is the inner activation with deeper commitment, because faith without corresponding action in works of obedience is dead (James 2:18-26).

Faith pleases our heavenly Father, and to diligently seek Him reveals a trusting and tenacious heart. He longs to release favor and blessing to His children, and He will, but He knows what is best and when is best. He certainly pours out the rain on the just and the unjust (Matthew 5:45). However, I believe His favor is reserved for the obedient. Consider Isaiah 1:19 in light of God's favor relative to our obedience: "If you are willing and obedient, you shall eat the good of the land." When He speaks instructions, it is prudent to obey in the best and quickest way we know how.

Faith in God is to embrace Him as Truth, trusting Him with a sure hope that He fulfills His promises. Faith believes what is not necessarily seen with the natural eyes and is an assurance of those things for which we hope (Hebrews 11:1). By faith we have righteousness and right standing with God. Trust on the other hand is from our heart and reveals through our actions that we truly possess faith and are obeying what we hear from the Spirit of God. When we have faith, we have a mental and emotional acknowledgment and acceptance of God, who is unseen. Faith has potential to move mountains. Trust, however, touches the heart of God because it motivates us to obey and reveals intimacy with Him. He is stirred by anyone trusting Him in obedience. Yes, God is immutable and never changes, yet somehow we touch the heart of God with our trust in Him when we actively obey His Word and His personal initiatives to us in our walk with Him.

Faith in our hearts toward God also helps us to trust Him in the ongoing plan He has for our lives. "Faith is what happens when I join my heart with God's and believe for something great" (Schatzline 2015, 171). God has plans and purposes for each one of us and the "something great" just might be to overcome in an area of our lives in order to step into His greater purposes. As we join our faith with God's we are well able to prevail over every obstacle.

Joining our hearts with God's involves abiding and intimacy. Hopefully we all desire to believe for something great that God will do through our lives. Greatness looks different for every person. I cannot be Smith Wigglesworth or Billy Graham. Greatness to God is in our obedience to serve, whatever the capacity. He is in the small beginnings and what might be considered as mundane or inconsequential, and He is in the great things of His Kingdom. Nothing is insignificant to God.

Obedience is better than sacrifice (1ˢᵗ Samuel 15:22). We obey Him, trusting He will reward our faithful efforts, even when we don't know the results of that obedience. He sees our hearts and motives and knows our personalities and potentials. Through our obedience greater trust in Him is established. He leads us to accomplish His will, and to have joy in Him while doing His bidding. In fact, the greater our intimacy with the Father, the greater our trust becomes as we delight in Him, which leads us to experience the desires of our hearts.

Trust with Total Reliance

One time while driving my car I saw a hawk swooping up from his dive with a snake in its talons. This thrilled my heart. God knows my fascination with regal birds, and as that hawk soared upward, I absolutely sensed the Lord saying, "I have dealt with the serpent (Satan) on your behalf." Immediately a Scripture came to mind: "But those who wait on the LORD shall renew their strength. They shall mount up with wings like eagles. They shall run and not be weary. They shall walk and not faint" (Isaiah 40:31). God was expressing to me that I could rely upon Him in dealing with the enemy on my behalf. From this experience my heart was encouraged to believe, to wait on Him, to run and not be weary in my faith, and to trust Him.

Trusting God is both an act of the will and of the heart. When faith moves to trust it is an experience of love from the heart, of intimacy in reliance, and of total dependence upon God. Is it possible to have faith with no love? Yes, "If I have all faith so as to move mountains, but *have not love*, I am nothing" (1 Corinthians 13:2). Is it possible to have faith with love and limited trust? Consider Thomas, who had been a faithful disciple in his relationship with Jesus: he had grown to love Jesus, but said unless he saw the nail prints and was able to put his hand into the Lord's side, he would not believe that Jesus had risen from the dead (John 20:25). His declaration of doubt revealed his trust was in development. To believe or have faith infers trust, commitment and being able to entrust oneself (Strong). Thomas struggled in his heart because his faith was in transition toward the deeper levels of trust.

Let us not be too harsh with Thomas. I personally do not like to call him Doubting Thomas as he is often labeled. Like most of us at various times, he was leaning upon his own limited understanding, and his love for Jesus had not transformed into total trust just yet. Our love for God grows, and eventually becomes wholehearted, so our trust level will also progressively deepen. Love and trust are intimately related, for if we truly love Jesus we will trust Him when our experiences are difficult or not pleasant or not lining up with our perceptions of how things should work out. Faith and trust working from our love for Him and His love for us become the foundation of our relationship with the Lord and our intimacy with Him. When we trust God wholeheartedly our faith works in and through the deeper reaches of our love for Him (Galatians 5:6b), always leading to deeper trust.

Without faith it is impossible to please God. When we lovingly, conscientiously, and wholeheartedly seek Him we will find Him and the reward of intimacy with the Lord becomes our delightful experience. Then we will discover what is forever true: knowing and trusting God personally leads us into the Secret Place of total reliance on Him, a place of steadfastness, security, joy, peace, and love.

TRUST AND STEWARDSHIP

So then each of us shall give account of himself to God.
Romans 14:12

E ach individual has a different level of faith. Scripture calls this the measure of faith from which one operates; according to the measure of faith we prophecy, minister, teach, exhort, lead, have mercy, or give (Romans 12:3-8).

There are additional measures in the Kingdom of God relative to the grace gifts in the Body of Christ: "But to each one of us grace was given according to the measure of Christ's gift" (Ephesians 4:7). What we do with the gift has to do with trust, obedience, sacrifice, counting the cost, diligence, and loyalty to Christ and His call upon our lives. Our faith is a gift from God, and trust is our response back to Him (Manning, 2000). God's grace is progressively provided for every level of faith, and we reveal our level of faith by trust.

The word used for *measure* in both references above is *metron* in the Greek, meaning measure or limited portion or degree (Strong). By implication it also indicates one's sphere of influence, or jurisdictional authority. Christ's gifts to us are provided along with the grace to empower each one of us in exercising that gift. In other words, we are entrusted with certain abilities with corresponding responsibilities. Both the Father and the Son discharge Holy Spirit to dispense His gifts to us for our stewardship of them within the bounds of His provision, His will, and our individual capability. What does this mean regarding trust? God entrusts His gifts to us and expects stewardship of them within the measure of faith provided, with the potential for that faith to grow and increase. We trust Holy Spirit for the operation of our gifts in our life's experiences and the function of these gifts in the management and stewardship of His grace (Ephesians 3:2).

Trust and Obey

Jesus told a parable to illustrate stewardship. The story involved three different men who were given talents (large sums of money) by their master before he went on a long journey. All three understood what was expected of them. To the first one the master gave five talents, to the second he gave two, and to the third he gave one as each was given *according to his own ability* (Matthew 25:15). The first and second acted in faith with what was given. They trusted their master for their reward as they obeyed. Their actions revealed their trust, as they invested their talents, which resulted in an increase. However, the third person merely took his talent and buried it.

When the master returned he blessed and honored the two servants who showed initiative with what was entrusted to them. The servant with five had yielded an increase of five. The servant with two had yielded two. The master was not happy, however, with the third servant who buried his talent, and did nothing with it because, as he said, he was afraid to step out in faith, which revealed his lack of trust in his master. The master sternly rebuked him for this, took the one talent from him and gave that talent to the one who had invested and gained five. Jesus finished the parable with these words, "For to everyone who has, more will be given, and he will have abundance; but from him who does not have, even what he has will be taken away. And cast the unprofitable servant into the outer darkness. There will be weeping and gnashing of teeth" (Matthew 25:29-30). The two obedient and trustworthy men acted upon what was provided with diligence and they experienced blessings and acknowledgment of a job well done, but the lazy, unproductive man acted in doubt and fear; punishment was his reward.

This story illustrates how three men were in similar crucibles, each with different approaches and results. We do not know how the two studious men invested or what they had to go through during the absence of their master. They obviously operated in faith using what had been entrusted into their care, trusting that their efforts would yield what their master desired. In other words, they trusted their master's confidence in them within the sphere of their abilities and acted accordingly. The lazy servant had no faith in his own ability, nor did he trust his master. When confronted, he stated that he thought the master was a hard man who reaped where he did not sow; as a result, the servant hid the talent in order to be able to give it back. The other two more industrious and obedient men also knew their master, yet they stepped up to the assignment with faith and trust that would yield fruit for their efforts.

We all have been given gifts and abilities, and grace to grow in faith and trust in the function and operation of those gifts. We must not trust exclusively in ourselves, but trust in Him and His trust in us. This story not only illustrates but emphasizes that we absolutely must trust our heavenly Father in our effort to be obedient in His initiatives, and to trust ourselves to be obedient in stewardship. Someday we will give an account to the Lord for our lives. We have been blessed with great potential to invest ourselves in cooperation with God, to co-labor with Him, so we must step up in faith and trust Him as we apply ourselves with diligence and confidence in the Lord who will work through our efforts.

To invest in ourselves simply means personal application by seeking the Lord daily in extended times of prayer, learning to hear His Voice, being diligent in study and meditation of His Word, and learning from the examples of more seasoned and mature Christians. As an illustration, suppose a person has a call from God to go into pastoral ministry. Obviously, he or she would not immediately become a pastor. Remember, God makes or prepares the person before He opens an opportunity for ministry. Pastors must go through a preparation process as Scripture instructs (1 Timothy 3:1-7; Titus 1:5-9; Hebrews 6:12). The person also needs to be recognized by the church as one who is called by God, and he or she should be under the authority of a seasoned mentor in order to be trained (2 Timothy 2:2, 14-17). One cannot over-emphasize the diligent study of the Word of God while in the spirit and attitude of prayer to be able to correctly minister the principles of Scripture (1 Timothy 3:16).

Being trained to hear from the Spirit of God is vital for meaningful ministry. All the above stipulations are really tests and become crucibles of trust for the person of God, whether called to the ministry, or to serve in God's Kingdom in whatever capacity. But the most important ingredient in any ministry or service is love, and learning to hear the Voice of God, which actually originates in His love for us and in our love for Him.

We are all called to believe, to witness, and to pray; we are instructed to grow in the grace and knowledge of Jesus Christ and have been endowed with God's divine nature. We will also be accountable to God for how we loved others in the use of our gifts.

Our love for Jesus should motivate us to seek out just what our gift is and what sphere of influence God has allotted for us, seeking the Master's initiative in activation and investment, just like the two obedient servants.

Faith and hope becomes the doorway toward trust, which is the inner chamber of our bond, the inner working in the Secret Place of our relationship with our Heavenly Father. Faith pleases God, but whatever is not of faith is actually sin (Romans 14:23). Trust is much deeper, more relational, more on the heart level of stepping out in confidence, in love, and in intimacy.

When a person steps out in an act of faith, trust is being revealed and modeled. Scripture says that one can have faith, but to show faith in action reveals its genuineness: "But someone will say, "You have faith, and I have works. Show me your faith without your works, and I will show you my faith by my works" (James 2:18). Action reveals the trust that comes from faith. Actions speak louder than words; obedience reveals our faith in the deeper level of trust.

Step out of the Boat

Jesus had instructed His disciples to get into their boat and proceed to the other side of the sea without Him, because He had plans to go off by Himself to pray privately. Later, as the disciples were moving along on the water a storm came. Jesus had finished praying and was actually walking on the water as if to go on around them. The disciples saw Jesus and did not recognize Him, thinking He was a ghost. Jesus assured them it was Him saying, "Be of good cheer. It is I, do not be afraid." Peter, uncertain it was Jesus, said, "Lord, if it is You, command me to come to You on the water" (Matthew 14:27, 28). Jesus indicated for him to come.

Peter modeled trust when he stepped out of the boat and actually walked on the water—until he took his eyes off Jesus because he became distracted by the fierce wind. Beginning to sink, he cried out to Jesus. "And immediately Jesus stretched out His hand and caught him, and said to him, 'O you of little faith, why did you doubt?' And when they got into the boat, the wind ceased. Then those who were in the boat came and worshiped Him, saying, 'Truly You are the Son of God'" (Matthew 14:31-33). Peter trusted Jesus when he activated his faith, which according to Jesus was little, but incredible because he really *walked* on the water. He had grown to love Jesus, and in that love it was his trust of Jesus that motivated him to step out of the boat onto the water.

Our Lord will sometimes challenge us to get out of our boat to follow Him. He does this for our own good so we will stretch our faith, grow in our trust of Him, and yield our hearts more in our willingness to follow Him. He might ask us to do something way out of our comfort zone. He may ask of us to become missionaries in a foreign land, or to go on a short mission trip to another country, or to witness on the streets, or simply to offer to pray for a server at the restaurant or someone in the isle of a store.

The Lord challenged me to go on a mission trip to a Central American country that is closed to the Gospel. As part of a team, we not only smuggled Bibles and Christian teaching aids through customs and immigration, we also brought cloths, bottles of Tylenol and hydrogen peroxide—things difficult to get in that particular country. We spent a week there ministering, fellowshipping, worshiping the Lord, and praying together with pastors and leaders, and distributing Bibles to their underground churches. The joy in those people was amazing and contagious. I naively thought I was going as a blessing, but I ended up receiving such a blessing from these wonderful Christians, more than I could have realized. This trip was, up to this point, one of the highlights of my life as a disciple of Jesus and a minister of the Gospel. I am so glad I followed the Lord's prompting to go. In a very small way, I stepped out of the boat.

TRUST WITH CHILDLIKE FAITH

Assuredly, I say to you, unless you are
converted and become as little children,
you will by no means enter the kingdom of heaven.
Therefore whoever humbles himself as this little child
is the greatest in the kingdom of heaven.
Matthew 18:3-4

Remain childlike and simple in your walk with me...
Only look at everything through the eyes and the heart of a
trusting child
Graham Cooke

T rue spiritual understanding can only come from God and
His Word: "The entrance of your words gives light; it gives
understanding to the simple" (Psalm 119:130). The word translated,
entrance, from the Hebrew, *pethach*, means opening, unfolding,
or disclosure (Strong). The unfolding of God's Word, involves
teaching, discussing, reading, and hearing, bringing enlightenment to open-hearted people. Holy Spirit then brings insights and
understandings into our minds in order for faith and deeper trust

to develop in our hearts. When truth enters our hearts it is like a light coming on, becoming revelation and applicable truth.

Romans 10:17 says, "So then faith comes by hearing, and hearing by the word of God." We hear the Word of God by reading and meditating on Scripture. We listen as the Word is preached through anointed ministers who rightly divide the Word of Truth. We discuss the Word with others, keeping ourselves accountable in a small group. Each one of us must be diligent to read and study, seeking Holy Spirit guidance in order gain insight from Scripture (2 Timothy 2:15). As we look into the Bible with wholehearted attention, it humbles us as Holy Spirit leads us into all truth in intimate trust in the Lord in every area of our lives.

Faith *comes* by hearing the Word, but we *build up* our faith through praying in the Holy Spirit: "But you, beloved, building yourselves up on your most holy faith, *praying in the Holy Spirit,* keep yourselves in the love of God, looking for the mercy of our Lord Jesus Christ unto eternal life" (Jude 20, 21). What does it mean to pray in the Holy Spirit? Romans 8:26-27 speaks of praying in the Holy Spirit:

> Likewise the Spirit also helps in our weaknesses. For we do not know what we should pray for as we ought, but the Spirit Himself makes intercession for us with *groanings* which cannot be uttered. Now He who searches the hearts knows what the mind of the Spirit is, because He makes intercession for the saints according to the will of God.

Sometimes we do not know in our rational minds just what we should pray. Perhaps you have experienced—like me—a longing to pray and your mind or thoughts do not exactly know how to pray for that situation or person. Our inner cries to the Lord are often released in groanings and are unintelligible. "God is so good that He will look at us, even when we're so lost we cannot put a prayer into words, and say, 'Just groan, I'll understand what you mean, I promise.' God can and does interpret our groans" (Cooke 2015, 22). These groanings originate from our spirit in union with Holy Spirit, yet are released out from our soul. Our Father is in perfect union with His Spirit, and because we are one with Holy Spirit (1 Corinthians 6:17), our inner cries in prayer are released to the Father.

Jesus taught that if we believe in Him, out of our inner most being something wonderful would be released:

> On the last day, that great day of the feast, Jesus stood and cried out, saying, 'If anyone thirsts, let him come to Me and drink. He who believes in Me, as the Scripture has said, *out of his heart will flow rivers of living water.*' But this He spoke concerning the Spirit, whom those believing in Him *would receive*; for the Holy Spirit was not yet given, because Jesus was not yet glorified" (John 7:37-3).

Jesus said something would transpire as we believe and receive, with the result that from deep within our beings would flow waters that are alive and real. John, the inspired writer expanded on what Jesus meant, that because of receiving Holy Spirit infilling, our hearts will flow with rivers of release.

Jesus' words do not specifically address prayer, but they truly apply. Because He did say we ought to pray and not lose heart (Luke 18:1). Years later, the apostle Paul caught this same theme when he wrote: "Be anxious for nothing, but in everything by prayer and supplication, with thanksgiving, let your requests be made known to God; and the peace of God, which surpasses all understanding, will guard your hearts and minds through Christ Jesus." (Philippians 4:6). Paul also wrote 1 Thessalonians 5:17 exhorting us to pray without ceasing. The reasons for prayer are many, but mainly for communion and abiding with our Lord. We can become anxious and faint in adversity if we do not pray and trust while abiding in Christ. However, we are invited and encouraged to be in the spirit and attitude of prayer continually, bringing our thoughts and petitions before God to experience the peace of God, as we abide in Christ; and this includes walking in, and being led by His Spirit.

Scripture mentions various ways to pray: "For if *I pray in a tongue*, my spirit prays, but my understanding is unfruitful. What is the conclusion then? *I will pray with the spirit*, and I will also pray with the understanding. I will sing with the spirit, and I will also sing with the understanding" (1 Corinthians 14:14-16). We pray with our spirits, which Scripture indicates is in a tongue, and we also pray with our understanding. Both are wonderfully accepted by God!

Please allow grace here as I realize some do not necessarily acknowledge tongues as a viable expression of prayer today. Whether one believes and practices speaking and praying in tongues or not, it is Scriptural: "Therefore, brethren, desire earnestly to prophesy, and do not forbid to speak with tongues. Let all things be done decently and in order" (1 Corinthians 14:39-40). Scripture indicates when and how to use tongues in a public setting, but my focus here is on private intimacy with God. Both speaking in tongues and praying in tongues are from God, encouraged in Scripture as spiritual gifts, viable in the church, and praying God's will (1 Corinthians 12:10; 14:14; Romans 8:27).

A public release of a tongue, or privately praying in the Spirit are both humble acts of trust and total reliance upon Holy Spirit. Private praying in tongues is a wonderful way to humble ourselves before God. Childlike faith does not necessarily mean one has to pray in tongues; however, childlike faith is released when we submit ourselves to pray in the Spirit.

Admittedly, praying in tongues sounds strange, even ridiculous to our intellect, but like hearing God in silence is a gift, so tongues are a gift from God as one is filled with Holy Spirit (Acts 2:4; 10:46; 19:6). John the Baptist said, "I indeed baptize you with water; but One mightier than I is coming, whose sandal strap I am not worthy to loose. He will baptize you with the Holy Spirit and fire" (Luke 3:16). Jesus is the One who baptizes in Holy Spirit. The Spirit is the One who gives us the utterance as we yield our tongues to His control (Acts 2:4).

It takes being baptized in the Spirit and a yielding, a humbling of the will and the intellect to the Spirit of God in order to allow our spirits to pray in tongues. In my experience, I yield my mind and heart to Holy Spirit and words come forth out of my mouth with groanings and mutterings too deep for the native tongue to express or my mind to understand—tongues.

We pray from the depths of our being, and we are to pray wholeheartedly and fervently. James 5:16b says, "The effective, fervent prayer of a righteous man avails much." Thank God being righteous is based on faith in Jesus Christ and the cleansing power of His blood, not on the manner in which one prays. And thank the Lord for His Spirit within that helps us pray.

Experiencing the desperate unction to pray, but not knowing what to pray is where praying in the Spirit truly helps our weaknesses. When praying in tongues we are totally dependent and reliant upon Holy Spirit. Our intellects are in a place of active rest as our spirits pray through tongues. The rationalistic mind says this is futile. Paul says as much in 1 Corinthians 14:14, "but my understanding is unfruitful," as he prayed in tongues. This is where true submission and childlike faith are activated and are necessary.

To **pray** in the Spirit is both cognitive and spiritual, but the power of the Spirit comes from the spiritual, not the cognitive. Praying in Holy Spirit provides unction, fervor, and empowerment, and it helps build up our most holy faith. Praying in the Spirit reinforces our faith, edifying our hearts, thus building our trust in the Lord.

Romans 8:27 says the Lord also searches and examines us because God is holy and He desires our hearts to be pure and holy so our prayers will come from pure, childlike faith. He knows our motives, our attitudes, and our character traits. Therefore, we allow Holy Spirit to search our hearts for us to be cleansed and His purity to be interposed into our hearts as we surrender to pray. This encourages submission to God, building trust as Holy Spirit helps us pray with our spirits and not only our feeble, intellectual efforts. By faith we trust Holy Spirit to always pray the perfect will of God, and that is just what He does (Romans 8:27).

The devil hates when we pray in tongues, because whether he can understand tongues or not, (I believe he cannot) he incites division and confusion in the Body of Christ over this Scriptural and spiritual reality. Satan's goal is to steal, kill, and destroy, and, in the case of tongues, he will cause a divisive spirit, which is most often in the form of an intellectual, or a rationalistic doctrinal attitude—which, sadly, is really pride—to manifest.

Satan, who is crafty and subtle, obviously understands our native-tongue prayers and I believe he attempts to implement strategies against our heart cries to God. Our words have meaning and power when praying by the Spirit, either in our native tongue or in our heavenly language. God hears the faintest cry when we release it in faith and hopeful desperation. However praying in the Spirit is where our spirits truly are built up, releasing God-pleasing faith.

Therefore, when we pray with our mental ability it is important to speak Scriptural truth, declaring and proclaiming the manifold wisdom of God as we pray His Word out loud, because the powers of darkness are also listening (Ephesians 3:10). On the other hand, 1 Corinthians 14:2 says, "For he who speaks in a tongue does not speak to men but to God, for no one understands him; however, in the spirit he speaks mysteries."

When praying in tongues, we are praying directly to our Father. Praying in this manner edifies our own spirits, or inner man, and it comes out of us in a language only understood by God. From praying by faith in an unknown tongue, He will implement His perfect will accordingly. Another wonderful advantage to praying in the Spirit is God will also bring revelation to our minds. The Lord brings insights and interpretations as they are needed and as we ask of Him (1 Corinthians 14:13). So, with childlike faith we pray with our understanding and we also pray in tongues to speak to God and build up our most holy faith. From the perspective of our minds and our flesh, praying in tongues truly is a crucible of trust.

Doorway into the Unseen

Trust is the doorway by which we enter into the deeper spiritual realm. Our faith starts as we are born again by Holy Spirit, thus entering into something greater—the beginning of transformation into the image of Jesus Christ. Just like Jesus, God's Beloved Son in whom He was well pleased, so we enter into that place of the Father being pleased with us because we are in His Son, Jesus Christ. Having faith in Jesus Christ leads us into that deeper, ongoing relationship with the Father, potentially the same as Jesus enjoyed with the Father while here on earth.

To know Jesus as Savior requires faith. To believe Jesus Christ is the Son of Man and the Son of God (His humanity intermixed with His divinity) is to grow into the deeper mystery of trust, which is Christ in us (individually and corporately) as our Hope of glory. He is our Savior and Lord and so much more. His Spirit in us is the Treasure in our earthen vessels. He is our Wonderful Counselor, our Everlasting Father, Our Prince of Peace, our Friend, our Brother, our Companion, our Master, our Bridegroom, our Judge, and He is our very Life. He is our Secret Place and our Hiding Place as we dwell under the Shadow of His Wings. These metaphors only attempt to express the reality of the unseen, yet show the very real essence of who God is and just how much our Lord loves us and takes care of us. Individually we are one with Him; corporately we are one with Him as the Body of Christ.

Growing faith draws us to absolutely trust God, believing in what cannot be seen with the natural eye. Faith becomes assurance that the things for which we hope and pray actually will come to pass according to God's will (Hebrews 11:1). These things are invisible, not yet seen in our current experience. We believe God for our requests before they actually transpire because Jesus said we should. "Therefore I say to you, whatever things you ask when you pray, believe that you receive them, and you will have them" (Mark 11:24). We see through the eyes of faith. With God nothing is impossible to the person who believes! He will open the eyes of our understanding to the unseen realm as we seek Him and as we grow in His Spirit.

Dr. Mark Chirona, an anointed man of God, scholar and teacher, has a sermon series called "The Issachar Legacy." In it he speaks of faith, hope, and love with regard to the unseen: "Faith *perceives* the invisible. Hope *believes* the invisible. Love *trusts* the invisible." There is a dynamic relationship within our faith, our hope, and our love, with love being the greatest. Notice also the progression from perception to belief and then to trust. We have faith in God, who is not seen, but certainly sensed. We accept Him for Who He is as we believe His promises. We have hope in

God who will not disappoint because His love has been poured out into our hearts by the Holy Spirit (Romans 5:5). The spiritual realities of faith, hope, and love take place in our hearts, affecting our minds, wills, and emotions, ever transforming us to greater trust in the Living God. We enjoy intimacy with Him even though He is invisible, because by faith He causes us to dwell righteously in His presence.

Trusting in the unseen also involves vulnerability, total reliance, and submission with childlike faith. God's Spirit is the Invisible One within us who leads us to grow. "Once you develop faith, you eventually move to the next level: trust. Trust is what happens when you not only believe something will happen, but you also move forward without doubting that God has it" (Schatzline, 2015, 171-172).

When we hear someone say, "I've got this," it indicates they have things under control. God says the same thing in His plans for us. He has us in the palm of His hand, while taking care of every detail. The unseen becomes seen as He progressively fulfills our calling and empowers us to accomplish His will in our lives. In the progressive manifestation of His will, we grow more like Jesus. At each new level of the unseen, trust grows all the more while God reveals new and different aspects of Himself to us.

Complete trust is not always easy, but is within our grasp, because our unseen God is working in us to will and to do according to His good pleasure (Philippians 2:13). In every aspect of His will for our lives, we learn deeper trust. He will accomplish all His good plans for our lives because He says so and His Word will not return to Him empty.

The Journey of Trust

And He said to them, "Take nothing for the journey,
neither staffs nor bag nor bread nor money;
and do not have two tunics apiece."
Luke 9:3

"Draw near to God and He will draw near to you."
James 4:8

When we were born again our journey of trust and abiding in Christ began. Faith was birthed in our hearts in seed form and began to grow and mature. It continues to move toward the full harvest of a personal, most holy faith, which in completion leads us to total abandon in trust in God and His will. We progressively grow "from faith to faith" (Romans 1:17), which transitions into the deeper, living and loving, cycle of trust through reoccurring experiences in the Spirit of God. Our life's journey in Christ leads us to grow from trust, to deeper trust, to absolute abandoned trust.

Proverbs 3:5 says, "Trust in the LORD *with all your heart* and lean not upon your own understanding." Trust comes from leaning on God and His Word wholeheartedly, not on our own understanding. God encourages us to gain understanding and He provides for us as we seek: "Wisdom is the principal thing; therefore get wisdom. And in all your getting, get understanding" (Proverbs 4:7). However, we must resist natural understanding from the rationalistic, reasoning, and analytical aspects of the mind. God gives spiritual understanding in abundance to the hungry, seeking heart.

The one place in Scripture where it encourages us to reason says, "'Come now, and *let us reason together*,' says the LORD, 'Though your sins are like scarlet, They shall be as white as snow; Though they are red like crimson, they shall be as wool'" (Isaiah 1:18).

Notice God says our reasoning is to be together with Him, not apart with our own cognitive abilities. This can only be accomplished by yielded abiding and intimacy with Holy Spirit and presenting our intellect to Him as we think and meditate upon His Word.

Reasoning in our own minds apart from God leads to soulish and intellectual understanding, which leads to pride, not spiritual insight and revelation. The natural mind does not receive the things of the Spirit of God (1 Corinthians 2:14). If we continually and consistently—in surrender— present our limited understanding to God, Holy Spirit will enlighten our hearts in line with God's Word. Our trust is then based on what God says, and our love and our relationship with the Lord, not our intellectual understanding. Trust precedes understanding, and then He provides true spiritual enlightenment in our hearts, imparting the Mind of Christ as we seek Him wholeheartedly.

As we grow in knowing Christ, learning to trust Him more, He takes us on a journey of abiding in closer intimacy because He loves us with passion. Faith is the entry point of this intimacy and God's gift to us (Ephesians 2:8). Faith continually transitions us into this wonderful journey of trust as we get to know Him more intimately. We continually activate our cycle of trust, perpetuated when we intentionally and consistently draw near to God, knowing that He will draw near to us. In reality, He is the One drawing us into this extraordinary journey. When we abide with Him in trust, He abides with us continually. Drawing near to God is our journey—which is simply being present with Him, consciously and willingly throughout our day and our life. Walking with Holy Spirit as our constant Companion takes us deeper into the heart of God, and in doing so, He manifests more of Christ in and through our lives, thus we grow as sons being transformed more and more into the image of Christ Jesus.

The Hall of Trust

Now faith is the substance of things hoped for,
the evidence of things not seen.
Hebrews 11:1

My very good friend Jim, of whom I wrote earlier, was buried in a National Military Cemetery. While waiting for his memorial service, I could not help but notice row upon row of grave stones marked "Unknown Soldier." I paused to wonder of all the untold stories, acts of heroism, and the terrors of war. Truly I beheld a hall of trust as each of these gave their lives for their country.

Throughout history God's people have also been through challenges, trials, tests, and tribulations. Hebrews 11 is considered the "Faith Chapter" with testimonies of many faithful saints from the Old Testament. Scripture records their experiences and trials as they obtained a good testimony of faith by keeping their trust in God while not actually receiving the promises. They saw the promises from afar, embracing, and confessing them. In like manner, we should embrace our promises, confessing them as reality. They believed God's promises and trusted Him, and are excellent examples of going through incredible crucibles of trust.

Their testimony was steadfast faith in God's faithfulness and trustfulness, but there is also a mystery in their experiences. Those of the Old Covenant were to wait for those of the New Covenant so that both can be made perfect together and inherit the promise. What promise? God combines all things that involve the Kingdom of God in Christ Jesus (Hebrews 11:13, 39, 40). No matter what trial we may face, God is leading us to overcome by trusting Christ so all things will culminate in Him. This pledge from Almighty God is about the eternal Kingdom of God in Christ Jesus. His plan in His promise is to raise individuals up as sons and daughters to be kings and priests unto the Lord Most High (Revelation 1:6; 5:10).

Many of God's people partially received the promises with the sure hope of total consummation of all God promised, but died in faith going through their crucibles of trust. I believe they are cheering us on from their vantage point of the spirit realm as we face our own battles of faith and our own crucibles of trust. Hebrews 12:1-2 says,

> Therefore we also, since we are surrounded by so great a cloud of witnesses, let us lay aside every weight, and the sin which so easily ensnares us, and let us run with endurance the race that is set before us, looking unto Jesus, the author and finisher of our faith, who for the joy that was set before Him endured the cross, despising the shame, and has sat down at the right hand of the throne of God.

Our place of trust is to follow Jesus who went through the ultimate crucible of trust as He endured the cross. We do so by keeping our focus on Him and following His example of total reliance upon the Father and the example of all those who have gone before us in faith (Hebrews 6:12). This is the only way to run the race through to victory because God will always lead us through to triumph as we are in Christ (2 Corinthians 2:14). Victory over death, hell, and the grave was Jesus' triumph in His resurrection; He becomes our victory because we trust in Him.

Jesus came to fulfill the Father's will, which was to reveal the glory of God, to destroy all the works of the devil, and to lay down His life for the sins of the world. In the Garden of Gethsemane, Jesus experienced what is called His passion. Jesus anguished in

His soul and went through the yielding of His will. As a man, in His flesh He certainly did not desire to go through the cruelty of the cross. Even as He despised the shame of it, He overcame His own will in the flesh by the Spirit. In His fervor, He experienced hematidrosis sweating great drops intermingled with blood, because His anxiety level and tension of soul were so traumatic. I believe He won the victory over the cross in that moment. He resolved in His heart to go through what He knew was foretold to redeem humanity (Psalm 22; Isaiah 53) as He said, "Father, if it is Your will, take this cup away from Me; nevertheless not My will, but Yours, be done. Then an angel appeared to Him from heaven, strengthening Him, and being in agony, He prayed more earnestly. Then His sweat became like great drops of blood falling to the ground" (Luke 22:42, 44).

What He did for us goes beyond encouragement, and provides inspiration for us as we follow Him going through whatever crucibles we face. God's process of trust leads us to be like Jesus. His willingness to lay down His life for us by going through the brutality of crucifixion for our sin causes us fall to our knees in humble adoration and worship. He is worthy of all praise! As the Moravian Cry resounds, "May the Lamb that was slain, receive the reward of His sufferings."

PRESS INTO GOD'S REST

There remains therefore a rest for the people of God.
For he who has entered His rest has himself also
ceased from his works as God did from His.
Let us therefore be diligent to enter that rest,
lest anyone fall according to the same example of disobedience.
Hebrews 4:9-11

I enjoy vacationing with my wife and family. It is a time of much needed rest, relaxation, recreation, and just getting away from the routines of life. However, going on vacation involves planning and preparation. I know of some people who seem to enjoy the planning as much as the actual vacation. Diligent effort is put forth in finding accommodations, in where to eat, and in setting a daily itinerary. Others like to go and enjoy making plans as each day unfolds. I am sort of in the middle. For example, I enjoy golf, and it saves much hassle to have my tee times arranged in advance. However, I also like to go expecting to find adventure in the experience of not knowing exactly what we will enjoy that day. That is the way of the Spirit in our lives.

For a successful vacation, on the other hand, there is the need to set aside enough for expenses, do the necessary packing, set things in order for while we're away, and do anything else that needs to be done before departure. My wife wants to come back home to a clean house. I agree. It takes some diligence to properly prepare for vacation and to have peace of mind in enjoying it while spending time away from home.

Diligence, however, implies effort, intent, and hard work. As contradictory as it sounds, we are encouraged to be diligent to enter into God's rest. Indeed, many of God's truths are paradoxical. For instance, Jesus said in Matthew 10:39, "He who finds his life will lose it, and he who loses his life for My sake will find it." He is not just referring to eternal life. Most people desire to find their lives in the manner they want to live, not to lose it. Jesus is really saying one must lose the old life of sin and selfishness in order to obtain that which is necessary to enjoy the benefits of the new life in Him.

As Jesus said, "Come to Me, all you who labor and are heavy laden, and I will give you rest. Take My yoke upon you and learn from Me, for I am gentle and lowly in heart, and you will find rest for your souls. For My yoke is easy and My burden is light" (Matthew 11:28-30).

Taking Jesus' yoke means we give up ours by giving up our lives for Him. We let go of our burdens and efforts in dealing with them by taking His burden and find rest for our souls. Losing our life to find it correlates with entering into His rest with His burden and yoke. The Lord spoke to me regarding this and said, "You are so hard on yourself. You have allowed a mindset of concern in your thinking that causes that tightness and strain on your mind. Relax, My son. Enjoy My peace today and from now on. Come to Me to learn how to enjoy My rest. Enter into My finished works."

When considering what it means to take His yoke, oxen plowing come to mind. There is effort and labor for these oxen in a yoke, but one ox is more dominant and stronger, so the other learns to yield while yoked. Jesus' yoke is easy and His burden is light. He is the Mighty One who takes the brunt of the burden as we rely upon Him; He makes our part easier.

As we rest in Christ Jesus and walk with Him, we just walk along with Him in the journey. If we resist His lead and exert our own effort in the yoke, we lose the rhythm of Jesus, and will likely lose our balance spiritually and stumble in the natural. In a physical yoke one's neck would most likely become chaffed from going against the rhythm of the other. Spiritually, our hearts and minds will find unrest and lack of peace as we go against Jesus' steadiness and consistency. In staying in step with Jesus, allowing Him to take the lead and the brunt of the load, we sense ease in our burden. We experience the ability to walk along in unity and in sync with Him.

In contrast, another type of yoke is that of bondage and slavery to sin or of oppression. Jesus says His yoke is bearable, easier, and lighter because He is the one bearing it, not us. He breaks the yoke of bondage over our lives by us entering His rest, letting Him take the burden while we experience His peace is the way He intends for us to live. His yoke is easier because He does all the pulling His way. Jesus is the Way, the Truth, and the Life for us, so taking His yoke is the true way and life for us. In order to apply what it means to take His yoke, we trust Him as we abide in Him by casting all our cares and burdens upon Him because He cares for us so much (1 Peter 5:7).

Diligent in Rest

The word for "diligent" in the Greek is *spoudazō*, meaning to "endeavor, to make an effort, to make haste, to exert oneself, to be zealous, and to labor" (Strong). What effort must there be in taking Jesus' yoke or entering God's rest? We must come to Jesus, denying ourselves and learn from Him. The answer lies in yielding and intentionally trusting God. It means to deliberately put on the Lord Jesus Christ, letting His love and character become our own (Romans 13:14). Diligence in this case becomes an act of the will in losing our lives for His sake in order to find life in Him. Then we enter His rest because we are no longer striving; we enter His life of rest experiencing inner peace. Entering His rest requires effort of mind, taking every thought captive in surrender to the Mind of Christ, and allowing Him to live through us.

Conversely, the Greek word for rest, *katapausis* means "repose, a putting to rest or resting" (Strong). Hebrews 4:11 says, "Let us therefore be diligent to enter that rest, lest anyone fall according to the same example of disobedience." We are encouraged to enter God's rest, which indicates action on our part, or else we could fall according the same disobedience as the Children of Israel. The writer of Hebrews is referring to Psalm 95:11, which says that God swore that those Israelites who disobeyed and grumbled in the wilderness would not enter His rest. Why? They did not mix hearing the good news of God's promises with faith (Hebrews 4:1-3). They angered God because of their unbelieving attitudes and behavior. Christians potentially can also not enter God's rest when they fall victim to unbelief and complaining (Philippians 2:14; James 5:9). We simply will not experience God's rest and peace when we allow these negative characteristics to exist in our hearts. Christians can live frustrated and disruptive lives if they are not careful to trust Christ, taking His yoke, and entering into His rest. As I have testified earlier, having a grumbling attitude is certainly not restful, nor healthy. God is serious about His children entering His rest because He desires for us to enjoy His peace and His joy.

The word for rest in the Hebrew language is *menuchah*, which means much the same as the Greek word for rest, but it adds one very important component, "an abode or a place of rest" (Strong). What this means for us is to abide in that place of God's rest as a habitation. He invites us to enter and enjoy His place of rest, to enjoy His presence in fellowship and intimacy in our everyday lives, even while we are in our crucibles of trust. God created us for His good pleasure, and when His kids learn to enjoy His rest and peace, even during trials, He is pleased and we grow. Because He is the God of Peace, that place of rest is truly being rest-assured in Him, trusting and not leaning upon our own understanding. It is a paradigm of rest, a lifestyle of respite in Christ.

Jesus is Immanuel, God with us. Christ in us is our hope of glory; Christ is our peace. He is our Prince of Peace, drawing us into His peace. There is no other way to truly enter into God's rest, except through Christ. He created us to experience His peace and to find rest only in Him. He wants us to have a mindset and lifestyle of trust and reliance, truly the Secret Place of the Most High in which David loved to dwell (Psalm 91).

Ever Growing in the Lord

Years ago my good friend, mentor, and pastor at that time, Brother Gerry Claybrook, told me of a visit he made to Miss Bonnie, an elderly saint in the church. This precious lady was blind and would walk along the railroad tracks to go to church on Sunday morning, knowing exactly how many steps to take and where to turn to arrive at the building. The day of his visit he asked her how she was doing. Her response to him has always amazed and inspired me. She smiled and said, "Brother Gerry, I am ever growing in the Lord." She was truly remarkable in her trust in God and her faithfulness to Him.

Miss Bonnie's testimony was trust, rest, and maturity in Christ. May this be my testimony! For her, and all of us, knowing the Lord leads to continued growth in Him. When I think of her attitude, these words of Bill and Gloria Gaither's song "The Longer I Serve Him" come to mind: "Since I started for the Kingdom, since my life He controls, since I gave my heart to Jesus, the longer I serve Him the sweeter He grows."

I love that about Jesus. He grows sweeter to us as we get to know Him more intimately. He never changes, but He continues to reveal nuances of His love and personality to us leading us into deeper intimacy, and His Spirit guides us into all truth, leading us in His way everlasting. Trust, admiration, worship, and particularly, love are our true responses as we grow to rest more and more in Him. He is infinitely faithful, trustworthy, and His love knows no bounds.

Joy in the
Crucible of Trust

He who dwells in the secret place of the Most High
shall abide under the shadow of the Almighty.
I will say of the LORD, "He is my refuge and my fortress;
My God, in Him I will trust. Psalm 91:1-2

Throughout *The Crucible of Trust*, I have written that life just has a way of bringing trials and tests that give opportunity to grow our faith toward deeper trust in the Lord. God is faithful and He is directly involved with us through all of life's ups and downs. Concerns, troubles, and conflicts are all part of our experience in life, but as we present ourselves and all our concerns while in the crucible of life to Abba (our Heavenly Papa) in love, trust, submission, and expectancy, He will always come through in ways that are best. If we are sensitive to His presence, His joy is revealed inside our hearts, and we truly experience His strength. God strengthens our spirits as we count it all joy while in the crucible of trust, because He truly is right there with us strengthening and guiding our hearts. His joy becomes our joy, and our joy becomes complete in Him (John 15:11).

We often need to stir up God's joy within when under strong attack or in conflicting situations. How do we activate His joy? What can we do to rouse ourselves, activating our shield of faith to withstand all the darts of the enemy? For joy to be our experience we learn to rejoice. We rest in Christ, entrusting all our concerns to Him. By faith, we let joy arise from our inner man, because our eyes are on Jesus, not on self or situations: "Though now you do not see Him yet believing, you rejoice with joy inexpressible and full of glory, receiving the end of your faith—the salvation of you souls" (1 Peter 1:8-9). Let gladness of heart manifest by choosing joy knowing it is part of our inheritance and integral in our relationship of intimacy with our Lord.

When life hits us hard, this does take a little effort of the will, but this is where the divine nature can override natural inclinations. Joy unspeakable is inside each born again child of God in the Person of Holy Spirit. We learn to meditate upon this joy and we also learn to have perpetual delight in our Lord. "Rejoice in the Lord always. Again I will say, rejoice!" (Philippians 4:4). Let's continually rejoice in Him.

When I was in prayer one day the Lord impressed upon my heart that my concerns are His concerns, my challenges are His challenges—which is true for all His children. He promises to take us through whatever we face. Psalm 34:19 says, "Many are the afflictions of the righteous, but the LORD delivers him out of them all." So how do we grab hold of His peace and comfort with joy during trials, temptations, tests, or afflictions?

The answers are not always easy, but God provides for us in every situation if we only seek Him. The Lord gave me a system regarding how to be led by Holy Spirit, which I call my P's of spiritual protocol: Pause, Present, Pray, Perceive, Peace, and Proceed. This practice can be learned and activated instantly in all situations. Simply slow down and pause your mind and heart attitude before

God. Present your mind, will, and emotions—your heart—to Holy Spirit, in recognition of His Presence within. Pray and commune with Him, asking and seeking His help, guidance, counsel, or whatever else that is needed. Perceive His response. Usually a Scripture will come to mind. Then look for His peace to enter your heart and proceed. If peace is not present, then perhaps He is placing a check in your spirit to refrain or to proceed with caution and discretion. In this way the Lord leads our hearts with inner activation of walking in the Spirit while being led by peace.

The Lord promises that He is always with us. His yearning desire is that we are not only aware of Him, but that we involve and embrace His Spirit in everything we face. The Lord does not intend us to experience mere existence apart from Him in our lives. He wants us to enjoy the abundant life of dwelling in the Secret Place with Him. God loves us as His dear children and He enjoys our presence as we seek Him. He loves our approach to Him for fellowship and intimacy; knowing this experientially really changes our perspective regarding being in God's Presence.

Our Father plans to bring total fulfillment to our lives and fill them with all His fullness as we fellowship with Him in deep and abiding gladness. Jesus came to give us the abundant life of His Spirit which is a pleasurable and wonderful experience of walking with Him, even in our crucibles. His presence becomes our pleasure. He has great plans for us and yearns for us to enjoy life in Him, the "exceedingly abundantly above all that we ask or think" kind of life (Ephesians 3:20). In all these blessings He desires our daily communion, our constant abiding, and our reliance upon Him. We delight in Him and He delights in us as His beloved children.

Abundant Life in Christ

No matter what we face, we have Christ in us, the hope of glory (Colossians 1:27). The Secret Place with Him is really His presence within us. A story of David found in 1 Samuel 30 illustrates how to activate trust for victory in any attack. David and his men had gone out from the city of Ziklag, leaving the women and children there with all their belongings. While they were away the Amalekites came and burned the city taking captive all the women and children. When David and his men returned, they were met with intense turmoil and grief as they realized what happened to the wives and children. 1 Samuel 30:6 records, "Now David was greatly distressed, for the people spoke of stoning him, because the soul of all the people was grieved, every man for his sons and his daughters. But *David strengthened himself in the LORD his God*."

David was in a crucible of trial in which he had to trust in the Lord because his life was in jeopardy. I asked the Lord how David strengthened himself. The key was he did so "in the Lord his God." To strengthen himself, David stirred up not only his faith, but he drew from the Lord what was needed. The word *strengthened* in Hebrew is *chazaq*, meaning to fasten upon, to seize, and be strong, indicating courage and help, also meaning to bind, to be obstinate, and to conquer (Strong). David courageously conquered his deep distress by exercising his trust in God by obstinate reliance, resilience of heart, and drawing upon the Lord his God for his strength. He exercised his faith in the Lord by binding himself with the Lord.

We must follow David's example to be strong in the Lord by also binding ourselves with the power of His might that is within our hearts. His power is in us by the presence of Holy Spirit (Ephesians 3:16; Colossians 1:11; Philippians 4:13). We also are encouraged to stand while in our crucibles of trust by putting on the whole armor of God (Ephesians 6:10-18).

Because David modeled how to overcome and what it means to be in a crucible of trust while dwelling in the Secret Place, we also have that same ability. All during his life David rejoiced before God, even in his trials, focusing upon the Lord. "But as for me, I will trust in You O God." David's focus was continually upon the Lord:

> I have set the LORD always before me; because He is at my right hand I shall not be moved. Therefore my heart is glad, and my glory rejoices. My flesh also will rest in hope. For You will not leave my soul in Sheol, nor will You allow Your Holy One to see corruption. You will show me the path of life. In Your presence is fullness of joy; at Your right hand are pleasures forevermore (Psalm 16:8-11).

Truly we can enjoy our journey of trust today as we keep our hearts focused upon Jesus, for as Dr. Virkler says, "Whatever you focus upon grows within; what grows within you become."

God's plans are for us to live the dream of abundant life with Him. His plans are to prosper us, to give us a future, and to bring us to the expected end (Jeremiah 29:11). These plans include our maturity and fulfillment, going through whatever happens, knowing all things work together for the good of those who love the Lord, leading us to transformation into Christ's likeness (Romans 8:28-29).

Financial prosperity is only a small part, as He will supply all our needs according to His riches in glory (Philippians 4:19). Spiritual prosperity in becoming complete and mature in Him is His goal for us. We are to grow in godliness, generosity of soul toward others, and living out of the Fruit of the Spirit in communion with Christ. We are to have child-like wonder knowing that in Christ life is better than good; life is to be fun and enjoyable, a fantastic adventure that thrills and fulfills our godly desires as we submit to our Father. Trials, conflicts, and persecutions come our way as we walk with the Lord, but communion and intimacy are catalysts to ignite that place of fulfillment as we are in Christ. The spark of His divine nature within us leads us in triumph no matter what we face, because we are born of His Spirit; we are children of the Most High God.

As we focus upon Jesus, our hearts are drawn to Him. With our attention on Him a wonderful thing transpires. His influence upon our hearts leads us to becoming more like Him. His Spirit within us constantly infuses us with His light as we focus upon His life; He is alive within us. We actually will grow brighter and brighter in our path until the full day (Proverbs 4:18). The closer we draw to Him, the brighter our lives will become, because our demeanors and countenances will truly reflect Jesus Christ.

As we grow from glory to glory, Holy Spirit transforms us as partakers of the divine nature, the very Nature of God. Because of the divine nature within us Holy Spirit activates the divine empowerment of God. We overcome any and every trial, test, or temptation as partakers of that very nature of God. Whatever crucible we find ourselves within, we are in the Secret Place. We keep pressing in and giving our hearts to Him so that His divine nature can have preeminence in our lives. When we yield and acknowledge our ineptitude, His Spirit brings inner strength to us because God's strength is made perfect in our weakness (2 Corinthians 12:9).

Imagine the joy and glory Jesus enjoyed with the Father before He became a man. Let us also consider the joy that was set before Him as He faced the ultimate crucible of trust, the cross. Can we imagine His ability to see into the future and seeing Himself coming into His full glory again? Can we imagine His joy as He sees us, His Bride, the church spotless, pure, and without blemish? Let the cry of the Moravians be our cry: "May the Lamb that was slain receive the reward of His sufferings." They sold themselves into slavery so they could lead slaves to Christ who had no other opportunity to hear the Gospel to Christ.

For Jesus, seeing all His disciples becoming mature sons and daughters of the Father, manifesting His Life upon the earth, is His reward and exceedingly great joy. His motivation was that joy as He faced crucifixion. His joy is also our motivation as we take up and endure our crosses, entering our crucibles of trust.

As we look with the eyes of faith into the future with joy set before us, we are humbled before a gracious and merciful Father. Ponder the reality of His great joy. Let us endure the circumstances of our crucibles of trust in order to reap the benefits of trust, "till we all come to the unity of the faith and of the knowledge of the Son of God, to a perfect man, to the measure of the stature of the fullness of Christ; that we should no longer be children, tossed to and fro and carried about with every wind of doctrine, by the trickery of men, in the cunning craftiness of deceitful plotting, but, speaking the truth in love, may grow up in all things into Him who is the head — Christ" (Ephesians 4:13-16).

No matter what we face in life we can carry the presence of the Lord. Psalm 16:11 says, "You will show me the path of life; in Your presence is fullness of joy; at Your right hand are pleasures forevermore." In His path of life, God uses whatever we encounter, whether trial, test, or temptation for our good, which leads to further joy as we are conformed into the image of Christ. Whatever furnace of affliction we find ourselves in, He is with us and within us. He is our strength, our shield, and our joy. Psalm 3:3 says, "But You, O LORD, are a shield for me, My glory and the One who lifts up my head." As He lifts our heads, we are being transformed into His very image. As long as we live on this earth, any crucible of trust we find ourselves in is truly the Secret Place of the Most High.

APPENDIX A

HEARING GOD'S VOICE

Hearing God's voice is directly related to learning to trust Him implicitly, especially when things do not go as planned. Recognizing He knows best while in trials and tests is trust in a nutshell.

Hearing God's voice through direct communion with His Spirit brings comfort and guidance through every difficulty in life. Learning to hear the Spirit of God is not as difficult as one might imagine. Indeed, a child can learn to hear God's voice. Jesus requires child-like faith, like young Samuel who heard the Spirit of God (1Samuel 3:1-21). How much more should Christians know how to hear the voice of the Spirit of God in their daily walk?

In their book, *4 Keys to Hearing God's Voice*, Drs. Mark and Patti Virkler present the truth that Christians can, and should learn to hear the Lord in their daily lives. "Hearing God's voice is a simple as quieting oneself down, fixing one's eyes on Jesus, tuning to spontaneity, and writing" (2010, 27). For three teaching sessions from Dr. Virkler regarding how to gain the tools to hearing God's voice access http://www.cwgministries.org/Four-Keys-to-Hearing-Gods-Voice.

It takes just a very small adjustment to be able to learn this wonderful communication with God. He speaks through many avenues, namely, His Word, His Spirit, nature, parents, ministers, and authorities. But He also speaks to the heart, the mind, and the spirit. Preparing and expecting to hear God's voice are important keys. One can tune in to His Spirit because He is always communicating. Jesus taught, "My sheep hear My voice and I know them, and they follow Me" (John 10:27). We are Jesus' sheep as His disciples. He longs for His disciples to hear Him continuously. He has much to speak to us into every area of our lives.

The principles of hearing God's voice are seen in Habakkuk 2:1, 2: "I will stand at my guard post and position myself at the rampart to watch and see what He would speak to me and how I would reply when rebuked. The Lord answered me and said, 'Record the vision and write it on tablets that the one who reads may run.'"

This verse is a good example of how God can get us to a place of being able to receive His revelation(s). It exemplifies the principles of quieting oneself down, focusing upon God (or Christ Jesus), tuning to spontaneity, and journaling from flowing thoughts. Habakkuk seemed to have learned to write down his thoughts when getting quiet before the Lord. He knew God was speaking through these meditations. Many others in Scripture, such as David, Asaph, the sons of Korah, Solomon, and Elijah, also exemplified this principle in quieting themselves as they focused upon the Lord. Our Lord Jesus would often get up before dawn to go out in quietude with His Father. This in turn becomes a standard of how we can truly hear the voice of God.

One of the important factors regarding hearing and recognizing God's voice is to know of His loving nature. He will not lash out. He will not condemn. He will not discredit or discourage. He may chastise or reprove, but always done as a loving Father. He is a good, good Father and communicates with His children with words that come from His Fountain of Life. Jesus said the Words He speaks are Spirit and life (John 6:63). In other words, what He speaks brings life the hearer.

The Four Keys

1. Recognize God's voice as spontaneous thoughts that light upon the mind.
    - God will interpose His words into my heart as I meditate upon Him.

2. Become still.
    - Learning to quiet the mind and heart is very important to hearing God's voice. To quiet the mind get away from the television or other stimuli; find a quiet place or room to pray and journal; listen to quiet instrumental music or soaking music; let peace umpire your heart.

3. Look for vision as you pray
    - God will place pictures on the gallery of my mind as I focus upon Him. This also includes listening to hear. God will sort of think His thoughts into my mind. This is the primary way God speaks to me personally. I sense His thoughts as I journal.

4. Two-way journaling
    - I like to start by writing out a question of God. For instance, "Lord what are we doing today?" or, "What are we focusing on today?" Then I just write as thoughts come in spontaneity. Within the heart of every believer of Jesus Christ are rivers. John 7:38-39 records, "'He who believes in Me, as the Scripture has said, out of

his heart will flow rivers of living water.' But this He spoke concerning the Spirit, whom those believing in Him would receive; for the Holy Spirit was not yet given, because Jesus was not yet glorified." It is from these rivers, that God puts into our hearts His spontaneous thoughts.

In their book, the Virklers also present the four keys in a different order to allow an easy way for God's voice to be recognizable. The principles are the same as I have delineated above. God speaks to your heart as you:

1. Quiet yourself before the Lord,
2. Fix your eyes upon Jesus (tune in to His vision),
3. Tune in to spontaneity,
4. Begin writing or journaling.

The written Scripture is considered as the *Logos,* the Greek for word for *Word.* The Bible is the written Word of God. Another word in the Greek for word is *rhema,* the spoken or understood Word of the Lord. When I journal, it comes from rhema. It is not Scripture, but as I learn to allow initiated flow in journaling as I fix my eyes on Jesus, I am hearing God's voice. When I journal, or write out spontaneous thoughts that come upon my mind, if they truly are from the Spirit of God, these will not violate or contradict Scripture. Indeed, these will be in accordance with Scripture.

Safeguards

When one seeks to hear God's voice, they are actually entering into the spirit world. Some fear seeking to hear God's voice thinking they will be deceived by evil spirits. This is a possibility, but as disciples of Jesus we can hear His voice and we will be able to discern the voice of a stranger (John 10:5). To understand how to recognize God's voice is to realize He loves us so much more than we can comprehend.

To prophesy under the Holy Spirit's influence is likened unto God's voice, which is why all prophesy should be judged (1 Corinthians 14:29). According to 1 Corinthians 14:3, the one who prophesies speaks edification, exhortation, and comfort. God's voice is the same. God desires to build us up, to bring consolation, and to admonish us. God is love, yet at times He is firm to lead us to obedience. He is never condemning, but He will bring conviction of sin, and He will bring correction. However, His reproof is always done in love. He may bring a loving rebuke, but He will also affirm, hearten, and enlighten us as His children. He always draws us to Himself, to His heart of compassion for communion, to intimacy, and to oneness with Him. His language is the language of love, and His approach to us is always from His heart of mercy, grace, and tender loving kindness.

God's voice can also be recognized in respect to His covenant names, some are listed below:

- Jehovah—jirah (I am the LORD who provides);
- Jehovah—rapha (I am the LORD who heals);
- Jehovah—raah (I am the LORD your Shepherd);
- Jehovah—nissi (I am the LORD your banner);
- Jehovah—shalom (I am the LORD your peace); and several others.

There are also other important safeguards that should be incorporated in our journaling experience. The Virklers write of these safeguards for when we explore the world of the spirit:

- We must have salvation in Christ Jesus having our sins washed by His Blood, born again by the Spirit of God;
- We must accept the Bible as the inerrant written Word of God;
- We must be committed to knowing God's Word and immerse ourselves in it with—love and respect toward God—an ongoing, systematic study with meditation upon its truths;
- We must be submissive to the revealed Word, as God opens our eyes to His Word;
- We should have two or three spiritual advisors to whom we can submit our journaling for input and verification that we are hearing from the Spirit (I read mine to my wife also);
- We should have a working knowledge of the Word of God, having read through the Bible or studied and meditated upon it over time;
- We should be accountable to someone or several others within the Body of Christ;
- We must have humility and a childlike approach to God and His revelations;
- We must be teachable with openness and flexibility.

In regard to having a spiritual advisor, the Lord will lead you to one as you pray and seek His will. Just as there are safeguards to hearing God's voice, there are guidelines in seeking out a good spiritual advisor. The person:

- Must be a close friend who is trustworthy, knows you very well and shows concern.
- Must have a Biblical orientation toward all aspects of life.

- Must have an ability to sense the Holy Spirit's voice in their heart.
- Must be committed and be willing to invest time and effort into your life.
- Must also be one who receives counsel (has spiritual advisors)
- Must be ahead of your personal spirituality or maturity.

God earnestly desires communion with His children. He has given us the ability to hear His voice. As we learn the simple way of the Spirit, we enter into a lifestyle of communion with God that will encourage, uplift, edify, and comfort. We truly have an ongoing opportunity to fellowship with the Father and the Son of God in direct communion (1 John 1:1-4). We have the privilege to live a life of hearing His voice and communing through the inward dwelling of His Spirit.

APPENDIX B

The Lord has shown me that many will benefit from my admitting this sin and being set free from its bondage. Whatever is willingly brought into the Light of Christ, He will heal and restore. Praise His Name! He makes all things new as He restores our souls. He uplifts while He cleanses, by His blood, leading us to repentance and on to freedom, making our hearts pure. He sets the captives of sin free so they may walk in His liberty. From inner brokenness and self-degradation He renews our hearts and restores our souls by activating this deliverance so we can not only live free, but also minister His life to others.

For any who needs deliverance from any type of habitual sin, I encourage you to pray and ask God to lead you to a mature, anointed person who will love you and be gracious. If you are a man your mentor must be a man. If you are a woman your mentor must be a woman. The signal that he or she is the right person is the love and grace in which they extend in response to your confession. I also believe, if one seeks for it, there are anointed support groups. I recommend the Conquer Series (https://conquerseries.com/resources/); also the books *Undefiled,* by Dr. Harry Shaumburg; and *Prayers that Heal the Heart,* by Drs. Mark and Patti Virkler. They are very helpful in pointing to God as the answer for being set free. His will is our liberation from sin. He did just that for me. He will do the same for anyone else.

My prayer is that my testimony ministers reconciliation to others. There is great gratitude in my heart toward my heavenly Father's mercy and grace. He forgives, and He delivers from sin. It is hard to wrap my mind around the truth that God called me into ministry when I was so sinful, but the gifts and calling of God are without repentance (Romans 11:29). Indeed, He calls the unqualified to bring them to that place of surrender to allow His redeeming grace to cleanse them for service and bring them into qualification. This was all part God's plan to get me to a place of yieldedness and total reliance upon Him in this crucible of trust as the process of development—even when I was unfaithful and disobedient. God is indeed gracious and merciful to restore and renew.

WORKS CITED

Blackaby, Henry and King, Claude: 2008, *Experiencing God: Knowing and Doing the Will of God.* Nashville: B&H Publishing Group.

Baptist Hymnal: 1975, Nashville, Convention Press.

Chisholm, Thomas: 1923, *Great is Thy Faithfulness.*

Havergal, Francis R.: 1874, *Take My Live, and Let it Be.*

Robinson, Robert: 1758, *Come Thou Fount of Every Blessing.*

Wesley, Charles: 1739, *O For a Thousand Tongues to Sing.*

Bounds, E.M.: 2000, *The Complete Works of E.M. Bounds on Prayer:* Peabody: Prince Press.

Brunner, John: 2015, *Battlefield Verses*, Chesterfield, MO: Veritas Works.

Chironna, Mark: 2017, *The Issachar Legacy*, Longwood: Mark Chironna Ministries.

Conquer Series: https://conquerseries.com/resources/

Cooke, Graham: 2015, *Crafted Prayer: The Joy of Getting Your Prayers Answered*, Vancouver: Brilliant Book House.

Faust, James E.: Brainy Quote, copyright 2001-2020. https://www.brainyquote.com/quotes/james_e_faust_621149.

Gaither, Bill and Gloria: 1965, *The Longer I Serve Him*, The Sweeter He Grows, Hanna Sheet Music

Hamon, Bill Dr.: November 8, 2009, *The Ten M's of Ministry*: Webmaster@inJesus.com. http://injesus.com/message-archives/prophetic/Foundations/the-ten-ms-of-ministry-by-bill-hamon

Herbert, Frank: 1965, *Dune*, New York: Berkley.

Kronstadt, John: A-Z Quotes, https://www.azquotes.com/quote/883876

Manning, Brennan: 1986, *The Relentless Tenderness of Jesus*, Grand Rapid: Revell.

1996, *The Signature of Jesus*, New York: Waterbrook Multnomah Books.

2000, *Ruthless Trust*, New York: HarperCollins Publisher.

Meese, David: "Learning to Trust," Track 2 on *Learning to Trust*, Star Song, 1989, Cassette.

"His Love is Reaching," Track 5 on *Candle in the Rain*, Myrrh, 1987, Cassette.

Mother Theresa: A-Z quotes, https://www.azquotes.com/author/14530-Mother_Teresa/tag/silence

Murray, Andrew: 1981, *Absolute Surrender*, Springdale, Whitaker House.

Ridlon, Elizabeth J.: 2005, *God Meets all Our Needs: Finding Contentment by Trusting God to Meet our Needs*, Kearney: Morris Press.

Schatzline, Pat: 2015, *Unqualified*, Lake Mary: Charisma House

Shaumburg, Harry: 2009, *Undefiled*, Chicago: Moody.

Spurgeon, Charles H.: 1865, *Morning and Evening*. Morning entry for September 9.

Strong's Exhaustive Concordance, 1890, BibleSoft PC Study Bible 4.2b. 1988-2004

Talbot, John Michael: 2013, *The Jesus Prayer: A Cry for Mercy, A Path of Renewal.* Downers Grove, InterVarsity Press

Webster, Noah: 1828, *The American Dictionary of the English Language.* San Francisco, Republished in Facsimile Edition by Foundation For American Christian Education.

Virkler, Mark and Patti: 2001, *Prayers That Heal the Heart*, Alachua, FL: Bridge-Logos

Virkler, Mark and Patti: 2010, *4 Keys to Hearing God's Voice*, Shippensburg: Destiny Image Publishers, Inc.

Virkler, Mark Dr.: 2014, "How to Have Mountain Moving Faith." YouTube.com. https://www.youtube.com/watch?v=21tUzdgAq2I

2017. "Perfect Peace When your Imagination is…" The Elijah List. http://elijahlist.com/words/display_word.html4?ID=17608